THE ART OF
COMPUTER PROGRAMMING

VOLUME 4, FASCICLE 2

Generating All Tuples
and Permutations

DONALD E. KNUTH *Stanford University*

ADDISON–WESLEY

Upper Saddle River, NJ · Boston · Indianapolis · San Francisco
New York · Toronto · Montréal · London · Munich · Paris · Madrid
Capetown · Sydney · Tokyo · Singapore · Mexico City

For sales outside the U.S., please contact:

> International Sales
> `international@pearsoned.com`

Visit us on the Web: `www.awprofessional.com`

Internet page `http://www-cs-faculty.stanford.edu/~knuth/taocp.html` contains
current information about this book and related books.

See also `http://www-cs-faculty.stanford.edu/~knuth/sgb.html` for information
about *The Stanford GraphBase*, including downloadable software for dealing with the
graphs used in many of the examples in Chapter 7.

And see `http://www-cs-faculty.stanford.edu/~knuth/mmix.html` for basic information about the MMIX computer.

PREFACE

*I am grateful to all my friends,
and record here and now my most especial appreciation
to those friends who, after a decent interval,
stopped asking me, "How's the book coming?"*
— PETER J. GOMES, *The Good Book* (1996)

THIS BOOKLET is Fascicle 2 of *The Art of Computer Programming*, Volume 4: *Combinatorial Algorithms*. As explained in the preface to Fascicle 1 of Volume 1, I'm circulating the material in this preliminary form because I know that the task of completing Volume 4 will take many years; I can't wait for people to begin reading what I've written so far and to provide valuable feedback.

There will also be a Fascicle 1 for Volume 4. But I've written Fascicle 2 first. Experienced programmers will understand that the initialization of a program usually can't be written properly until after the main body has been fleshed out.

To put the material in context, this fascicle contains Sections 7.2.1.1 and 7.2.1.2 of a long, long chapter on combinatorial searching. Chapter 7 will eventually fill three volumes (namely Volumes 4A, 4B, and 4C), assuming that I'm able to remain healthy. It will begin with a short review of graph theory, with emphasis on some highlights of significant graphs in The Stanford GraphBase, from which I will be drawing many examples. Then comes Section 7.1, which deals with bitwise manipulation and with algorithms relating to Boolean functions. Section 7.2 is about generating all possibilities, and it begins with Section 7.2.1: Generating Basic Combinatorial Patterns. That sets the stage for the main contents of the present booklet, namely Section 7.2.1.1 (where I get the ball rolling by dealing with the generation of n-tuples) and Section 7.2.1.2 (which extends the ideas to permutations). Then will come Section 7.2.1.3 (about combinations), Section 7.2.1.4 (about integer partitions), and Section 7.2.1.5 (about set partitions), all in Fascicle 3. Section 7.2.1.6 (about trees) and Section 7.2.1.7 (about the history of combinatorial generation) will comprise Fascicle 4. Section 7.2.2 will deal with backtracking in general. And so it will go on, if all goes well; an outline of the entire Chapter 7 as currently envisaged appears on the `taocp` webpage that is cited on page ii.

I had great pleasure writing this material, akin to the thrill of excitement that I felt when writing Volume 2 many years ago. As in Volume 2, where I found to my delight that the basic principles of elementary probability theory and number theory arose naturally in the study of algorithms for random number generation and arithmetic, I learned while preparing Section 7.2.1 that the basic principles of elementary combinatorics arise naturally and in a highly motivated way when we study algorithms for combinatorial generation. Thus, I found once again that a beautiful story was "out there" waiting to be told.

My original intention was to devote far less space to this topic. But when I saw how fundamental the ideas were for combinatorial studies in general, I knew that I could never be happy unless I covered the basics quite thoroughly. Therefore I've done my best to build a solid foundation of theoretical and practical ideas that will support many kinds of reliable superstructures.

The topic of combinatorial generation has not only given me a chance to discuss important mathematical theories, it also has led to other kinds of fun, because of its many connections to amusing games and puzzles. Good puzzles are great aids to education, and I intend to continue focusing on recreational topics throughout Volume 4.

> *The average boy who abhors square root or algebra*
> *finds delight in working puzzles which involve similar*
> *principles, and may be led into a course of study*
> *which would develop the mathematical and inventive bumps*
> *in a way to astonish the family phrenologist.*
> — SAM LOYD, *The World of Puzzledom* (1896)

I shall happily pay a finder's fee of $2.56 for each error in this fascicle when it is first reported to me, whether that error be typographical, technical, or historical. The same reward holds for items that I forgot to put in the index. And valuable suggestions for improvements to the text are worth 32¢ each. (Furthermore, if you find a better solution to an exercise, I'll actually reward you with immortal glory instead of mere money, by publishing your name in the eventual book:−)

I wish to thank Yoichi Hariguchi for helping me to build and rebuild the computer on which this booklet was written. And I also want to thank Frank Ruskey for bravely foisting an early draft of this material on college students and for telling me about his classroom experiences.

Notations that are used here and not otherwise explained can be found in the Index to Notations at the end of Volumes 1, 2, or 3. Those indices point to the places where further information is available. Of course Volume 4 will some day contain its own Index to Notations.

Machine-language examples in all future editions of *The Art of Computer Programming* will be based on the MMIX computer, which is defined in Section 1.3.1′ of Volume 1, Fascicle 1. Cross-references to Sections 1.3.1′, 1.3.2′, 1.4.1′, 1.4.2′, and 1.4.3′ in the present booklet refer to that fascicle.

Cross references to yet-unwritten material sometimes appear as '00' in the following pages; this impossible value is a placeholder for the actual numbers to be supplied later.

Happy reading!

Stanford, California   D. E. K.
December 2004

CONTENTS

> *I thought it worth a Dayes labour,*
> *to write something on this Art or Science,*
> *that the Rules thereof might not be lost and obscured.*
> — RICHARD DUCKWORTH, *Tintinnalogia* (1668)

CHAPTER SEVEN

COMBINATORIAL SEARCHING

 *The opening sections of this chapter will appear in Volume 4, Fascicle 1, planned for publication in 2006.*

7.2. GENERATING ALL POSSIBILITIES

All present or accounted for, sir.
— Traditional American military saying

All present and correct, sir.
— Traditional British military saying

7.2.1. Generating Basic Combinatorial Patterns

OUR GOAL in this section is to study methods for running through all of the possibilities in some combinatorial universe, because we often face problems in which an exhaustive examination of all cases is necessary or desirable. For example, we might want to look at all permutations of a given set.

Some authors call this the task of *enumerating* all of the possibilities; but that's not quite the right word, because "enumeration" most often means that we merely want to *count* the total number of cases, not that we actually want to look at them all. If somebody asks you to enumerate the permutations of $\{1, 2, 3\}$, you are quite justified in replying that the answer is $3! = 6$; you needn't give the more complete answer $\{123, 132, 213, 231, 312, 321\}$.

Other authors speak of *listing* all the possibilities; but that's not such a great word either. No sensible person would want to make a list of the $10! = 3{,}628{,}800$ permutations of $\{0, 1, 2, 3, 4, 5, 6, 7, 8, 9\}$ by printing them out on thousands of sheets of paper, nor even by writing them all in a computer file. All we really want is to have them present momentarily in some data structure, so that a program can examine each permutation one at a time.

So we will speak of *generating* all of the combinatorial objects that we need, and *visiting* each object in turn. Just as we studied algorithms for tree traversal in Section 2.3.1, where the goal was to visit every node of a tree, we turn now to algorithms that systematically traverse a combinatorial space of possibilities.

He's got 'em on the list—
he's got 'em on the list;
And they'll none of 'em be missed—
they'll none of 'em be missed.
— WILLIAM S. GILBERT, The Mikado (1885)

7.2.1.1. Generating all n-tuples. Let's start small, by considering how to run through all 2^n strings that consist of n binary digits. Equivalently, we want to visit all n-tuples $(a_1, \ldots, a_n)$ where each a_j is either 0 or 1. This task is also, in essence, equivalent to examining all subsets of a given set $\{x_1, \ldots, x_n\}$, because we can say that x_j is in the subset if and only if $a_j = 1$.

Of course such a problem has an absurdly simple solution. All we need to do is start with the binary number $(0 \ldots 00)_2 = 0$ and repeatedly add 1 until we reach $(1 \ldots 11)_2 = 2^n - 1$. We will see, however, that even this utterly trivial problem has astonishing points of interest when we look into it more deeply. And our study of n-tuples will pay off later when we turn to the generation of more difficult kinds of patterns.

In the first place, we can see that the binary-notation trick extends to other kinds of n-tuples. If we want, for example, to generate all $(a_1, \ldots, a_n)$ in which each a_j is one of the decimal digits $\{0, 1, 2, 3, 4, 5, 6, 7, 8, 9\}$, we can simply count from $(0 \ldots 00)_{10} = 0$ to $(9 \ldots 99)_{10} = 10^n - 1$ in the decimal number system. And if we want more generally to run through all cases in which

$$0 \le a_j < m_j \qquad \text{for } 1 \le j \le n, \tag{1}$$

where the upper limits m_j might be different in different components of the vector $(a_1, \ldots, a_n)$, the task is essentially the same as repeatedly adding unity to the number

$$\begin{bmatrix} a_1, & a_2, & \ldots, & a_n \\ m_1, & m_2, & \ldots, & m_n \end{bmatrix} \tag{2}$$

in a mixed-radix number system; see Eq. 4.1–(9) and exercise 4.3.1–9.

We might as well pause to describe the process more formally:

Algorithm M (*Mixed-radix generation*). This algorithm visits all n-tuples that satisfy (1), by repeatedly adding 1 to the mixed-radix number in (2) until overflow occurs. Auxiliary variables a_0 and m_0 are introduced for convenience.

M1. [Initialize.] Set $a_j \leftarrow 0$ for $0 \le j \le n$, and set $m_0 \leftarrow 2$.

M2. [Visit.] Visit the n-tuple $(a_1, \ldots, a_n)$. (The program that wants to examine all n-tuples now does its thing.)

M3. [Prepare to add one.] Set $j \leftarrow n$.

M4. [Carry if necessary.] If $a_j = m_j - 1$, set $a_j \leftarrow 0$, $j \leftarrow j - 1$, and repeat this step.

M5. [Increase, unless done.] If $j = 0$, terminate the algorithm. Otherwise set $a_j \leftarrow a_j + 1$ and go back to step M2. ∎

Algorithm M is simple and straightforward, but we shouldn't forget that nested loops are even simpler, when n is a fairly small constant. When $n = 4$, we could for example write out the following instructions:

$$\begin{aligned}
&\text{For } a_1 = 0, 1, \ldots, m_1 - 1 \text{ (in this order) do the following:} \\
&\quad \text{For } a_2 = 0, 1, \ldots, m_2 - 1 \text{ (in this order) do the following:} \\
&\qquad \text{For } a_3 = 0, 1, \ldots, m_3 - 1 \text{ (in this order) do the following:} \\
&\qquad\quad \text{For } a_4 = 0, 1, \ldots, m_4 - 1 \text{ (in this order) do the following:} \\
&\qquad\qquad \text{Visit } (a_1, a_2, a_3, a_4).
\end{aligned} \tag{3}$$

These instructions are equivalent to Algorithm M, and they are easily expressed in any programming language.

Gray binary code. Algorithm M runs through all $(a_1, \ldots, a_n)$ in lexicographic order, as in a dictionary. But there are many situations in which we prefer to visit those n-tuples in some other order. The most famous alternative arrangement is the so-called Gray binary code, which lists all 2^n strings of n bits in such a way

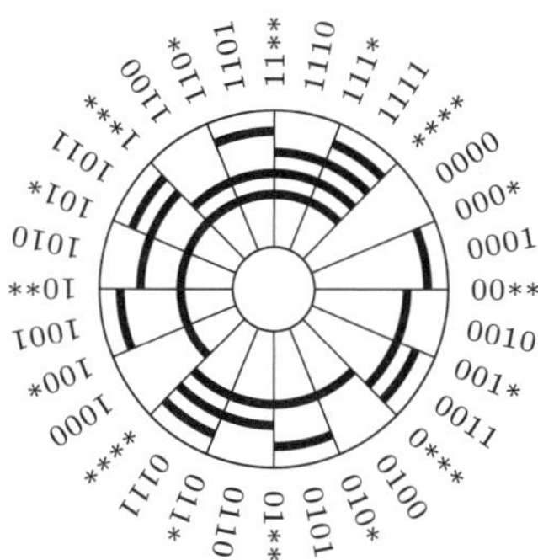

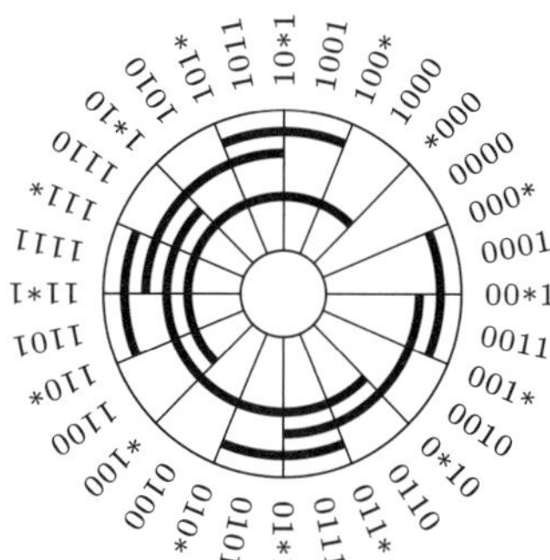

Fig. 10. (a) Lexicographic binary code.   (b) Gray binary code.

that only one bit changes each time, in a simple and regular way. For example, the Gray binary code for $n = 4$ is

$$0000, 0001, 0011, 0010, 0110, 0111, 0101, 0100,$$
$$1100, 1101, 1111, 1110, 1010, 1011, 1001, 1000. \tag{4}$$

Such codes are especially important in applications where analog information is being converted to digital or vice versa. For example, suppose we want to identify our current position on a rotating disk that has been divided into 16 sectors, using four sensors that each distinguish black from white. If we use lexicographic order to mark the tracks from 0000 to 1111, as in Fig. 10(a), wildly inaccurate measurements can occur at the boundaries between sectors; but the code in Fig. 10(b) never gives a bad reading.

Gray binary code can be defined in many equivalent ways. For example, if Γ_n stands for the Gray binary sequence of n-bit strings, we can define Γ_n recursively by the two rules

$$\Gamma_0 = \epsilon;$$
$$\Gamma_{n+1} = 0\Gamma_n, \; 1\Gamma_n^R. \tag{5}$$

Here ϵ denotes the empty string, $0\Gamma_n$ denotes the sequence Γ_n with 0 prefixed to each string, and $1\Gamma_n^R$ denotes the sequence Γ_n in *reverse order* with 1 prefixed to each string. Since the last string of Γ_n equals the first string of Γ_n^R, it is clear from (5) that exactly one bit changes in every step of Γ_{n+1} if Γ_n enjoys the same property.

Another way to define the sequence $\Gamma_n = g(0), g(1), \ldots, g(2^n - 1)$ is to give an explicit formula for its individual elements $g(k)$. Indeed, since Γ_{n+1} begins with $0\Gamma_n$, the infinite sequence

$$\Gamma_\infty = g(0), g(1), g(2), g(3), g(4), \ldots$$
$$= (0)_2, (1)_2, (11)_2, (10)_2, (110)_2, \ldots \tag{6}$$

is a permutation of all the nonnegative integers, if we regard each string of 0s and 1s as a binary integer with optional leading 0s. Then Γ_n consists of the first 2^n elements of (6), converted to n-bit strings by inserting 0s at the left if needed.

When $k = 2^n + r$, where $0 \le r < 2^n$, relation (5) tells us that $g(k)$ is equal to $2^n + g(2^n - 1 - r)$. Therefore we can prove by induction on n that the integer k whose binary representation is $(\dots b_2 b_1 b_0)_2$ has a Gray binary equivalent $g(k)$ with the representation $(\dots a_2 a_1 a_0)_2$, where

$$a_j = b_j \oplus b_{j+1}, \qquad \text{for } j \ge 0. \tag{7}$$

(See exercise 6.) For example, $g\big((111001000011)_2\big) = (100101100010)_2$. Conversely, if $g(k) = (\dots a_2 a_1 a_0)_2$ is given, we can find $k = (\dots b_2 b_1 b_0)_2$ by inverting the system of equations (7), obtaining

$$b_j = a_j \oplus a_{j+1} \oplus a_{j+2} \oplus \cdots, \qquad \text{for } j \ge 0; \tag{8}$$

this infinite sum is really finite because $a_{j+t} = 0$ for all large t.

One of the many pleasant consequences of Eq. (7) is that $g(k)$ can be computed very easily with bitwise arithmetic:

$$g(k) = k \oplus \lfloor k/2 \rfloor. \tag{9}$$

Similarly, the inverse function in (8) satisfies

$$g^{[-1]}(l) = l \oplus \lfloor l/2 \rfloor \oplus \lfloor l/4 \rfloor \oplus \cdots; \tag{10}$$

this function, however, requires more computation (see exercise 7.1–00). We can also deduce from (7) that, if k and k' are any nonnegative integers,

$$g(k \oplus k') = g(k) \oplus g(k'). \tag{11}$$

Yet another consequence is that the $(n+1)$-bit Gray binary code can be written

$$\Gamma_{n+1} = 0\Gamma_n, \ (0\Gamma_n)\oplus 110\dots 0;$$

this pattern is evident, for example, in (4). Comparing with (5), we see that reversing the order of Gray binary code is equivalent to complementing the first bit:

$$\Gamma_n^R = \Gamma_n \oplus 1\overbrace{0\dots 0}^{n-1}. \tag{12}$$

The exercises below show that the function $g(k)$ defined in (7), and its inverse $g^{[-1]}$ defined in (8), have many further properties and applications of interest. Sometimes we think of these as functions taking binary strings to binary strings; at other times we regard them as functions from integers to integers, via binary notation, with leading zeros irrelevant.

Gray binary code is named after Frank Gray, a physicist who became famous for helping to devise the method long used for compatible color television broadcasting [*Bell System Tech. J.* **13** (1934), 464–515]. He invented Γ_n for applications to pulse code modulation, a method for analog transmission of digital signals [see *Bell System Tech. J.* **30** (1951), 38–40; *U.S. Patent 2632058* (17 March 1953); W. R. Bennett, *Introduction to Signal Transmission* (1971), 238–240]. But the idea of "Gray binary code" was known long before he worked on it; for example, it appeared in *U.S. Patent 2307868* by George Stibitz (12 January 1943). More significantly, Γ_5 was used in a telegraph machine demonstrated in 1878 by Émile Baudot, after whom the term "baud" was later named. At about the same time, a similar but less systematic code for telegraphy was independently devised by Otto Schäffler [see *Journal Télégraphique* **4** (1878), 252–253; *Annales Télégraphiques* **6** (1879), 361, 382–383].*

In fact, Gray binary code is implicitly present in a classic toy that has fascinated people for centuries, now generally known as the "Chinese ring puzzle" in English, although Englishmen used to call it the "tiring irons." Figure 11 shows a seven-ring example. The challenge is to remove the rings from the bar, and the rings are interlocked in such a way that only two basic types of move are possible (although this may not be immediately apparent from the illustration):

a) The rightmost ring can be removed or replaced at any time;
b) Any other ring can be removed or replaced if and only if the ring to its right is on the bar and all rings to the right of that one are off.

We can represent the current state of the puzzle in binary notation, writing 1 if a ring is on the bar and 0 if it is off; thus Fig. 11 shows the rings in state 1011000. (The second ring from the left is encoded as 0, because it lies entirely above the bar.)

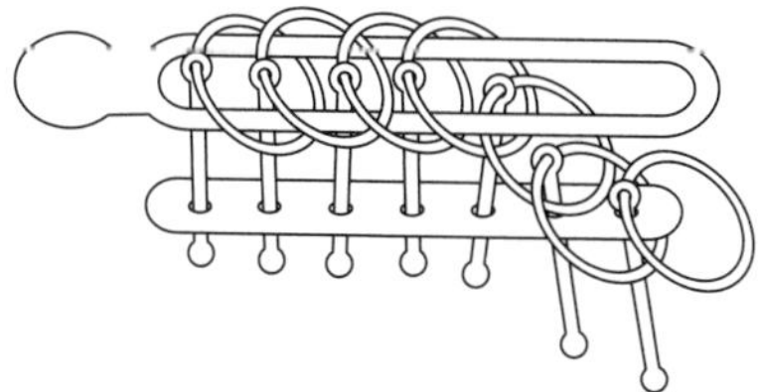

Fig. 11.
The Chinese ring puzzle.

A French magistrate named Louis Gros demonstrated an explicit connection between Chinese rings and binary numbers, in a booklet called *Théorie du Baguenodier* [sic] (Lyon: Aimé Vingtrinier, 1872) that was published anonymously. If the rings are in state $a_{n-1}\ldots a_0$, and if we define the binary number $k = (b_{n-1}\ldots b_0)_2$ by Eq. (8), he showed that exactly k more steps are necessary and sufficient to solve the puzzle. Thus Gros is the true inventor of Gray binary code.

*Certainly no home should be without
this fascinating, historic, and instructive puzzle.*

— HENRY E. DUDENEY (1901)

When the rings are in any state other than $00\ldots0$ or $10\ldots0$, exactly two moves are possible, one of type (a) and one of type (b). Only one of these moves advances toward the desired goal; the other is a step backward that will need to be undone. A type (a) move changes k to $k \oplus 1$; thus we want to do it when k is odd, since this will decrease k. A type (b) move from a position that ends in $(10^{j-1})_2$ for $1 \le j < n$ changes k to $k \oplus (1^{j+1})_2 = k \oplus (2^{j+1} - 1)$. When k

---

* Some authors have asserted that Gray code was invented by Elisha Gray, who developed a printing telegraph machine at the same time as Baudot and Schäffler. Such claims are untrue, although Elisha did get a raw deal with respect to priority for inventing the telephone [see L. W. Taylor, *Amer. Physics Teacher* **5** (1937), 243–251].

is even, we want $k \oplus (2^{j+1} - 1)$ to equal $k - 1$, which means that k must be a multiple of 2^j but not a multiple of 2^{j+1}; in other words,

$$j = \rho(k), \tag{13}$$

where ρ is the "ruler function" of Eq. 7.1–(oo). Therefore the rings follow a nice pattern when the puzzle is solved properly: If we number them $0, 1, \ldots, n - 1$ (starting at the free end), the sequence of ring moves on or off the bar is the sequence of numbers that ends with $\ldots, \rho(4), \rho(3), \rho(2), \rho(1)$.

Going backwards, successively putting rings on or off until we reach the ultimate state $10 \ldots 0$ (which, as John Wallis observed in 1693, is more difficult to reach than the supposedly harder state $11 \ldots 1$), yields an algorithm for counting in Gray binary code:

Algorithm G (*Gray binary generation*). This algorithm visits all binary n-tuples $(a_{n-1}, \ldots, a_1, a_0)$ by starting with $(0, \ldots, 0, 0)$ and changing only one bit at a time, also maintaining a parity bit a_∞ such that

$$a_\infty = a_{n-1} \oplus \cdots \oplus a_1 \oplus a_0. \tag{14}$$

It successively complements bits $\rho(1)$, $\rho(2)$, $\rho(3)$, $\ldots$, $\rho(2^n - 1)$ and then stops.

G1. [Initialize.] Set $a_j \leftarrow 0$ for $0 \le j < n$; also set $a_\infty \leftarrow 0$.

G2. [Visit.] Visit the n-tuple $(a_{n-1}, \ldots, a_1, a_0)$.

G3. [Change parity.] Set $a_\infty \leftarrow 1 - a_\infty$.

G4. [Choose j.] If $a_\infty = 1$, set $j \leftarrow 0$. Otherwise let $j \ge 1$ be minimum such that $a_{j-1} = 1$. (After the kth time we have performed this step, $j = \rho(k)$.)

G5. [Complement coordinate j.] Terminate if $j = n$; otherwise set $a_j \leftarrow 1 - a_j$ and return to G2. ∎

The parity bit a_∞ comes in handy if we are computing a sum like

$$X_{000} - X_{001} - X_{010} + X_{011} - X_{100} + X_{101} + X_{110} - X_{111}$$

or

$$X_\emptyset - X_a - X_b + X_{ab} - X_c + X_{ac} + X_{bc} - X_{abc},$$

where the sign depends on the parity of a binary string or the number of elements in a subset. Such sums arise frequently in "inclusion-exclusion" formulas such as Eq. 1.3.3–(29). The parity bit is also necessary, for efficiency: Without it we could not easily choose between the two ways of determining j, which correspond to performing a type (a) or type (b) move in the Chinese ring puzzle. But the most important feature of Algorithm G is that step G5 makes only a single coordinate change. Therefore only a simple change is usually needed to the terms X that we are summing, or to whatever other structures we are concerned with as we visit each n-tuple.

> *It is impossible, of course, to remove all ambiguity in the lowest-order digit*
> *except by a scheme like one the Irish railways are said to have used*
> *of removing the last car of every train*
> *because it is too susceptible to collision damage.*
> — G. R. STIBITZ and J. A. LARRIVEE, *Mathematics and Computers* (1957)

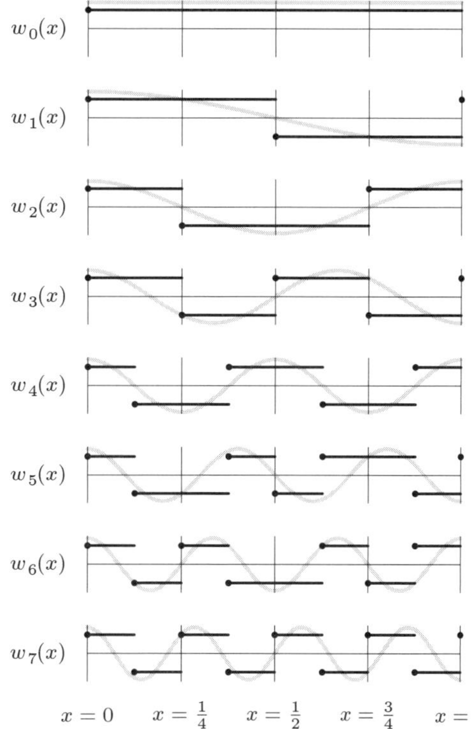

Fig. 12. Walsh functions $w_k(x)$ for $0 \le k < 8$, with the analogous trigonometric functions $\sqrt{2}\cos k\pi x$ shown in gray for comparison.

Another key property of Gray binary code was discovered by J. L. Walsh in connection with an important sequence of functions now known as *Walsh functions* [see *Amer. J. Math.* **45** (1923), 5–24]. Let $w_0(x) = 1$ for all real numbers x, and

$$w_k(x) = (-1)^{\lfloor 2x \rfloor \lceil k/2 \rceil}\, w_{\lfloor k/2 \rfloor}(2x), \qquad \text{for } k > 0. \tag{15}$$

For example, $w_1(x) = (-1)^{\lfloor 2x \rfloor}$ changes sign whenever x is an integer or an integer plus $\frac{1}{2}$. It follows that $w_k(x) = w_k(x+1)$ for all k, and that $w_k(x) = \pm 1$ for all x. More significantly, $w_k(0) = 1$ and $w_k(x)$ has *exactly k sign changes in the interval* $(0 \mathinner{.\,.} 1)$, so that it approaches $(-1)^k$ as x approaches 1 from the left. Therefore $w_k(x)$ behaves rather like a trigonometric function $\cos k\pi x$ or $\sin k\pi x$, and we can represent other functions as a linear combination of Walsh functions in much the same way as they are traditionally represented as Fourier series. This fact, together with the simple discrete nature of $w_k(x)$, makes Walsh functions extremely useful in computer calculations related to information transmission, image processing, and many other applications.

Figure 12 shows the first eight Walsh functions together with their trigonometric cousins. Engineers commonly call $w_k(x)$ the Walsh function of *sequency k*, by analogy with the fact that $\cos k\pi x$ and $\sin k\pi x$ have *frequency $k/2$*. [See, for example, the book *Sequency Theory: Foundations and Applications* (New York: Academic Press, 1977), by H. F. Harmuth.]

Although Eq. (15) may look formidable at first glance, it actually provides an easy way to see by induction why $w_k(x)$ has exactly k sign changes as claimed. If k is even, say $k = 2l$, we have $w_{2l}(x) = w_l(2x)$ for $0 \le x < \frac{1}{2}$; the effect is simply to compress the function $w_l(x)$ into half the space, so $w_{2l}(x)$ has accumulated l sign changes so far. Then $w_{2l}(x) = (-1)^l w_l(2x) = (-1)^l w_l(2x - 1)$ in the range $\frac{1}{2} \le x < 1$; this concatenates another copy of $w_l(2x)$, flipping the sign if necessary to avoid a sign change at $x = \frac{1}{2}$. The function $w_{2l+1}(x)$ is similar, but it *forces* a sign change when $x = \frac{1}{2}$.

What does this have to do with Gray binary code? Walsh discovered that his functions could all be expressed neatly in terms of simpler functions called *Rademacher functions* [Hans Rademacher, *Math. Annalen* **87** (1922), 112–138],

$$r_k(x) = (-1)^{\lfloor 2^k x \rfloor}, \tag{16}$$

which take the value $(-1)^{c-k}$ when $(\ldots c_2 c_1 c_0 . c_{-1} c_{-2} \ldots)_2$ is the binary representation of x. Indeed, we have $w_1(x) = r_1(x)$, $w_2(x) = r_1(x) r_2(x)$, $w_3(x) = r_2(x)$, and in general

$$w_k(x) = \prod_{j \ge 0} r_{j+1}(x)^{b_j \oplus b_{j+1}} \qquad \text{when } k = (b_{n-1} \ldots b_1 b_0)_2. \tag{17}$$

(See exercise 33.) Thus the exponent of $r_{j+1}(x)$ in $w_k(x)$ is the jth bit of the Gray binary number $g(k)$, according to (7), and we have

$$w_k(x) = r_{\rho(k)+1}(x) w_{k-1}(x), \qquad \text{for } k > 0. \tag{18}$$

Equation (17) implies the handy formula

$$w_k(x) w_{k'}(x) = w_{k \oplus k'}(x), \tag{19}$$

which is much simpler than the corresponding product formulas for sines and cosines. This identity follows easily because $r_j(x)^2 = 1$ for all j and x, hence $r_j(x)^{a \oplus b} = r_j(x)^{a+b}$. It implies in particular that $w_k(x)$ is *orthogonal* to $w_{k'}(x)$ when $k \ne k'$, in the sense that the average value of $w_k(x) w_{k'}(x)$ is zero. We also can use (17) to define $w_k(x)$ for fractional values of k like $1/2$ or $13/8$.

The *Walsh transform* of 2^n numbers $(X_0, \ldots, X_{2^n-1})$ is the vector defined by the equation $(x_0, \ldots, x_{2^n-1})^T = W_n (X_0, \ldots, X_{2^n-1})^T$, where W_n is the $2^n \times 2^n$ matrix having $w_j(k/2^n)$ in row j and column k, for $0 \le j, k < 2^n$. For example, Fig. 12 tells us that the Walsh transform when $n = 3$ is

$$\begin{pmatrix} x_{000} \\ x_{001} \\ x_{010} \\ x_{011} \\ x_{100} \\ x_{101} \\ x_{110} \\ x_{111} \end{pmatrix} = \begin{pmatrix} 1 & 1 & 1 & 1 & 1 & 1 & 1 & 1 \\ 1 & 1 & 1 & 1 & \bar{1} & \bar{1} & \bar{1} & \bar{1} \\ 1 & 1 & \bar{1} & \bar{1} & \bar{1} & \bar{1} & 1 & 1 \\ 1 & 1 & \bar{1} & \bar{1} & 1 & 1 & \bar{1} & \bar{1} \\ 1 & \bar{1} & \bar{1} & 1 & 1 & \bar{1} & \bar{1} & 1 \\ 1 & \bar{1} & \bar{1} & 1 & \bar{1} & 1 & 1 & \bar{1} \\ 1 & \bar{1} & 1 & \bar{1} & \bar{1} & 1 & \bar{1} & 1 \\ 1 & \bar{1} & 1 & \bar{1} & 1 & \bar{1} & 1 & \bar{1} \end{pmatrix} \begin{pmatrix} X_{000} \\ X_{001} \\ X_{010} \\ X_{011} \\ X_{100} \\ X_{101} \\ X_{110} \\ X_{111} \end{pmatrix}. \tag{20}$$

(Here $\bar{1}$ stands for -1, and the subscripts are conveniently regarded as binary strings 000–111 instead of as the integers 0–7.) The *Hadamard transform* is defined similarly, but with the matrix H_n in place of W_n, where H_n has $(-1)^{j\cdot k}$ in row j and column k; here '$j\cdot k$' denotes the dot product $a_{n-1}b_{n-1}+\cdots+a_0b_0$ of the binary representations $j=(a_{n-1}\ldots a_0)_2$ and $k=(b_{n-1}\ldots b_0)_2$. For example, the Hadamard transform for $n=3$ is

$$
\begin{pmatrix} x'_{000} \\ x'_{001} \\ x'_{010} \\ x'_{011} \\ x'_{100} \\ x'_{101} \\ x'_{110} \\ x'_{111} \end{pmatrix}
=
\begin{pmatrix}
1 & 1 & 1 & 1 & 1 & 1 & 1 & 1 \\
1 & \bar{1} & 1 & \bar{1} & 1 & \bar{1} & 1 & \bar{1} \\
1 & 1 & \bar{1} & \bar{1} & 1 & 1 & \bar{1} & \bar{1} \\
1 & \bar{1} & \bar{1} & 1 & 1 & \bar{1} & \bar{1} & 1 \\
1 & 1 & 1 & 1 & \bar{1} & \bar{1} & \bar{1} & \bar{1} \\
1 & \bar{1} & 1 & \bar{1} & \bar{1} & 1 & \bar{1} & 1 \\
1 & 1 & \bar{1} & \bar{1} & \bar{1} & \bar{1} & 1 & 1 \\
1 & \bar{1} & \bar{1} & 1 & \bar{1} & 1 & 1 & \bar{1}
\end{pmatrix}
\begin{pmatrix} X_{000} \\ X_{001} \\ X_{010} \\ X_{011} \\ X_{100} \\ X_{101} \\ X_{110} \\ X_{111} \end{pmatrix}. \tag{21}
$$

This is the same as the discrete Fourier transform on an n-dimensional cube, Eq. 4.6.4–(38), and we can evaluate it quickly "in place" by adapting the method of Yates discussed in Section 4.6.4:

Given	First step	Second step	Third step
X_{000}	$X_{000}+X_{001}$	$X_{000}+X_{001}+X_{010}+X_{011}$	$X_{000}+X_{001}+X_{010}+X_{011}+X_{100}+X_{101}+X_{110}+X_{111}$
X_{001}	$X_{000}-X_{001}$	$X_{000}-X_{001}+X_{010}-X_{011}$	$X_{000}-X_{001}+X_{010}-X_{011}+X_{100}-X_{101}+X_{110}-X_{111}$
X_{010}	$X_{010}+X_{011}$	$X_{000}+X_{001}-X_{010}-X_{011}$	$X_{000}+X_{001}-X_{010}-X_{011}+X_{100}+X_{101}-X_{110}-X_{111}$
X_{011}	$X_{010}-X_{011}$	$X_{000}-X_{001}-X_{010}+X_{011}$	$X_{000}-X_{001}-X_{010}+X_{011}+X_{100}-X_{101}-X_{110}+X_{111}$
X_{100}	$X_{100}+X_{101}$	$X_{100}+X_{101}+X_{110}+X_{111}$	$X_{000}+X_{001}+X_{010}+X_{011}-X_{100}-X_{101}-X_{110}-X_{111}$
X_{101}	$X_{100}-X_{101}$	$X_{100}-X_{101}+X_{110}-X_{111}$	$X_{000}-X_{001}+X_{010}-X_{011}-X_{100}+X_{101}-X_{110}+X_{111}$
X_{110}	$X_{110}+X_{111}$	$X_{100}+X_{101}-X_{110}-X_{111}$	$X_{000}+X_{001}-X_{010}-X_{011}-X_{100}-X_{101}+X_{110}+X_{111}$
X_{111}	$X_{110}-X_{111}$	$X_{100}-X_{101}-X_{110}+X_{111}$	$X_{000}-X_{001}-X_{010}+X_{011}-X_{100}+X_{101}+X_{110}-X_{111}$

Notice that the rows of H_3 are a permutation of the rows of W_3. This is true in general, so we can obtain the Walsh transform by permuting the elements of the Hadamard transform. Exercise 36 discusses the details.

Going faster. When we're running through 2^n possibilities, we usually want to reduce the computation time as much as possible. Algorithm G needs to complement only one bit a_j per visit to $(a_{n-1},\ldots,a_0)$, but it loops in step G4 while choosing an appropriate value of j. Another approach has been suggested by Gideon Ehrlich [*JACM* **20** (1973), 500–513], who introduced the notion of *loopless* combinatorial generation: With a loopless algorithm, the number of operations performed between successive visits is required to be bounded in advance, so there never is a long wait before a new pattern has been generated.

We learned some tricks in Section 7.1 about quick ways to determine the number of leading or trailing 0s in a binary number. Those methods could be used in step G4 to make Algorithm G loopless, assuming that n isn't unreasonably large. But Ehrlich's method is quite different, and much more versatile, so it provides us with a new weapon in our arsenal of techniques for efficient computation. Here is how his approach can be used to generate binary n-tuples [see Bitner, Ehrlich, and Reingold, *CACM* **19** (1976), 517–521]:

Algorithm L (*Loopless Gray binary generation*). This algorithm, like Algorithm G, visits all binary n-tuples $(a_{n-1}, \ldots, a_0)$ in the order of the Gray binary code. But instead of maintaining a parity bit, it uses an array of "focus pointers" $(f_n, \ldots, f_0)$, whose significance is discussed below.

L1. [Initialize.] Set $a_j \leftarrow 0$ and $f_j \leftarrow j$ for $0 \le j < n$; also set $f_n \leftarrow n$. (A loopless algorithm is allowed to have loops in its initialization step, as long as the initial setup is reasonably efficient; after all, every program needs to be loaded and launched.)

L2. [Visit.] Visit the n-tuple $(a_{n-1}, \ldots, a_1, a_0)$.

L3. [Choose j.] Set $j \leftarrow f_0$, $f_0 \leftarrow 0$. (If this is the kth time we are performing the present step, j is now equal to $\rho(k)$.) Terminate if $j = n$; otherwise set $f_j \leftarrow f_{j+1}$ and $f_{j+1} \leftarrow j + 1$.

L4. [Complement coordinate j.] Set $a_j \leftarrow 1 - a_j$ and return to L2. ∎

For example, the computation proceeds as follows when $n = 4$. Elements a_j have been underlined in this table if the corresponding bit b_j is 1 in the binary string $b_3b_2b_1b_0$ such that $a_3a_2a_1a_0 = g(b_3b_2b_1b_0)$:

a_3	0	0	0	0	0	0	0	0	1	1	1	1	1	1	1	1
a_2	0	0	0	0	1	1	1	1	1	1	1	1	0	0	0	0
a_1	0	0	1	1	1	1	0	0	0	0	1	1	1	1	0	0
a_0	0	1	1	0	0	1	1	0	0	1	1	0	0	1	1	0
f_3	3	3	3	3	3	3	3	3	4	4	4	4	3	3	3	3
f_2	2	2	2	2	3	3	2	2	2	2	2	2	4	4	2	2
f_1	1	1	2	1	1	1	3	1	1	1	2	1	1	1	4	1
f_0	0	1	0	2	0	1	0	3	0	1	0	2	0	1	0	4

Although the binary number $k = (b_{n-1} \ldots b_0)_2$ never appears explicitly in Algorithm L, the focus pointers f_j represent it implicitly in a clever way, so that we can repeatedly form $g(k) = (a_{n-1} \ldots a_0)_2$ by complementing bit $a_{\rho(k)}$ as we should. Let's say that a_j is *passive* when it is underlined, *active* otherwise. Then the focus pointers satisfy the following invariant relations:

1) If a_j is passive and a_{j-1} is active, then f_j is the smallest index $j' > j$ such that $a_{j'}$ is active. (Bits a_n and a_{-1} are considered to be active for purposes of this rule, although they aren't really present in the algorithm.)

2) Otherwise $f_j = j$.

Thus, the rightmost element a_j of a block of passive elements $a_{i-1} \ldots a_{j+1}a_j$, with decreasing subscripts, has a focus f_j that points to the element a_i just to the left of that block. All other elements a_j have f_j pointing to themselves.

In these terms, the first two operations '$j \leftarrow f_0$, $f_0 \leftarrow 0$' in step L3 are equivalent to saying, "Set j to the index of the rightmost active element, and activate all elements to the right of a_j." Notice that if $f_0 = 0$, the operation $f_0 \leftarrow 0$ is redundant; but it doesn't do any harm. The other two operations of L3, '$f_j \leftarrow f_{j+1}$, $f_{j+1} \leftarrow j + 1$', are equivalent to saying, "Make a_j passive," because we know that a_j and a_{j-1} are both active at this point in the computation.

(Again the operation $f_{j+1} \leftarrow j+1$ might be harmlessly redundant.) The net effect of activation and passivation is therefore equivalent to counting in binary notation, as in Algorithm M, with 1-bits passive and 0-bits active.

Algorithm L is almost blindingly fast, because it does only five assignment operations and one test for termination between each visit to a generated n-tuple. But we can do even better. In order to see how, let's consider an application to recreational linguistics: Rudolph Castown, in *Word Ways* **1** (1968), 165–169, noted that all 16 of the ways to intermix the letters of `sins` with the corresponding letters of `fate` produce words that are found in a sufficiently large dictionary of English: `sine`, `sits`, `site`, etc.; and all but three of those words (namely `fane`, `fite`, and `sats`) are sufficiently common as to be unquestionably part of standard English. Therefore it is natural to ask the analogous question for five-letter words: What two strings of five letters will produce the maximum number of words in the Stanford GraphBase, when letters in corresponding positions are swapped in all 32 possible ways?

To answer this question, we need not examine all $\binom{26}{2}^5 = 3{,}625{,}908{,}203{,}125$ essentially different pairs of strings; it suffices to look at all $\binom{5757}{2} = 16{,}568{,}646$ pairs of words in the GraphBase, provided that at least one of those pairs produces at least 17 words, because every set of 17 or more five-letter words obtainable from two five-letter strings must contain two that are "antipodal" (with no corresponding letters in common). For every antipodal pair, we want to determine as rapidly as possible whether the 32 possible subset-swaps produce a significant number of English words.

Every 5-letter word can be represented as a 25-bit number using 5 bits per letter, from `"a"` = 00000 to `"z"` = 11001. A table of 2^{25} bits or bytes will then determine quickly whether a given five-letter string is a word. So the problem is reduced to generating the bit patterns of the 32 potential words obtainable by mixing the letters of two given words, and looking those patterns up in the table. We can proceed as follows, for each pair of 25-bit words w and w':

W1. [Check the difference.] Set $z \leftarrow w \oplus w'$. Reject the word pair (w, w') if $\big((z-m) \oplus z \oplus m\big) \wedge m' \neq 0$, where $m = 2^{20} + 2^{15} + 2^{10} + 2^5 + 1$ and $m' = 2^5 m$; this test eliminates cases where w and w' have a common letter in some position. (See 7.1–(oo); it turns out that 10,614,085 of the 16,568,646 word pairs have no such common letters.)

W2. [Form individual masks.] Set $m_0 \leftarrow z \wedge (2^5 - 1)$, $m_1 \leftarrow z \wedge (2^{10} - 2^5)$, $m_2 \leftarrow z \wedge (2^{15} - 2^{10})$, $m_3 \leftarrow z \wedge (2^{20} - 2^{15})$, and $m_4 \leftarrow z \wedge (2^{25} - 2^{20})$, in preparation for the next step.

W3. [Count words.] Set $l \leftarrow 1$ and $A_0 \leftarrow w$; the variable l will count how many words starting with w we have found so far. Then perform the operations $swap(4)$ defined below.

W4. [Print a record-setting solution.] If l exceeds or equals the current maximum, print A_j for $0 \le j < l$. ∎

The heart of this high-speed method is the sequence of operations $swap(4)$, which should be expanded inline (for example with a macro-processor) to eliminate all unnecessary overhead. It is defined in terms of the basic operation

$sw(j)$: Set $w \leftarrow w \oplus m_j$. Then if w is a word, set $A_l \leftarrow w$ and $l \leftarrow l + 1$.

Given $sw(j)$, which flips the letters in position j, we define

$$
\begin{aligned}
swap(0) &= sw(0); \\
swap(1) &= swap(0), sw(1), swap(0); \\
swap(2) &= swap(1), sw(2), swap(1); \\
swap(3) &= swap(2), sw(3), swap(2); \\
swap(4) &= swap(3), sw(4), swap(3).
\end{aligned}
\tag{22}
$$

Thus $swap(4)$ expands into a sequence of 31 steps $sw(0)$, $sw(1)$, $sw(0)$, $sw(2)$, $\ldots$, $sw(0) = sw(\rho(1))$, $sw(\rho(2))$, $\ldots$, $sw(\rho(31))$; these steps will be used 10 million times. We clearly gain speed by embedding the ruler function values $\rho(k)$ directly into our program, instead of recomputing them repeatedly for each word pair via Algorithm M, G, or L.

The winning pair of words generates a set of 21, namely

$$
\begin{array}{ccccccc}
\texttt{ducks} & \texttt{ducky} & \texttt{duces} & \texttt{dunes} & \texttt{dunks} & \texttt{dinks} & \texttt{dinky} \\
\texttt{dines} & \texttt{dices} & \texttt{dicey} & \texttt{dicky} & \texttt{dicks} & \texttt{picks} & \texttt{picky} \\
\texttt{pines} & \texttt{piney} & \texttt{pinky} & \texttt{pinks} & \texttt{punks} & \texttt{punky} & \texttt{pucks}
\end{array}
\tag{23}
$$

If, for example, $w = \texttt{ducks}$ and $w' = \texttt{piney}$, then $m_0 = \texttt{s} \oplus \texttt{y}$, so the first operation $sw(0)$ changes $\texttt{ducks}$ to $\texttt{ducky}$, which is seen to be a word. The next operation $sw(1)$ applies m_1, which is $\texttt{k} \oplus \texttt{e}$ in the next-to-last letter position, so it produces the nonword $\texttt{ducey}$. Another application of $sw(0)$ changes $\texttt{ducey}$ to $\texttt{duces}$ (a legal term generally followed by the word $\texttt{tecum}$). And so on. All word pairs can be processed by this method in at most a few seconds.

Further streamlining is also possible. For example, once we have found a pair that yields k words, we can reject later pairs as soon as they generate $33 - k$ nonwords. But the method we've discussed is already quite fast, and it demonstrates the fact that even the loopless Algorithm L can be beaten.

Fans of Algorithm L may, of course, complain that we have speeded up the process only in the small special case $n = 5$, while Algorithm L solves the generation problem for n in general. A similar idea does, however, work also for general values of $n > 5$: We can expand out a program so that it rapidly generates all 32 settings of the rightmost bits $a_4 a_3 a_2 a_1 a_0$, as above; then we can apply Algorithm L after every 32 steps, using it to generate successive changes to the other bits $a_{n-1} \ldots a_5$. This approach reduces the amount of unnecessary work done by Algorithm L by nearly a factor of 32.

Other binary Gray codes. The Gray binary code $g(0)$, $g(1)$, $\ldots$, $g(2^n - 1)$ is only one of many ways to traverse all possible n-bit strings while changing only a single bit at each step. Let us say that, in general, a "Gray cycle" on binary n-tuples is *any* sequence $(v_0, v_1, \ldots, v_{2^n-1})$ that includes every n-tuple and has the property that v_k differs from $v_{(k+1) \bmod 2^n}$ in just one bit position. Thus, in the terminology of graph theory, a Gray cycle is an oriented Hamiltonian

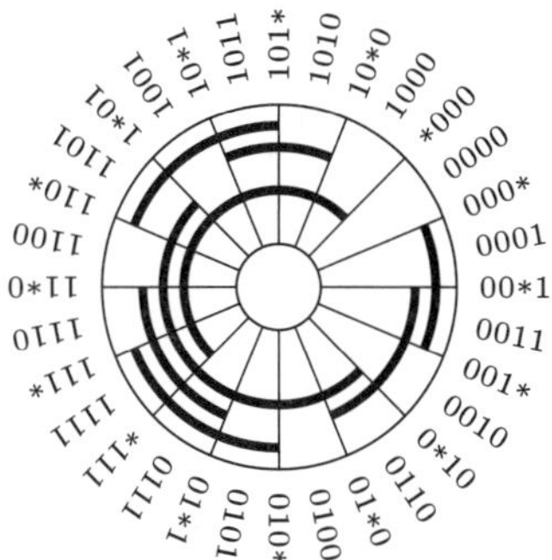

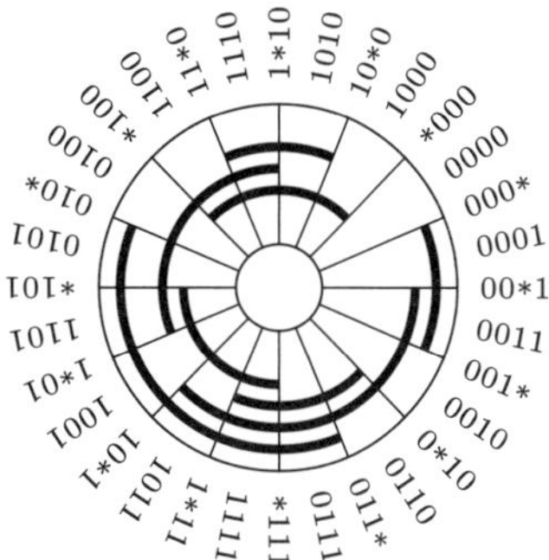

Fig. 13. (a) Complementary Gray code.   (b) Balanced Gray code.

cycle on the n-cube. We can assume that subscripts have been chosen so that $v_0 = 0\ldots0$.

If we think of the v's as binary numbers, there are integers $\delta_0 \ldots \delta_{2^n-1}$ such that

$$v_{(k+1)\bmod 2^n} = v_k \oplus 2^{\delta_k}, \qquad \text{for } 0 \le k < 2^n; \tag{24}$$

this so-called "delta sequence" is another way to describe a Gray cycle. For example, the delta sequence for standard Gray binary when $n = 3$ is 01020102; it is essentially the ruler function $\delta_k = \rho(k+1)$ of (13), but the final value δ_{2^n-1} is $n-1$ instead of n, so that the cycle closes. The individual elements δ_k always lie in the range $0 \le \delta_k < n$, and they are called "coordinates."

Let $d(n)$ be the number of different delta sequences that define an n-bit Gray cycle, and let $c(n)$ be the number of "canonical" delta sequences in which each coordinate k appears before the first appearance of $k + 1$. Then $d(n) = n!\,c(n)$, because every permutation of the coordinate numbers in a delta sequence obviously produces another delta sequence. The only possible canonical delta sequences for $n \le 3$ are easily seen to be

$$00; \qquad 0101; \qquad 01020102 \quad \text{and} \quad 01210121. \tag{25}$$

Therefore $c(1) = c(2) = 1$, $c(3) = 2$; $d(1) = 1$, $d(2) = 2$, and $d(3) = 12$. A straightforward computer calculation, using techniques for the enumeration of Hamiltonian cycles that we will study later, establishes the next values,

$$\begin{aligned}
c(4) &= 112; & d(4) &= 2688; \\
c(5) &= 15{,}109{,}096; & d(5) &= 1{,}813{,}091{,}520.
\end{aligned} \tag{26}$$

No simple pattern is evident, and the numbers grow quite rapidly (see exercise 45); therefore it's a fairly safe bet that nobody will ever know the exact values of $c(8)$ and $d(8)$.

Since the number of possibilities is so huge, people have been encouraged to look for Gray cycles that have additional useful properties. For example, Fig. 13(a) shows a 4-bit Gray cycle in which every string $a_3a_2a_1a_0$ is diametrically opposite to its complement $\bar{a}_3\bar{a}_2\bar{a}_1\bar{a}_0$. Such coding schemes are possible whenever the number of bits is even (see exercise 49).

An even more interesting Gray cycle, found by G. C. Tootill [*Proc. IEE* **103**, Part B Supplement (1956), 435], is shown in Fig. 13(b). This one has the same number of changes in each of the four coordinate tracks, hence all coordinates share equally in the activities. Gray cycles that are balanced in a similar way can in fact be constructed for all larger values of n, by using the following versatile method to extend a cycle from n bits to $n + 2$ bits:

Theorem D. *Let $\alpha_1 j_1 \alpha_2 j_2 \ldots \alpha_l j_l$ be a delta sequence for an n-bit Gray cycle, where each j_k is a single coordinate, each α_k is a possibly empty sequence of coordinates, and l is odd. Then*

$$\alpha_1(n{+}1)\alpha_1^R n\alpha_1$$
$$j_1\alpha_2 n\alpha_2^R(n{+}1)\alpha_2 \; j_2\alpha_3(n{+}1)\alpha_3^R n\alpha_3 \;\ldots\; j_{l-1}\alpha_l(n{+}1)\alpha_l^R n\alpha_l \qquad (27)$$
$$(n{+}1)\alpha_l^R j_{l-1}\alpha_{l-1}^R \ldots \alpha_2^R j_1 \alpha_1^R n$$

is the delta sequence of an $(n + 2)$-bit Gray cycle.

For example, if we start with the sequence $010\underline{2}010\underline{2}$ for $n = 3$ and let the three underlined elements be j_1, j_2, j_3, the new sequence (27) for a 5-bit cycle is

$$01410301020131024201043401020103. \qquad (28)$$

Proof. Let α_k have length m_k and let v_{kt} be the vertex reached if we start at $0\ldots0$ and apply the coordinate changes $\alpha_1 j_1 \ldots \alpha_{k-1} j_{k-1}$ and the first t of α_k. We need to prove that all vertices $00v_{kt}$, $01v_{kt}$, $10v_{kt}$, and $11v_{kt}$ occur when (27) is used, for $1 \le k \le l$ and $0 \le t \le m_k$. (The leftmost coordinate is $n{+}1$.)

Starting with $000\ldots0 = 00v_{10}$, we proceed to obtain the vertices

$$00v_{11}, \ldots, 00v_{1m_1}, 10v_{1m_1}, \ldots, 10v_{10}, 11v_{10}, \ldots, 11v_{1m_1};$$

then j_1 yields $11v_{20}$, which is followed by

$$11v_{21}, \ldots, 11v_{2m_2}, 10v_{2m_2}, \ldots, 10v_{20}, 00v_{20}, \ldots, 00v_{2m_2};$$

then comes $00v_{30}$, etc., and we eventually reach $11v_{lm_l}$. The glorious finale then uses the third line of (27) to generate all the missing vertices $01v_{lm_l}, \ldots, 01v_{10}$ and take us back to $000\ldots0$. $\blacksquare$

The *transition counts* $(c_0, \ldots, c_{n-1})$ of a delta sequence are defined by letting c_j be the number of times $\delta_k = j$. For example, (28) has transition counts $(12, 8, 4, 4, 4)$, and it arose from a sequence with transition counts $(4, 2, 2)$. If we choose the original delta sequence carefully and underline appropriate elements j_k, we can obtain transition counts that are as equal as possible:

Corollary B. *For all $n \ge 1$, there is an n-bit Gray cycle with transition counts $(c_0, c_1, \ldots, c_{n-1})$ that satisfy the condition*

$$|c_j - c_k| \le 2 \qquad \text{for } 0 \le j < k < n. \qquad (29)$$

(This is the best possible balance condition, because each c_j must be an even number, and we must have $c_0 + c_1 + \cdots + c_{n-1} = 2^n$. Indeed, condition (29) holds if and only if $n - r$ of the counts are equal to $2q$ and r are equal to $2q + 2$, where $q = \lfloor 2^{n-1}/n \rfloor$ and $r = 2^{n-1} \bmod n$.)

Proof. Given a delta sequence for an n-bit Gray cycle with transition counts $(c_0, \ldots, c_{n-1})$, the counts for cycle (27) are obtained by starting with the values $(c'_0, \ldots, c'_{n-1}, c'_n, c'_{n+1}) = (4c_0, \ldots, 4c_{n-1}, l+1, l+1)$, then subtracting 2 from c'_{j_k} for $1 \le k < l$ and subtracting 4 from c'_{j_l}. For example, when $n = 3$ we can obtain a balanced 5-bit Gray cycle having transition counts $(8 - 2, 16 - 10, 8, 6, 6) = (6, 6, 8, 6, 6)$ if we apply Theorem D to the delta sequence $\underline{01}2\underline{1}0\underline{1}2\underline{1}$. Exercise 51 works out the details for other values of n. ∎

Another important class of n-bit Gray cycles in which each of the coordinate tracks has equal responsibility arises when we consider *run lengths*, namely the distances between consecutive appearances of the same δ value. Standard Gray binary code has run length 2 in the least significant position, and this can lead to a loss of accuracy when precise measurements need to be made [see, for example, the discussion by G. M. Lawrence and W. E. McClintock, *Proc. SPIE* **2831** (1996), 104–111]. But all runs have length 4 or more in the remarkable 5-bit Gray cycle whose delta sequence is

$$(0123042103210423)^2. \tag{30}$$

Let $r(n)$ be the maximum value r such that an n-bit Gray cycle can be found in which all runs have length $\ge r$. Clearly $r(1) = 1$, and $r(2) = r(3) = r(4) = 2$; and it is easy to see that $r(n)$ must be less than n when $n > 2$, hence (30) proves that $r(5) = 4$. Exhaustive computer searches establish the values $r(6) = 4$ and $r(7) = 5$. Indeed, a fairly straightforward backtrack calculation for the case $n = 7$ needs a tree of only about 60 million nodes to determine that $r(7) < 6$, and exercise 61(a) constructs a 7-bit cycle with no run shorter than 5. The exact values of $r(n)$ are unknown for $n \ge 8$; but $r(10)$ is almost certainly 8, and interesting constructions are known by which we can prove that $r(n) = n - O(\log n)$ as $n \to \infty$. (See exercises 60–64.)

***Binary Gray paths.** We have defined an n-bit Gray cycle as a way to arrange all binary n-tuples into a sequence $(v_0, v_1, \ldots, v_{2^n-1})$ with the property that v_k is adjacent to v_{k+1} in the n-cube for $0 \le k < 2^n$, and such that v_{2^n-1} is also adjacent to v_0. The cyclic property is nice, but not always essential; and sometimes we can do better without it. Therefore we say that an n-bit *Gray path*, also commonly called a *Gray code*, is any sequence that satisfies the conditions of a Gray cycle except that the last element need not be adjacent to the first. In other words, a Gray cycle is a Hamiltonian *cycle* on the vertices of the n-cube, but a Gray code is simply a Hamiltonian *path* on that graph.

The most important binary Gray paths that are not also Gray cycles are n-bit sequences $(v_0, v_1, \ldots, v_{2^n-1})$ that are *monotonic*, in the sense that

$$\nu(v_k) \le \nu(v_{k+2}) \qquad \text{for } 0 \le k < 2^n - 2. \tag{31}$$

(Here, as elsewhere, we use ν to denote the "weight" or the "sideways sum" of a binary string, namely the number of 1s that it has.) Trial and error shows that

Fig. 14. Examples of
8-bit Gray codes:

    a) standard;
    b) balanced;
    c) complementary;
    d) long-run;
    e) nonlocal;
    f) monotonic;
    g) trend-free.

(a)   (b)   (c)   (d)   (e)   (f)   (g)

there are essentially only two monotonic n-bit Gray codes for each $n \le 4$, one starting with 0^n and the other starting with $0^{n-1}1$. The two for $n = 3$ are

$$000, 001, 011, 010, 110, 100, 101, 111; \qquad (32)$$
$$001, 000, 010, 110, 100, 101, 111, 011. \qquad (33)$$

The two for $n = 4$ are slightly less obvious, but not really difficult to discover.

Since $\nu(v_{k+1}) = \nu(v_k) \pm 1$ whenever v_k is adjacent to v_{k+1}, we obviously can't strengthen (31) to the requirement that all n-tuples be strictly sorted by weight. But relation (31) is strong enough to determine the weight of each v_k, given k and the weight of v_0, because we know that exactly $\binom{n}{j}$ of the n-tuples have weight j.

Figure 14 summarizes our discussions so far, by illustrating seven of the zillions of Gray codes that make a grand tour through all 256 of the possible 8-bit bytes. Black squares represent ones and white squares represent zeros. Figure 14(a) is the standard Gray binary code, while Fig. 14(b) is balanced with exactly $256/8 = 32$ transitions in each coordinate position. Fig. 14(c) is a Gray code analogous to Fig. 13(a), in which the bottom 128 codes are complements of the top 128. In Fig. 14(d), the transitions in each coordinate position never occur closer than five steps apart; in other words, all run lengths are at least 5. The cycle in Fig. 14(e) is *nonlocal* in the sense of exercise 59. Fig. 14(f) shows a monotonic path for $n = 8$; notice how black it gets near the bottom. Finally, Fig. 14(g) illustrates a Gray code that is totally nonmonotonic, in the sense that the center of gravity of the black squares lies exactly at the halfway point in each column. Standard Gray binary code has this property in seven of the coordinate positions, but Fig. 14(g) achieves perfect black-white weight balance in all eight. Such codes are called *trend-free*; they are important in the design of agricultural and other experiments (see exercises 75 and 76).

Carla Savage and Peter Winkler [*J. Combinatorial Theory* **A70** (1995), 230–248] found an elegant way to construct monotonic binary Gray codes for all $n > 0$. Such paths are necessarily built from subpaths P_{nj} in which all transitions are between n-tuples of weights j and $j + 1$. Savage and Winkler defined suitable subpaths recursively by letting $P_{10} = 0, 1$ and, for all $n > 0$,

$$P_{(n+1)j} = 1P_{n(j-1)}^{\pi_n},\ 0P_{nj}; \qquad (34)$$
$$P_{nj} = \emptyset \quad \text{if } j < 0 \text{ or } j \ge n. \qquad (35)$$

Here π_n is a permutation of the coordinates that we will specify later, and the notation P^π means that every element $a_{n-1} \dots a_1 a_0$ of the sequence P is replaced by $b_{n-1} \dots b_1 b_0$, where $b_{j\pi} = a_j$. (We don't define P^π by letting $b_j = a_{j\pi}$, because we want $(2^j)^\pi$ to be $2^{j\pi}$.) It follows, for example, that

$$P_{20} = 0P_{10} = 00,\ 01 \qquad (36)$$

because $P_{1(-1)}$ is vacuous; also

$$P_{21} = 1P_{10}^{\pi_1} = 10,\ 11 \qquad (37)$$

because P_{11} is vacuous and π_1 must be the identity permutation. In general, P_{nj} is a sequence of n-bit strings containing exactly $\binom{n-1}{j}$ strings of weight j interleaved with $\binom{n-1}{j}$ strings of weight $j+1$.

Let α_{nj} and ω_{nj} be the first and last elements of P_{nj}. Then we easily find

$$\omega_{nj} = 0^{n-j-1}1^{j+1}, \qquad \text{for } 0 \le j < n; \tag{38}$$

$$\alpha_{n0} = 0^n, \qquad \text{for } n > 0; \tag{39}$$

$$\alpha_{nj} = 1\alpha_{(n-1)(j-1)}^{\pi_{n-1}}, \qquad \text{for } 1 \le j < n. \tag{40}$$

In particular, α_{nj} always has weight j, and ω_{nj} always has weight $j+1$. We will define permutations π_n of $\{0, 1, \ldots, n-1\}$ so that both of the sequences

$$P_{n0}, \; P_{n1}^R, \; P_{n2}, \; P_{n3}^R, \; \ldots \tag{41}$$

$$\text{and } P_{n0}^R, \; P_{n1}, \; P_{n2}^R, \; P_{n3}, \; \ldots \tag{42}$$

are monotonic binary Gray paths for $n = 1, 2, 3, \ldots$. In fact, the monotonicity is clear, so only the Grayness is in doubt; and the sequences (41), (42) link up nicely because the adjacencies

$$\alpha_{n0} \—\ \alpha_{n1} \—\ \cdots \—\ \alpha_{n(n-1)}, \qquad \omega_{n0} \—\ \omega_{n1} \—\ \cdots \—\ \omega_{n(n-1)} \tag{43}$$

follow immediately from (34), regardless of the permutations π_n. Thus the crucial point is the transition at the comma in formula (34), which makes $P_{(n+1)j}$ a Gray subpath if and only if

$$\omega_{n(j-1)}^{\pi_n} = \alpha_{nj} \qquad \text{for } 0 < j < n. \tag{44}$$

For example, when $n = 2$ and $j = 1$ we need $(01)^{\pi_2} = \alpha_{21} = 10$, by (38)–(40); hence π_2 must transpose coordinates 0 and 1. The general formula (see exercise 71) turns out to be

$$\pi_n = \sigma_n \pi_{n-1}^2, \tag{45}$$

where σ_n is the n-cycle $(n{-}1 \; \ldots \; 1\,0)$. The first few cases are therefore

$$\begin{aligned}
\pi_1 &= (0), & \pi_4 &= (0\,3), \\
\pi_2 &= (0\,1), & \pi_5 &= (0\,4\,3\,2\,1), \\
\pi_3 &= (0\,2\,1), & \pi_6 &= (0\,5\,2\,4\,1\,3);
\end{aligned}$$

no simple "closed form" for the magic permutations π_n is apparent. Exercise 73 shows that the Savage–Winkler codes can be generated efficiently.

Nonbinary Gray codes. We have studied the case of binary n-tuples in great detail, because it is the simplest, most classical, most applicable, and most thoroughly explored part of the subject. But of course there are numerous applications in which we want to generate $(a_1, \ldots, a_n)$ with coordinates in the more general ranges $0 \le a_j < m_j$, as in Algorithm M. Gray codes apply nicely to this case as well.

Consider, for example, decimal digits, where we want $0 \le a_j < 10$ for each j. Is there a decimal way to count that is analogous to the Gray binary code, changing only one digit at a time? Yes; in fact, *two* natural schemes are available. In the first, called *reflected Gray decimal*, the sequence for counting up to a thousand with 3-digit strings has the form

$$000, 001, \ldots, 009, 019, 018, \ldots, 011, 010, 020, 021, \ldots, 091, 090, 190, 191, \ldots, 900,$$

with each coordinate moving alternately from 0 up to 9 and then back down from 9 to 0. In the second, called *modular Gray decimal*, the digits always increase by 1 mod 10, therefore they "wrap around" from 9 to 0:

$$000, 001, \ldots, 009, 019, 010, \ldots, 017, 018, 028, 029, \ldots, 099, 090, 190, 191, \ldots, 900.$$

In both cases the digit that changes on step k is determined by the radix-ten ruler function $\rho_{10}(k)$, the largest power of 10 that divides k. Therefore each n-tuple of digits occurs exactly once: We generate 10^j different settings of the rightmost j digits before changing any of the others, for $1 \le j \le n$.

In general, the reflected Gray code in any mixed-radix system can be regarded as a permutation of the nonnegative integers, a function that maps an ordinary mixed-radix number

$$k = \begin{bmatrix} b_{n-1}, & \ldots, & b_1, & b_0 \\ m_{n-1}, & \ldots, & m_1, & m_0 \end{bmatrix} = b_{n-1}m_{n-2}\ldots m_1 m_0 + \cdots + b_1 m_0 + b_0 \qquad (46)$$

into its reflected-Gray equivalent

$$\hat{g}(k) = \begin{bmatrix} a_{n-1}, & \ldots, & a_1, & a_0 \\ m_{n-1}, & \ldots, & m_1, & m_0 \end{bmatrix} = a_{n-1}m_{n-2}\ldots m_1 m_0 + \cdots + a_1 m_0 + a_0, \qquad (47)$$

just as (7) does this in the special case of binary numbers. Let

$$A_j = \begin{bmatrix} a_{n-1}, & \ldots, & a_j \\ m_{n-1}, & \ldots, & m_j \end{bmatrix}, \qquad B_j = \begin{bmatrix} b_{n-1}, & \ldots, & b_j \\ m_{n-1}, & \ldots, & m_j \end{bmatrix}, \qquad (48)$$

with $A_n = B_n = 0$, so that when $0 \le j < n$ we have

$$A_j = m_j A_{j+1} + a_j \qquad \text{and} \qquad B_j = m_j B_{j+1} + b_j. \qquad (49)$$

The rule connecting the a's and b's is not difficult to derive by induction on $n - j$:

$$a_j = \begin{cases} b_j, & \text{if } B_{j+1} \text{ is even;} \\ m_j - 1 - b_j, & \text{if } B_{j+1} \text{ is odd.} \end{cases} \qquad (50)$$

(Here we are numbering the coordinates of the n-tuples $(a_{n-1}, \ldots, a_1, a_0)$ and $(b_{n-1}, \ldots, b_1, b_0)$ from right to left, for consistency with (7) and the conventions of mixed-radix notation in Eq. 4.1–(9). Readers who prefer notations like $(a_1, \ldots, a_n)$ can change j to $n - j$ in all the formulas if they wish.) Going the other way, we have

$$b_j = \begin{cases} a_j, & \text{if } a_{j+1} + a_{j+2} + \cdots \text{ is even;} \\ m_j - 1 - a_j, & \text{if } a_{j+1} + a_{j+2} + \cdots \text{ is odd.} \end{cases} \qquad (51)$$

Curiously, rule (50) and its inverse in (51) are exactly the same when all of the radices m_j are odd. In Gray ternary code, for example, when $m_0 = m_1 = \cdots = 3$, we have $\hat{g}\big((10010211012)_3\big) = (12210211010)_3$ and also $\hat{g}\big((12210211010)_3\big) =$

$(10010211012)_3$. Exercise 78 proves (50) and (51), and discusses similar formulas that hold in the modular case.

We can in fact generate such Gray sequences looplessly, generalizing Algorithms M and L:

Algorithm H (*Loopless reflected mixed-radix Gray generation*). This algorithm visits all n-tuples $(a_{n-1}, \ldots, a_0)$ such that $0 \le a_j < m_j$ for $0 \le j < n$, changing only one coordinate by ± 1 at each step. It maintains an array of focus pointers $(f_n, \ldots, f_0)$ to control the actions as in Algorithm L, together with an array of directions $(o_{n-1}, \ldots, o_0)$. We assume that each radix m_j is ≥ 2.

H1. [Initialize.] Set $a_j \leftarrow 0$, $f_j \leftarrow j$, and $o_j \leftarrow 1$, for $0 \le j < n$; also set $f_n \leftarrow n$.

H2. [Visit.] Visit the n-tuple $(a_{n-1}, \ldots, a_1, a_0)$.

H3. [Choose j.] Set $j \leftarrow f_0$ and $f_0 \leftarrow 0$. (As in Algorithm L, j was the rightmost active coordinate; all elements to its right have now been reactivated.)

H4. [Change coordinate j.] Terminate if $j = n$; otherwise set $a_j \leftarrow a_j + o_j$.

H5. [Reflect?] If $a_j = 0$ or $a_j = m_j - 1$, set $o_j \leftarrow -o_j$, $f_j \leftarrow f_{j+1}$, and $f_{j+1} \leftarrow j + 1$. (Coordinate j has thus become passive.) Return to H2. ∎

A similar algorithm generates the modular variation (see exercise 77).

***Subforests.** An interesting and instructive generalization of Algorithm H, discovered by Y. Koda and F. Ruskey [*J. Algorithms* **15** (1993), 324–340], sheds further light on the subject of Gray codes and loopless generation. Suppose we have a forest of n nodes, and we want to visit all of its "principal subforests," namely all subsets of nodes S such that if x is in S and x is not a root, the parent of x is also in S. For example, the 7-node forest has 33 such subsets, corresponding to the black nodes in the following 33 diagrams:

$$\tag{52}$$

Notice that if we read the top row from left to right, the middle row from right to left, and the bottom row from left to right, the status of exactly one node changes at each step.

If the given forest consists of degenerate nonbranching trees, the principal subforests are equivalent to mixed-radix numbers. For example, a forest like

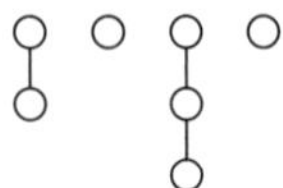

has $3 \times 2 \times 4 \times 2$ principal subforests, corresponding to 4-tuples (x_1, x_2, x_3, x_4) such that $0 \le x_1 < 3$, $0 \le x_2 < 2$, $0 \le x_3 < 4$, and $0 \le x_4 < 2$; the value of x_j is the number of nodes selected in the jth forest. When the algorithm of Koda and Ruskey is applied to such a forest, it will visit the subforests in the same order as the reflected Gray code on radices $(3, 2, 4, 2)$.

Algorithm K (*Loopless reflected subforest generation*). Given a forest whose nodes are $(1, \ldots, n)$ when arranged in postorder, this algorithm visits all binary n-tuples $(a_1, \ldots, a_n)$ such that $a_p \geq a_q$ whenever p is a parent of q. (Thus, $a_p = 1$ means that p is a node in the current subforest.) Exactly one bit a_j changes between one visit and the next. Focus pointers $(f_0, f_1, \ldots, f_n)$ analogous to those of Algorithm L are used together with additional arrays of pointers $(l_0, l_1, \ldots, l_n)$ and $(r_0, r_1, \ldots, r_n)$, which represent a doubly linked list called the "current fringe." The current fringe contains all nodes of the current subforest and their children; r_0 points to its leftmost node and l_0 to its rightmost.

An auxiliary array $(c_0, c_1, \ldots, c_n)$ defines the forest as follows: If p has no children, $c_p = 0$; otherwise c_p is the leftmost (smallest) child of p. Also c_0 is the leftmost root of the forest itself. When the algorithm begins, we assume that $r_p = q$ and $l_q = p$ whenever p and q are consecutive children of the same family. Thus, for example, the forest in (52) has the postorder numbering

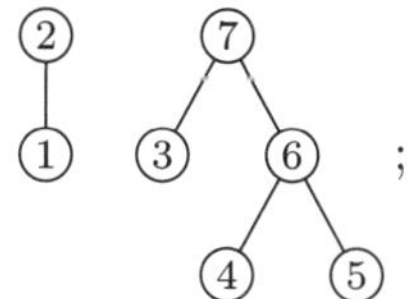

therefore we should have $(c_0, \ldots, c_7) = (2, 0, 1, 0, 0, 0, 4, 3)$ and $r_2 = 7$, $l_7 = 2$, $r_3 = 6$, $l_6 = 3$, $r_4 = 5$, and $l_5 = 4$ at the beginning of step K1 in this case.

K1. [Initialize.] Set $a_j \leftarrow 0$ and $f_j \leftarrow j$ for $1 \leq j \leq n$, thereby making the initial subforest empty and all nodes active. Set $f_0 \leftarrow 0$, $l_0 \leftarrow n$, $r_n \leftarrow 0$, $r_0 \leftarrow c_0$, and $l_{c_0} \leftarrow 0$, thereby putting all roots into the current fringe.

K2. [Visit.] Visit the subforest defined by $(a_1, \ldots, a_n)$.

K3. [Choose p.] Set $q \leftarrow l_0$, $p \leftarrow f_q$. (Now p is the rightmost active node of the fringe.) Also set $f_q \leftarrow q$ (thereby activating all nodes to p's right).

K4. [Check a_p.] Terminate the algorithm if $p = 0$. Otherwise go to K6 if $a_p = 1$.

K5. [Insert p's children.] Set $a_p \leftarrow 1$. Then, if $c_p \neq 0$, set $q \leftarrow r_p$, $l_q \leftarrow p - 1$, $r_{p-1} \leftarrow q$, $r_p \leftarrow c_p$, $l_{c_p} \leftarrow p$ (thereby putting p's children to the right of p in the fringe). Go to K7.

K6. [Delete p's children.] Set $a_p \leftarrow 0$. Then, if $c_p \neq 0$, set $q \leftarrow r_{p-1}$, $r_p \leftarrow q$, $l_q \leftarrow p$ (thereby removing p's children from the fringe).

K7. [Make p passive.] (At this point we know that p is active.) Set $f_p \leftarrow f_{l_p}$ and $f_{l_p} \leftarrow l_p$. Return to K2. $\blacksquare$

The reader is encouraged to play through this algorithm on examples like (52), in order to understand the beautiful mechanism by which the fringe grows and shrinks at just the right times.

***Shift register sequences.** A completely different way to generate all n-tuples of
m-ary digits is also possible: We can generate one digit at a time, and repeatedly
work with the n most recently generated digits, thus passing from one n-tuple
$(x_0, x_1, \ldots, x_{n-1})$ to another one $(x_1, \ldots, x_{n-1}, x_n)$ by shifting an appropriate
new digit in at the right. For example, Fig. 15 shows how all 5-bit numbers can
be obtained as blocks of 5 consecutive bits in a certain cyclic pattern of length 32.
This general idea has already been discussed in some of the exercises of Sections
2.3.4.2 and 3.2.2, and we now are ready to explore it further.

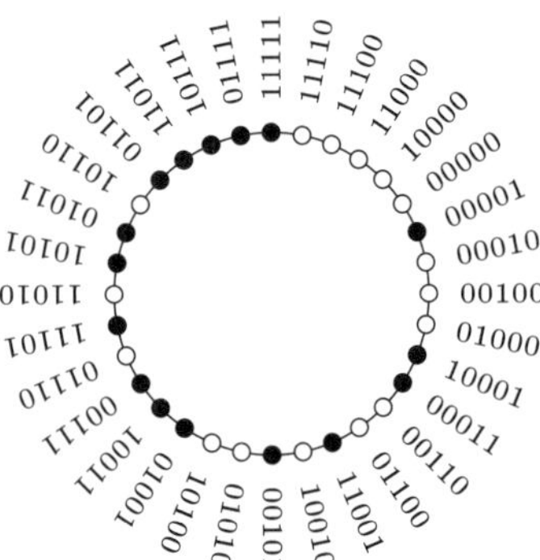

Fig. 15.

A de Bruijn cycle
for 5-bit numbers.

Algorithm S (*Generic shift register generation*). This algorithm visits all n-
tuples $(a_1, \ldots, a_n)$ such that $0 \le a_j < m$ for $1 \le j \le n$, provided that a suitable
function f is used in step S3.

S1. [Initialize.] Set $a_j \leftarrow 0$ for $-n < j \le 0$ and $k \leftarrow 1$.

S2. [Visit.] Visit the n-tuple $(a_{k-n}, \ldots, a_{k-1})$. Terminate if $k = m^n$.

S3. [Advance.] Set $a_k \leftarrow f(a_{k-n}, \ldots, a_{k-1})$, $k \leftarrow k + 1$, and return to S2. ∎

Every function f that makes Algorithm S valid corresponds to a cycle of
m^n radix-m digits such that every combination of n digits occurs consecutively
in the cycle. For example, the case $m = 2$ and $n = 5$ illustrated in Fig. 15
corresponds to the binary cycle

$$00000100011001010011101011011111; \tag{53}$$

and the first m^2 digits of the infinite sequence

$$00110212203132330414243440\ldots \tag{54}$$

yield an appropriate cycle for $n = 2$ and arbitrary m. Such cycles are commonly
called m-ary *de Bruijn cycles*, because N. G. de Bruijn treated the binary case
for arbitrary n in *Indagationes Mathematicæ* **8** (1946), 461–467.

Exercise 2.3.4.2–23 proves that exactly $m!^{m^{n-1}}/m^n$ functions f have the
required properties. That's a huge number, but only a few of those functions are
known to be efficiently computable. We will discuss three kinds of f that appear
to be the most useful.

Table 1

PARAMETERS FOR ALGORITHM A

$3:1$	$8:1,5$	$13:1,3$	$18:7$	$23:5$	$28:3$
$4:1$	$9:4$	$14:1,11$	$19:1,5$	$24:1,3$	$29:2$
$5:2$	$10:3$	$15:1$	$20:3$	$25:3$	$30:1,15$
$6:1$	$11:2$	$16:2,3$	$21:2$	$26:1,7$	$31:3$
$7:1$	$12:3,4$	$17:3$	$22:1,7$	$27:1,7$	$32:1,27$

The entries '$n:s$' or '$n:s,t$' mean that the polynomials $x^n + x^s + 1$ or $x^n + (x^s + 1)(x^t + 1)$ are primitive modulo 2. Additional values up to $n = 168$ have been tabulated by W. Stahnke, *Math. Comp.* **27** (1973), 977–980.

The first important case occurs when m is a prime number, and f is the almost-linear recurrence

$$f(x_1,\ldots,x_n) = \begin{cases} c_1, & \text{if } (x_1,x_2,\ldots,x_n) = (0,0,\ldots,0); \\ 0, & \text{if } (x_1,x_2,\ldots,x_n) = (1,0,\ldots,0); \\ (c_1x_1 + c_2x_2 + \cdots + c_nx_n) \bmod m, & \text{otherwise.} \end{cases} \qquad (55)$$

Here the coefficients $(c_1,\ldots,c_n)$ must be such that

$$x^n - c_nx^{n-1} - \cdots - c_2x - c_1 \qquad (56)$$

is a primitive polynomial modulo m, in the sense discussed following Eq. 3.2.2–(9). The number of such polynomials is $\varphi(m^n - 1)/n$, large enough to allow us to find one in which only a few of the c's are nonzero. [This construction goes back to a pioneering paper of Willem Mantel, *Nieuw Archief voor Wiskunde* (2) **1** (1897), 172–184.]

For example, suppose $m = 2$. We can generate binary n-tuples with a very simple loopless procedure:

Algorithm A (*Almost-linear bit-shift generation*). This algorithm visits all n-bit vectors, by using either a special offset s [Case 1] or two special offsets s and t [Case 2], as found in Table 1.

A1. [Initialize.] Set $(x_0, x_1,\ldots, x_{n-1}) \leftarrow (1,0,\ldots,0)$ and $k \leftarrow 0$, $j \leftarrow s$. In Case 2, also set $i \leftarrow t$ and $h \leftarrow s + t$.

A2. [Visit.] Visit the n-tuple $(x_{k-1},\ldots,x_0,x_{n-1},\ldots,x_{k+1},x_k)$.

A3. [Test for end.] If $x_k \neq 0$, set $r \leftarrow 0$; otherwise set $r \leftarrow r + 1$, and go to A6 if $r = n - 1$. (We have just seen r consecutive zeros.)

A4. [Shift.] Set $k \leftarrow (k - 1) \bmod n$ and $j \leftarrow (j - 1) \bmod n$. In Case 2 also set $i \leftarrow (i - 1) \bmod n$ and $h \leftarrow (h - 1) \bmod n$.

A5. [Compute a new bit.] Set $x_k \leftarrow x_k \oplus x_j$ [Case 1] or $x_k \leftarrow x_k \oplus x_j \oplus x_i \oplus x_h$ [Case 2]. Return to A2.

A6. [Finish.] Visit $(0,\ldots,0)$ and terminate. ∎

Appropriate offset parameters s and possibly t almost certainly exist for all n, because primitive polynomials are so abundant; for example, eight different choices of (s,t) would work when $n = 32$, and Table 1 merely lists the smallest.

However, a rigorous proof of existence in all cases lies well beyond the present state of mathematical knowledge.

Our first construction of de Bruijn cycles, in (55), was algebraic, relying for its validity on the theory of finite fields. A similar method that works when m is not a prime number appears in exercise 3.2.2–21. Our next construction, by contrast, will be purely combinatorial. In fact, it is strongly related to the idea of modular Gray m-ary codes.

Algorithm R (*Recursive de Bruijn cycle generation*). Suppose $f()$ is a coroutine that will output the successive digits of an m-ary de Bruijn cycle of length m^n, beginning with n zeros, when it is invoked repeatedly. This algorithm is a similar coroutine that outputs a cycle of length m^{n+1}, provided that $n \geq 2$. It maintains three private variables x, y, and t; variable x should initially be zero.

R1. [Output.] Output x. Go to R3 if $x \neq 0$ and $t \geq n$.

R2. [Invoke f.] Set $y \leftarrow f()$.

R3. [Count ones.] If $y = 1$, set $t \leftarrow t + 1$; otherwise set $t \leftarrow 0$.

R4. [Skip one?] If $t = n$ and $x \neq 0$, go back to R2.

R5. [Adjust x.] Set $x \leftarrow (x + y) \bmod m$ and return to R1. ∎

For example, let $m = 3$ and $n = 2$. If $f()$ produces the infinite 9-cycle

$$001102122\ 001102122\ 0\ldots, \tag{57}$$

then Algorithm R will produce the following infinite 27-cycle at step R1:

$$
\begin{aligned}
y &= \ 001021220011110212200102122\ 001\ldots \\
t &= \ 001001000012340010000100100\ 001\ldots \\
x &= 000110102220120020211122121\ 0001\ldots
\end{aligned}
$$

The proof that Algorithm R works correctly is interesting and instructive (see exercise 93). And the proof of the next algorithm, which *doubles* the window size n, is even more so (see exercise 95).

Algorithm D (*Doubly recursive de Bruijn cycle generation*). Suppose $f()$ and $f'()$ are coroutines that each will output the successive digits of an m-ary de Bruijn cycle of length m^n when invoked repeatedly, beginning with n zeros. (The two cycles are identical, but they must be generated by independent coroutines, because we will consume their values at different rates.) This algorithm is a similar coroutine that outputs a cycle of length m^{2n}. It maintains six private variables x, y, t, x', y', and t'; variables x and x' should initially be m.

The special parameter r must be set to a constant value such that

$$0 \leq r \leq m \qquad \text{and} \qquad \gcd(m^n - r,\ m^n + r) = 2. \tag{58}$$

The best choice is usually $r = 1$ when m is odd and $r = 2$ when m is even.

D1. [Possibly invoke f.] If $t \neq n$ or $x \geq r$, set $y \leftarrow f()$.

D2. [Count repeats.] If $x \neq y$, set $x \leftarrow y$ and $t \leftarrow 1$. Otherwise set $t \leftarrow t + 1$.

D3. [Output from f.] Output the current value of x.

D4. [Invoke f'.] Set $y' \leftarrow f'()$.

D5. [Count repeats.] If $x' \neq y'$, set $x' \leftarrow y'$ and $t' \leftarrow 1$. Otherwise set $t' \leftarrow t'+1$.

D6. [Possibly reject f'.] If $t' = n$ and $x' < r$ and either $t < n$ or $x' < x$, go to D4. If $t' = n$ and $x' < r$ and $x' = x$, go to D3.

D7. [Output from f'.] Output the current value of x'. Return to D3 if $t' = n$ and $x' < r$; otherwise return to D1. $\blacksquare$

The basic idea of Algorithm D is to output from $f()$ and $f'()$ alternately, making special adjustments when either sequence generates n consecutive x's for $x < r$. For example, when $f()$ and $f'()$ produce the 9-cycle (57), we take $r = 1$ and get

t in step D2: 12 31211112 12312111 12123121 11121231 21111212 ...
x in step D3: 00001102122 00011021 22000110 21220001 102122000 ...
t' in step D6: 1212111121212111121212111121212111121212111112121211112121 ...
x' in step D7: 0 11021220 11021220 11021220 11021220 11021220 1 ...;

so the 81-cycle produced in steps D3 and **D7** is $00001011012\ldots2222\,00001\ldots$.

The case $m = 2$ of Algorithm R was discovered by Abraham Lempel [*IEEE Trans.* **C-19** (1970), 1204–1209]; Algorithm D was not discovered until more than 25 years later [C. J. Mitchell, T. Etzion, and K. G. Paterson, *IEEE Trans.* **IT-42** (1996), 1472–1478]. By using them together, starting with simple coroutines for $n = 2$ based on (54), we can build up an interesting family of cooperating coroutines that will generate a de Bruijn cycle of length m^n for any desired $m \geq 2$ and $n \geq 2$, using only $O(\log n)$ simple computations for each digit of output. (See exercise 96.) Furthermore, in the simplest case $m = 2$, this combination "R&D method" has the property that its kth output can be computed directly, as a function of k, by doing $O(n \log n)$ simple operations on n-bit numbers. Conversely, given any n-bit pattern β, the position of β in the cycle can also be computed in $O(n \log n)$ steps. (See exercises 97–99.) No other family of binary de Bruijn cycles is presently known to have the latter property.

Our third construction of de Bruijn cycles is based on the theory of prime strings, which will be of great importance to us when we study pattern matching in Chapter 9. Suppose $\gamma = \alpha\beta$ is the concatenation of two strings; we say that α is a *prefix* of γ and β is a *suffix*. A prefix or suffix of γ is called *proper* if its length is positive but less than the length of γ. Thus β is a proper suffix of $\alpha\beta$ if and only if $\alpha \neq \epsilon$ and $\beta \neq \epsilon$.

Definition P. *A string is prime if it is nonempty and (lexicographically) less than all of its proper suffixes.*

For example, 01101 is not prime, because it is greater than 01; but 01102 is prime, because it is less than 1102, 102, 02, and 2. (We assume that strings are composed of letters, digits, or other symbols from a linearly ordered alphabet. Lexicographic or dictionary order is the normal way to compare strings, so we write $\alpha < \beta$ and say that α is less than β when α is lexicographically less than β. In particular, we always have $\alpha \leq \alpha\beta$, and $\alpha < \alpha\beta$ if and only if $\beta \neq \epsilon$.)

Prime strings have often been called *Lyndon words*, because they were introduced by R. C. Lyndon [*Trans. Amer. Math. Soc.* **77** (1954), 202–215]; Lyndon called them "standard sequences." The simpler term "prime" is justified because of the fundamental factorization theorem in exercise 101. We will, however, continue to pay respect to Lyndon implicitly by often using the letter λ to denote strings that are prime.

Several of the most important properties of prime strings were derived by Chen, Fox, and Lyndon in an important paper on group theory [*Annals of Math.* **68** (1958), 81–95], including the following easy but basic result:

Theorem P. *A nonempty string that is less than all its cyclic shifts is prime.*

(The cyclic shifts of $a_1 \ldots a_n$ are $a_2 \ldots a_n a_1$, $a_3 \ldots a_n a_1 a_2$, $\ldots$, $a_n a_1 \ldots a_{n-1}$.)

Proof. Suppose $\gamma = \alpha\beta$ is not prime, because $\alpha \neq \epsilon$ and $\gamma \geq \beta \neq \epsilon$; but suppose γ is also less than its cyclic shift $\beta\alpha$. Then the conditions $\beta \leq \gamma < \beta\alpha$ imply that $\gamma = \beta\theta$ for some string $\theta < \alpha$. Therefore, if γ is also less than its cyclic shift $\theta\beta$, we have $\theta < \alpha < \alpha\beta < \theta\beta$. But that is impossible, because α and θ have the same length. ∎

Let $L_m(n)$ be the number of m-ary primes of length n. Every string $a_1 \ldots a_n$, together with its cyclic shifts, yields d distinct strings for some divisor d of n, corresponding to exactly one prime of length d. For example, from 010010 we get also 100100 and 001001 by cyclic shifting, and the smallest of the periodic parts $\{010, 100, 001\}$ is the prime 001. Therefore we must have

$$\sum_{d\backslash n} dL_m(d) = m^n, \qquad \text{for all } m, n \geq 1. \tag{59}$$

This family of equations can be solved for $L_m(n)$ using exercise 4.5.3–28(a), and we obtain

$$L_m(n) = \frac{1}{n} \sum_{d\backslash n} \mu(d) m^{n/d}. \tag{60}$$

During the 1970s, Harold Fredricksen and James Maiorana discovered a beautifully simple way to generate all of the m-ary primes of length n or less, in increasing order [*Discrete Math.* **23** (1978), 207–210]. Before we are ready to understand their algorithm, we need to consider the *n-extension* of a nonempty string λ, namely the first n characters of the infinite string $\lambda\lambda\lambda\ldots$. For example, the 10-extension of 123 is 1231231231. In general if $|\lambda| = k$, its n-extension is $\lambda^{\lfloor n/k \rfloor}\lambda'$, where λ' is the prefix of λ whose length is $n \bmod k$.

Definition Q. *A string is preprime if it is a nonempty prefix of a prime, on some alphabet.*

Theorem Q. *A string of length $n > 0$ is preprime if and only if it is the n-extension of a prime string λ of length $k \leq n$. This prime string is uniquely determined.*

Proof. See exercise 105. ∎

Theorem Q states, in essence, that there is a one-to-one correspondence between primes of length $\leq n$ and preprimes of length n. The following algorithm generates all of the m-ary instances, in increasing order.

Algorithm F (*Prime and preprime string generation*). This algorithm visits all m-ary n-tuples $(a_1, \ldots, a_n)$ such that the string $a_1 \ldots a_n$ is preprime. It also identifies the index j such that $a_1 \ldots a_n$ is the n-extension of the prime $a_1 \ldots a_j$.

F1. [Initialize.] Set $a_1 \leftarrow \cdots \leftarrow a_n \leftarrow 0$ and $j \leftarrow 1$; also set $a_0 \leftarrow -1$.

F2. [Visit.] Visit $(a_1, \ldots, a_n)$ with index j.

F3. [Prepare to increase.] Set $j \leftarrow n$. Then if $a_j = m - 1$, decrease j until finding $a_j < m - 1$.

F4. [Add one.] Terminate if $j = 0$. Otherwise set $a_j \leftarrow a_j + 1$. (Now $a_1 \ldots a_j$ is prime, by exercise 105(a).)

F5. [Make n-extension.] For $k \leftarrow j + 1$, $\ldots$, n (in this order) set $a_k \leftarrow a_{k-j}$. Return to F2. ∎

For example, Algorithm F visits 32 ternary preprimes when $m = 3$ and $n = 4$:

$$
\begin{array}{llllllll}
0000 & 0011 & 0022 & 0111 & 0122 & 0212 & 1111 & 1212 \\
0001 & 0012 & 0101 & 0112 & 0202 & 0220 & 1112 & 1221 \\
0002 & 0020 & 0102 & 0120 & 0210 & 0221 & 1121 & 1222 \\
0010 & 0021 & 0110 & 0121 & 0211 & 0222 & 1122 & 2222
\end{array}
\qquad (61)
$$

(The digits preceding '$_\wedge$' are the prime strings 0, 0001, 0002, 001, 0011, $\ldots$, 2.)

Theorem Q explains why this algorithm is correct, because steps F3 and F4 obviously find the smallest m-ary prime of length $\leq n$ that exceeds the previous preprime $a_1 \ldots a_n$. Notice that after a_1 increases from 0 to 1, the algorithm proceeds to visit all the $(m - 1)$-ary primes and preprimes, increased by $1 \ldots 1$.

Algorithm F is quite beautiful, but what does it have to do with de Bruijn cycles? Here now comes the punch line: If we output the digits $a_1, \ldots, a_j$ in step F2 whenever j is a divisor of n, the sequence of all such digits forms a de Bruijn cycle! For example, in the case $m = 3$ and $n = 4$, the following 81 digits are output:

$$0\,0001\,0002\,0011\,0012\,0021\,0022\,01\,0102\,0111\,0112$$
$$0121\,0122\,02\,0211\,0212\,0221\,0222\,1\,1112\,1122\,12\,1222\,2. \qquad (62)$$

(We omit the primes 001, 002, 011, $\ldots$, 122 of (61) because their length does not divide 4.) The reasons underlying this almost magical property are explored in exercise 108. Notice that the cycle has the correct length, by (59).

There is a sense in which the outputs of this procedure are actually equivalent to the "granddaddy" of all de Bruijn cycle constructions that work for all m and n, namely the construction first published by M. H. Martin in *Bull. Amer. Math. Soc.* **40** (1934), 859–864: Martin's original cycle for $m = 3$ and $n = 4$ was $2222122202211 \ldots 10000$, the twos' complement of (62). In fact, Fredricksen and Maiorana discovered Algorithm F almost by accident while looking for a simple way to generate Martin's sequence. The explicit connection between their algorithm and preprime strings was not noticed until many years later, when Ruskey, Savage, and Wang carried out a careful analysis of the running time [*J. Algorithms* **13** (1992), 414–430]. The principal results of that analysis appear in exercise 107, namely

i) The average value of $n - j$ in steps F3 and F5 is approximately $1/(m-1)$.

ii) The total running time to produce a de Bruijn cycle like (62) is $O(m^n)$.

EXERCISES

1. [*10*] Explain how to generate all n-tuples $(a_1, \ldots, a_n)$ in which $l_j \le a_j \le u_j$, given lower bounds l_j and upper bounds u_j for each coordinate. (Assume that $l_j \le u_j$.)

2. [*15*] What is the 1000000th n-tuple visited by Algorithm M if $n = 10$ and $m_j = j$ for $1 \le j \le n$? *Hint:* $\left[\begin{smallmatrix} 0, & 0, & 1, & 2, & 3, & 0, & 2, & 7, & 1, & 0 \\ 1, & 2, & 3, & 4, & 5, & 6, & 7, & 8, & 9, & 10 \end{smallmatrix}\right] = 1000000.$

▶ **3.** [*M20*] How many times does Algorithm M perform step M4?

▶ **4.** [*18*] On most computers it is faster to count down to 0 rather than up to m. Revise Algorithm M so that it visits all n-tuples in the opposite order, starting with $(m_1 - 1, \ldots, m_n - 1)$ and finishing with $(0, \ldots, 0)$.

▶ **5.** [*20*] Algorithms such as the "fast Fourier transform" (exercise 4.6.4–14) often end with an array of answers in bit-reflected order, having $A[(b_0 \ldots b_{n-1})_2]$ in the place where $A[(b_{n-1} \ldots b_0)_2]$ is desired. What is a good way to rearrange the answers into proper order? [*Hint:* Reflect Algorithm M.]

6. [*M17*] Prove (7), the basic formula for Gray binary code.

7. [*20*] Figure 10(b) shows the Gray binary code for a disk that is divided into 16 sectors. What would be a good Gray-like code to use if the number of sectors were 12 or 60 (for hours or minutes on a clock), or 360 (for degrees in a circle)?

8. [*15*] What's an easy way to run through all n-bit strings of even parity, changing only two bits at each step?

9. [*16*] What move should follow Fig. 11, when solving the Chinese ring puzzle?

▶ **10.** [*M21*] Find a simple formula for the total number of steps A_n or B_n in which a ring is (a) removed or (b) replaced, in the shortest procedure for removing n Chinese rings. For example, $A_3 = 4$ and $B_3 = 1$.

11. [*M22*] (H. J. Purkiss, 1865.) The two smallest rings of the Chinese ring puzzle can actually be taken on or off the bar simultaneously. How many steps does the puzzle require when such accelerated moves are permitted?

▶ **12.** [*25*] The *compositions* of n are the sequences of positive integers that sum to n. For example, the compositions of 4 are 1111, 112, 121, 13, 211, 22, 31, and 4. An integer n has exactly 2^{n-1} compositions, corresponding to all subsets of the points $\{1, \ldots, n-1\}$ that might be used to break the interval $(0 \ldots n)$ into integer-sized subintervals.

a) Design a loopless algorithm to generate all compositions of n, representing each composition as a sequential array of integers $s_1 s_2 \ldots s_j$.

b) Similarly, design a loopless algorithm that represents the compositions implicitly in an array of pointers $q_0 q_1 \ldots q_t$, where the elements of the composition are $(q_0 - q_1)(q_1 - q_2) \ldots (q_{t-1} - q_t)$ and we have $q_0 = n$, $q_t = 0$. For example, the composition 211 would be represented under this scheme by the pointers $q_0 = 4$, $q_1 = 2$, $q_2 = 1$, $q_3 = 0$, and with $t = 3$.

13. [*21*] Continuing the previous exercise, compute also the multinomial coefficient $C = \binom{n}{s_1,\ldots,s_j}$ for use as the composition $s_1 \ldots s_j$ is being visited.

14. [*20*] Design an algorithm to generate all strings $a_1 \ldots a_j$ such that $0 \le j \le n$ and $0 \le a_i < m_i$ for $1 \le i \le j$, in lexicographic order. For example, if $m_1 = m_2 = n = 2$, your algorithm should successively visit ϵ, 0, 00, 01, 1, 10, 11.

▶ **15.** [*25*] Design a *loopless* algorithm to generate the strings of the previous exercise. All strings of the same length should be visited in lexicographic order as before, but strings of different lengths can be intermixed in any convenient way. For example, 0, 00, 01, ϵ, 10, 11, 1 is an acceptable order when $m_1 = m_2 = n = 2$.

16. [*23*] A loopless algorithm obviously cannot generate all binary vectors $(a_1, \ldots, a_n)$ in lexicographic order, because the number of coordinates a_j that need to change between successive visits is not bounded. Show, however, that loopless lexicographic generation does become possible if a *linked* representation is used instead of a sequential one: Suppose there are $2n + 1$ nodes $\{0, 1, \ldots, 2n\}$, each containing a LINK field. The binary n-tuple $(a_1, \ldots, a_n)$ is represented by letting

$$\text{LINK}(0) = 1 + na_1;$$
$$\text{LINK}(j - 1 + na_{j-1}) = j + na_j, \qquad \text{for } 1 < j \le n;$$
$$\text{LINK}(n + na_n) = 0;$$

the other n LINK fields can have any convenient values.

17. [*20*] A well-known construction called the *Karnaugh map* [M. Karnaugh, *Amer. Inst. Elect. Eng. Trans.* **72**, part I (1953), 593–599] uses Gray binary code in two dimensions to display all 4-bit numbers in a 4×4 torus:

0000	0001	0011	0010
0100	0101	0111	0110
1100	1101	1111	1110
1000	1001	1011	1010

(The entries of a torus "wrap around" at the left and right and also at the top and bottom — just as if they were tiles, replicated infinitely often in a plane.) Show that, similarly, all 6-bit numbers can be arranged in an 8×8 torus so that only one coordinate changes when we move north, south, east, or west from any point.

▶ **18.** [*20*] The *Lee weight* of a vector $u = (u_1, \ldots, u_n)$, where each component satisfies $0 \le u_j < m_j$, is defined to be

$$\nu_L(u) = \sum_{j=1}^{n} \min(u_j, m_j - u_j);$$

and the *Lee distance* between two such vectors u and v is

$$d_L(u, v) = \nu_L(u - v), \qquad \text{where } u - v = ((u_1 - v_1) \bmod m_1, \ldots, (u_n - v_n) \bmod m_n).$$

(This is the minimum number of steps needed to change u to v if we adjust some component u_j by ± 1 (modulo m_j) in each step.)

A quaternary vector has $m_j = 4$ for $1 \le j \le n$, and a binary vector has all $m_j = 2$. Find a simple one-to-one correspondence between quaternary vectors $u = (u_1, \ldots, u_n)$ and binary vectors $u' = (u'_1, \ldots, u'_{2n})$, with the property that $\nu_L(u) = \nu(u')$ and $d_L(u, v) = \nu(u' \oplus v')$.

19. [*21*] (*The octacode.*) Let $g(x) = x^3 + 2x^2 + x - 1$.

a) Use one of the algorithms in this section to evaluate $\sum z_{u_0} z_{u_1} z_{u_2} z_{u_3} z_{u_4} z_{u_5} z_{u_6} z_{u_\infty}$, summed over all 256 polynomials

$$(v_0 + v_1 x + v_2 x^2 + v_3 x^3)g(x) \bmod 4 = u_0 + u_1 x + u_2 x^2 + u_3 x^3 + u_4 x^4 + u_5 x^5 + u_6 x^6$$

for $0 \le v_0, v_1, v_2, v_3 < 4$, where u_∞ is chosen so that $0 \le u_\infty < 4$ and $(u_0 + u_1 + u_2 + u_3 + u_4 + u_5 + u_6 + u_\infty) \bmod 4 = 0$.

b) Construct a set of 256 16-bit numbers that differ from each other in at least six different bit positions. (Such a set, first discovered by Nordstrom and Robinson [*Information and Control* **11** (1967), 613–616], is essentially unique.)

20. [*M36*] The 16-bit codewords in the previous exercise can be used to transmit 8 bits of information, allowing transmission errors to be corrected if any one or two bits are corrupted; furthermore, mistakes will be detected (but not necessarily correctable) if any three bits are received incorrectly. Devise an algorithm that either finds the nearest codeword to a given 16-bit number u' or determines that at least three bits of u' are erroneous. How does your algorithm decode the number $(1100100100001111)_2$? [*Hint:* Use the facts that $x^7 \equiv 1$ (modulo $g(x)$ and 4), and that every quaternary polynomial of degree < 3 is congruent to $x^j + 2x^k$ (modulo $g(x)$ and 4) for some $j, k \in \{0, 1, 2, 3, 4, 5, 6, \infty\}$, where $x^\infty = 0$.]

21. [*M30*] A t-subcube of an n-cube can be represented by a string like $**10**0*$, containing t asterisks and $n - t$ specified bits. If all 2^n binary n-tuples are written in lexicographic order, the elements belonging to such a subcube appear in $2^{t'}$ clusters of consecutive entries, where t' is the number of asterisks that lie to the left of the rightmost specified bit. (In the example given, $n = 8$, $t = 5$, and $t' = 4$.) But if the n-tuples are written in Gray binary order, the number of clusters might be reduced. For example, the $(n-1)$-subcubes $*\ldots*0$ and $*\ldots*1$ occur in only $2^{n-2}+1$ and 2^{n-2} clusters, respectively, when Gray binary order is used, not in 2^{n-1} of them.

a) Explain how to compute $C(\alpha)$, the number of Gray binary clusters of the subcube defined by a given string α of asterisks, 0s, and 1s. What is $C(**10**0*)$?

b) Prove that $C(\alpha)$ always lies between $2^{t'-1}$ and $2^{t'}$, inclusive.

c) What is the average value of $C(\alpha)$, over all $2^{n-t}\binom{n}{t}$ possible t-subcubes?

▶ **22.** [*22*] A "right subcube" is a subcube such as $0110**$ in which all the asterisks appear after all the specified digits. Any binary trie (Section 6.3) can be regarded as a way to partition a cube into disjoint right subcubes, as in Fig. 16(a). If we interchange the left and right subtries of every right subtrie, proceeding downward from the root, we obtain a *Gray binary trie*, as in Fig. 16(b).

Prove that if the "lieves" of a Gray binary trie are traversed in order, from left to right, consecutive lieves correspond to adjacent subcubes. (Subcubes are adjacent if they contain adjacent vertices. For example, $00**$ is adjacent to $011*$ because the first contains 0010 and the second contains 0110; but $011*$ is not adjacent to $10**$.)

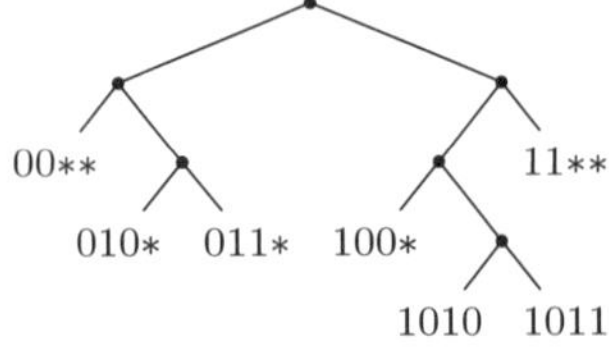

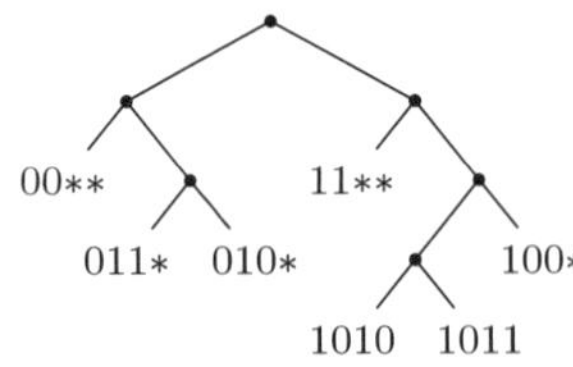

Fig. 16.   (a) Normal binary trie.   (b) Gray binary trie.

23. [*20*] Suppose $g(k) \oplus 2^j = g(l)$. What is a simple way to find l, given j and k?

24. [*M21*] Consider extending the Gray binary function g to all 2-adic integers (see exercise 4.1–31). What is the corresponding inverse function $g^{[-1]}$?

▶ **25.** [*M25*] Prove that if $g(k)$ and $g(l)$ differ in $t > 0$ bits, and if $0 \le k, l < 2^n$, then $\lceil 2^t/3 \rceil \le |k - l| \le 2^n - \lceil 2^t/3 \rceil$.

26. [*25*] (Frank Ruskey.) For which integers N is it possible to generate all of the nonnegative integers less than N in such a way that only one bit of the binary representation changes at each step?

▶ **27.** [*20*] Let $S_0 = \{1\}$ and $S_{n+1} = 1/(2 + S_n) \cup 1/(2 - S_n)$; thus, for example,

$$S_2 = \left\{ \cfrac{1}{2 + \cfrac{1}{2 + 1}}, \cfrac{1}{2 + \cfrac{1}{2 - 1}}, \cfrac{1}{2 - \cfrac{1}{2 + 1}}, \cfrac{1}{2 - \cfrac{1}{2 - 1}} \right\} = \left\{ \frac{3}{7}, \frac{1}{3}, \frac{3}{5}, 1 \right\},$$

and S_n has 2^n elements that lie between $\frac{1}{3}$ and 1. Compute the 10^{10}th smallest element of S_{100}.

28. [*M27*] A *median* of n-bit strings $\{\alpha_1, \ldots, \alpha_t\}$, where α_k has the binary representation $\alpha_k = a_{k(n-1)} \ldots a_{k0}$, is a string $\hat{\alpha} = a_{n-1} \ldots a_0$ whose bits a_j for $0 \le j < n$ agree with the majority of the bits a_{kj} for $1 \le k \le t$. (If t is even and the bits α_{kj} are half 0 and half 1, the median bit a_j can be either 0 or 1.) For example, the strings $\{0010, 0100, 0101, 1110\}$ have two medians, 0100 and 0110, which we can denote by 01*0.

    a) Find a simple way to describe the medians of $G_t = \{g(0), \ldots, g(t-1)\}$, the first t Gray binary strings, when $0 < t \le 2^n$.

    b) Prove that if $\alpha = a_{n-1} \ldots a_0$ is such a median, and if $2^{n-1} < t < 2^n$, then the string β obtained from α by complementing any bit a_j is also an element of G_t.

29. [*M24*] If integer values k are transmitted as n-bit Gray binary codes $g(k)$ and received with errors described by a bit pattern $p = (p_{n-1} \ldots p_0)_2$, the average numerical error is

$$\frac{1}{2^n} \sum_{k=0}^{2^n - 1} \left| (g^{[-1]}(k) \oplus p) - k \right|,$$

assuming that all values of k are equally likely. Show that this sum is equal to $\sum_{k=0}^{2^n-1} |(k \oplus p) - k|/2^n$, just as if Gray binary code were not used, and evaluate it explicitly.

▶ **30.** [*M27*] (*Gray permutation.*) Design a one-pass algorithm to replace the array elements $(X_0, X_1, X_2, \ldots, X_{2^n-1})$ by $(X_{g(0)}, X_{g(1)}, X_{g(2)}, \ldots, X_{g(2^n-1)})$, using only a constant amount of auxiliary storage. *Hint:* Considering the function $g(n)$ as a permutation of all nonnegative integers, show that the set

$$L = \left\{ 0, 1, (10)_2, (100)_2, (100*)_2, (100*0)_2, (100*0*)_2, \ldots \right\}$$

is the set of *cycle leaders* (the smallest elements of the cycles).

31. [*HM35*] (*Gray fields.*) Let $f_n(x) = g(r_n(x))$ denote the operation of reflecting the bits of an n-bit binary string as in exercise 5 and then converting to Gray binary code. For example, the operation $f_3(x)$ takes $(001)_2 \mapsto (110)_2 \mapsto (010)_2 \mapsto (011)_2 \mapsto (101)_2 \mapsto (111)_2 \mapsto (100)_2 \mapsto (001)_2$, hence all of the nonzero possibilities appear in a single cycle. Therefore we can use f_3 to define a field of 8 elements, with $\oplus$ as the addition operator and with multiplication defined by the rule

$$f_3^{[j]}(1) \times f_3^{[k]}(1) = f_3^{[j+k]}(1) = f_3^{[j]}(f_3^{[k]}(1)).$$

The functions f_2, f_5, and f_6 have the same nice property. But f_4 does not, because $f_4((1011)_2) = (1011)_2$.

Find all $n \le 100$ for which f_n defines a field of 2^n elements.

32. [*M20*] True or false: Walsh functions satisfy $w_k(-x) = (-1)^k w_k(x)$.

▶ **33.** [*M20*] Prove the Rademacher-to-Walsh law (17).

34. [*M21*] The *Paley functions* $p_k(x)$ are defined by

$$p_0(x) = 1 \qquad \text{and} \qquad p_k(x) = (-1)^{\lfloor 2x \rfloor k} p_{\lfloor k/2 \rfloor}(2x).$$

Show that $p_k(x)$ has a simple expression in terms of Rademacher functions, analogous to (17), and relate Paley functions to Walsh functions.

35. [*HM23*] The $2^n \times 2^n$ Paley matrix P_n is obtained from Paley functions just as the Walsh matrix W_n is obtained from Walsh functions. (See (20).) Find interesting relations between P_n, W_n, and the Hadamard matrix H_n. Prove that all three matrices are symmetric.

36. [*21*] Spell out the details of an efficient algorithm to compute the Walsh transform $(x_0, \ldots, x_{2^n-1})$ of a given vector $(X_0, \ldots, X_{2^n-1})$.

37. [*HM23*] Let z_{kl} be the location of the lth sign change in $w_k(x)$, for $1 \le l \le k$ and $0 < z_{kl} < 1$. Prove that $|z_{kl} - l/(k+1)| = O((\log k)/k)$.

▶ **38.** [*M25*] Devise a ternary generalization of Walsh functions.

▶ **39.** [*HM30*] (J. J. Sylvester.) The rows of $\left(\begin{smallmatrix} a & b \\ b & -a \end{smallmatrix}\right)$ are orthogonal to each other and have the same magnitude; therefore the matrix identity

$$(A\ B) \begin{pmatrix} a^2+b^2 & 0 \\ 0 & a^2+b^2 \end{pmatrix} \begin{pmatrix} A \\ B \end{pmatrix} = (A\ B) \begin{pmatrix} a & b \\ b & -a \end{pmatrix} \begin{pmatrix} a & b \\ b & -a \end{pmatrix} \begin{pmatrix} A \\ B \end{pmatrix}$$
$$= (Aa + Bb\ \ Ab - Ba) \begin{pmatrix} aA + bB \\ bA - aB \end{pmatrix}$$

implies the sum-of-two-squares identity $(a^2+b^2)(A^2+B^2) = (aA+bB)^2 + (bA-aB)^2$. Similarly, the matrix

$$\begin{pmatrix} a & b & c & d \\ b & -a & d & -c \\ d & c & -b & -a \\ c & -d & -a & b \end{pmatrix}$$

leads to the sum-of-four-squares identity

$$(a^2+b^2+c^2+d^2)(A^2+B^2+C^2+D^2) = (aA+bB+cC+dD)^2 + (bA-aB+dC-cD)^2$$
$$+ (dA + cB - bC - aD)^2 + (cA - dB - aC + bD)^2.$$

a) Attach the signs of the matrix H_3 in (21) to the symbols $\{a, b, c, d, e, f, g, h\}$, obtaining a matrix with orthogonal rows and a sum-of-eight-squares identity.

b) Generalize to H_4 and higher-order matrices.

▶ **40.** [*21*] Would the text's five-letter word computation scheme produce correct answers also if the masks in step W2 were computed as $m_j = x \wedge (2^{5j} - 1)$ for $0 \le j < 5$?

41. [*25*] If we restrict the five-letter word problem to the most common 3000 words — thereby eliminating `ducky`, `duces`, `dunks`, `dinks`, `dinky`, `dices`, `dicey`, `dicky`, `dicks`, `picky`, `pinky`, `punky`, and `pucks` from (23) — how many valid words can still be generated from a single pair?

42. [*35*] (M. L. Fredman.) Algorithm L uses $\Theta(n \log n)$ bits of auxiliary memory for focus pointers as it decides what Gray binary bit a_j should be complemented next. On each step L3 it examines $\Theta(\log n)$ of the auxiliary bits, and it occasionally changes $\Omega(\log n)$ of them.

Show that, from a theoretical standpoint, we can do better: The n-bit Gray binary code can be generated by changing at most 2 auxiliary bits between visits. (We still allow ourselves to examine $O(\log n)$ of the auxiliary bits on each step, so that we know which of them should be changed.)

43. [*47*] Determine $d(6)$, the number of 6-bit Gray cycles.

44. [*M37*] Show that arbitrary delta sequences for Gray cycles on $n - 1$ or $n - 2$ bits can be used to construct a large number of delta sequences for n-bit Gray cycles with the property that exactly (a) one or (b) two of the coordinate names occur only twice.

45. [*M25*] Prove that the sequence $d(n)$ has doubly exponential growth: There is a constant $A > 1$ such that $d(n) = \Omega(A^{2^n})$.

46. [*HM48*] Determine the asymptotic behavior of $d(n)^{1/2^n}$ as $n \to \infty$.

47. [*M46*] (Silverman, Vickers, and Sampson.) Let $S_k = \{g(0), \ldots, g(k-1)\}$ be the first k elements of the standard Gray binary code, and let $H(k, v)$ be the number of Hamiltonian paths in S_k that begin with 0 and end with v. Prove or disprove: $H(k, v) \le H(k, g(k-1))$ for all $v \in S_k$ that are adjacent to $g(k)$.

48. [*36*] Prove that $d(n) \le 4(n/2)^{2^n}$ if the conjecture in the previous exercise is true. [*Hint:* Let $d(n, k)$ be the number of n-bit Gray cycles that begin with $g(0) \ldots g(k-1)$; the conjecture implies that $d(n) \le c_{n1} \ldots c_{n(k-1)} d(n, k)$, where c_{nk} is the number of vertices adjacent to $g(k-1)$ in the n-cube but not in S_k.]

49. [*20*] Prove that for all $n \ge 1$ there is a $2n$-bit Gray cycle in which $v_{k+2^{2n-1}}$ is the complement of v_k, for all $k \ge 0$.

▶ **50.** [*21*] Find a construction like that of Theorem D but with l even.

51. [*M24*] Complete the proof of Corollary B to Theorem D.

52. [*M20*] Prove that if the transition counts of an n-bit Gray cycle satisfy $c_0 \le c_1 \le \cdots \le c_{n-1}$, we must have $c_0 + \cdots + c_{j-1} \ge 2^j$, with equality when $j = n$.

53. [*M46*] If the numbers $(c_0, \ldots, c_{n-1})$ are even and satisfy the condition of the previous exercise, is there always an n-bit Gray cycle with these transition counts?

54. [*M20*] (H. S. Shapiro, 1953.) Show that if a sequence of integers $(a_1, \ldots, a_{2^n})$ contains only n distinct values, then there is a subsequence whose product $a_{k+1} a_{k+2} \ldots a_l$ is a perfect square, for some $0 \le k < l \le 2^n$. However, this conclusion might not be true if we disallow the case $l = 2^n$.

55. [*47*] (F. Ruskey and C. Savage, 1993.) If $(v_0, \ldots, v_{2^n-1})$ is an n-bit Gray cycle, the pairs $\{\, \{v_{2k}, v_{2k+1}\} \mid 0 \le k < 2^{n-1} \,\}$ form a perfect matching between the vertices of even and odd parity in the n-cube. Conversely, does every such perfect matching arise as "half" of some n-bit Gray cycle?

56. [*M30*] (E. N. Gilbert, 1958.) Say that two Gray cycles are equivalent if their delta sequences can be made equal by permuting the coordinate names, or by reversing the cycle and/or starting the cycle at a different place. Show that the 2688 different 4-bit Gray cycles fall into just 9 equivalence classes.

57. [*32*] Consider a graph whose vertices are the 2688 possible 4-bit Gray cycles, where two such cycles are adjacent if they are related by one of the following simple transformations:

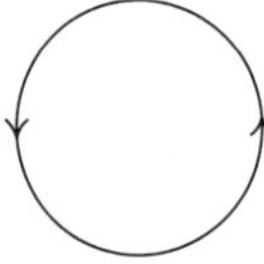  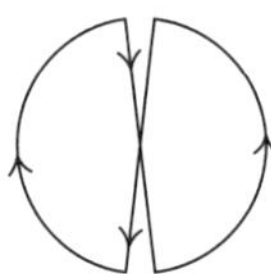  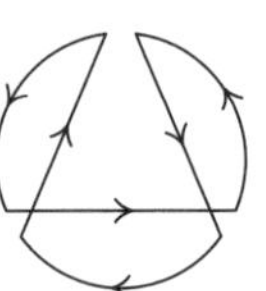 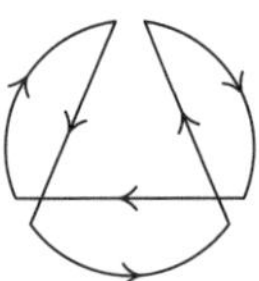

| Before | After Type 1 | After Type 2 | After Type 3 | After Type 4 |

(Type 1 changes arise when the cycle can be broken into two parts and reassembled with one part reversed. Types 2, 3, and 4 arise when the cycle can be broken into three parts and reassembled after reversing 0, 1, or 2 of the parts. The parts need not have equal size. Such transformations of Hamiltonian cycles are often possible.)

Write a program to discover which 4-bit Gray cycles are transformable into each other, by finding the connected components of the graph; restrict consideration to only one of the four types at a time.

▶ **58.** [*21*] Let α be the delta sequence of an n-bit Gray cycle, and obtain β from α by changing q occurrences of 0 to n, where q is odd. Prove that $\beta\beta$ is the delta sequence of an $(n+1)$-bit Gray cycle.

59. [*22*] The 5-bit Gray cycle of (30) is *nonlocal* in the sense that no 2^t consecutive elements belong to a single t-subcube, for $1 < t < n$. Prove that nonlocal n-bit Gray cycles exist for all $n \geq 5$. [*Hint:* See the previous exercise.]

60. [*20*] Show that the run-length-bound function satisfies $r(n+1) \geq r(n)$.

61. [*M30*] Show that $r(m+n) \geq r(m) + r(n) - 1$ if (a) $m = 2$ and $2 < r(n) < 8$; or (b) $m \leq n$ and $r(n) \leq 2^{m-3}$.

62. [*46*] Does $r(8) = 6$?

63. [*30*] (Luis Goddyn.) Prove that $r(10) \geq 8$.

▶ **64.** [*HM35*] (L. Goddyn and P. Gvozdjak.) An n-bit *Gray stream* is a sequence of permutations $(\sigma_0, \sigma_1, \ldots, \sigma_{l-1})$ where each σ_k is a permutation of the vertices of the n-cube, taking every vertex to one of its neighbors.

a) Suppose $(u_0, \ldots, u_{2^m-1})$ is an m-bit Gray cycle and $(\sigma_0, \sigma_1, \ldots, \sigma_{2^m-1})$ is an n-bit Gray stream. Let $v_0 = 0\ldots0$ and $v_{k+1} = v_k\sigma_k$, where $\sigma_k = \sigma_{k \bmod 2^m}$ if $k \geq 2^m$. Under what conditions is the sequence

$$W = (u_0v_0,\; u_0v_1,\; u_1v_1,\; u_1v_2,\; \ldots,\; u_{2^{m+n-1}-1}v_{2^{m+n-1}-1},\; u_{2^{m+n-1}-1}v_{2^{m+n-1}})$$

an $(m+n)$-bit Gray cycle?

b) Show that if m is sufficiently large, there is an n-bit Gray stream satisfying the conditions of (a) for which all run lengths of the sequence $(v_0, v_1, \ldots)$ are $\geq n - 2$.

c) Apply these results to prove that $r(n) \geq n - O(\log n)$.

65. [*30*] (Brett Stevens.) In Samuel Beckett's play *Quad*, the stage begins and ends empty; n actors enter and exit one at a time, running through all 2^n possible subsets, and the actor who leaves is always the one whose previous entrance was earliest. When $n = 4$, as in the actual play, some subsets are necessarily repeated. Show, however, that there is a perfect pattern with exactly 2^n entrances and exits when $n = 5$.

66. $[40]$ Is there a perfect Beckett–Gray pattern for 8 actors?

67. $[20]$ Sometimes it is desirable to run through all n-bit binary strings by changing as *many* bits as possible from one step to the next, for example when testing a physical circuit for reliable behavior in worst-case conditions. Explain how to traverse all binary n-tuples in such a way that each step changes n or $n-1$ bits, alternately.

68. $[21]$ Rufus Q. Perverse decided to construct an *anti-Gray* ternary code, in which each n-trit number differs from its neighbors in *every* digit position. Is such a code possible for all n?

▸ **69.** $[M25]$ Modify the definition of Gray binary code (7) by letting

$$h(k) = \left(\dots (b_6 \oplus b_5)(b_5 \oplus b_4)(b_4 \oplus b_3 \oplus b_2 \oplus b_0)(b_3 \oplus b_0)(b_2 \oplus b_1 \oplus b_0)b_1\right)_2,$$

when $k = (\dots b_5 b_4 b_3 b_2 b_1 b_0)_2$.

   a) Show that the sequence $h(0)$, $h(1)$, $\dots$, $h(2^n - 1)$ runs through all n-bit numbers in such a way that exactly 3 bits change each time, when $n > 3$.

   b) Generalize this rule to obtain sequences in which exactly t bits change at each step, when t is odd and $n > t$.

70. $[21]$ How many monotonic n-bit Gray codes exist for $n = 5$ and $n = 6$?

71. $[M22]$ Derive (45), the recurrence that defines the Savage–Winkler permutations.

72. $[20]$ What is the Savage–Winkler code from 00000 to 11111?

▸ **73.** $[32]$ Design an efficient algorithm to construct the delta sequence of an n-bit monotonic Gray code.

74. $[M25]$ (Savage and Winkler.) How far apart can adjacent vertices of the n-cube be, in a monotonic Gray code?

75. $[32]$ Find all 5-bit Gray paths v_0, $\dots$, v_{31} that are *trend-free*, in the sense that $\sum_{k=0}^{31} k(-1)^{v_{kj}} = 0$ in each coordinate position j.

76. $[M25]$ Prove that trend-free n-bit Gray codes exist for all $n \geq 5$.

77. $[21]$ Modify Algorithm H in order to visit mixed-radix n-tuples in *modular* Gray order.

78. $[M26]$ Prove the conversion formulas (50) and (51) for reflected mixed-radix Gray codes, and derive analogous formulas for the modular case.

▸ **79.** $[M22]$ When is the last n-tuple of the (a) reflected (b) modular mixed-radix Gray code adjacent to the first?

80. $[M20]$ Explain how to run through all divisors of a number, given its prime factorization $p_1^{e_1} \dots p_t^{e_t}$, repeatedly multiplying or dividing by a single prime at each step.

81. $[M21]$ Let (a_0, b_0), (a_1, b_1), $\dots$, (a_{m^2-1}, b_{m^2-1}) be the 2-digit m-ary modular Gray code. Show that, if $m > 2$, every edge $(x, y) \!-\! (x, (y+1) \bmod m)$ and $(x, y) \!-\! ((x+1) \bmod m, y)$ occurs in one of the two cycles

$$(a_0, b_0) \,\text{---}\, (a_1, b_1) \,\text{---}\, \cdots \,\text{---}\, (a_{m^2-1}, b_{m^2-1}) \,\text{---}\, (a_0, b_0),$$
$$(b_0, a_0) \,\text{---}\, (b_1, a_1) \,\text{---}\, \cdots \,\text{---}\, (b_{m^2-1}, a_{m^2-1}) \,\text{---}\, (b_0, a_0).$$

▸ **82.** $[M25]$ (G. Ringel, 1956.) Use the previous exercise to deduce that there exist four 8-bit Gray cycles that, together, cover all edges of the 8-cube.

83. $[41]$ Can four *balanced* 8-bit Gray cycles cover all edges of the 8-cube?

▶ **84.** [*25*] (Howard L. Dyckman.) Figure 17 shows a fascinating puzzle called Loony Loop or the Gordian Knot, in which the object is to remove a flexible cord from the rigid loops that surround it. Show that the solution to this puzzle is inherently related to the reflected Gray ternary code.

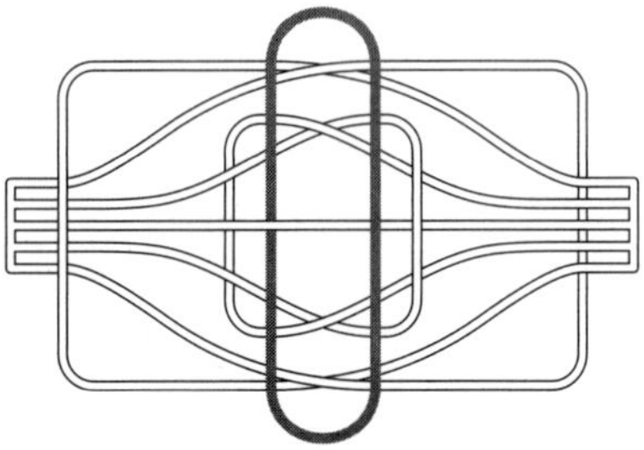

Fig. 17. The Loony Loop puzzle.

▶ **85.** [*M25*] (Dana Richards.) If $\Gamma = (\alpha_0, \ldots, \alpha_{t-1})$ is any sequence of t strings and $\Gamma' = (\alpha'_0, \ldots, \alpha'_{t'-1})$ is any sequence of t' strings, the *boustrophedon product* $\Gamma \boxtimes \Gamma'$ is the sequence of tt' strings that begins

$$(\alpha_0\alpha'_0, \ldots, \alpha_0\alpha'_{t'-1}, \alpha_1\alpha'_{t'-1}, \ldots, \alpha_1\alpha'_0, \alpha_2\alpha'_0, \ldots, \alpha_2\alpha'_{t'-1}, \alpha_3\alpha'_{t'-1}, \ldots)$$

and ends with $\alpha_{t-1}\alpha'_0$ if t is even, $\alpha_{t-1}\alpha'_{t'-1}$ if t is odd. For example, the basic definition of Gray binary code in (5) can be expressed in this notation as $\Gamma_n = (0,1) \boxtimes \Gamma_{n-1}$ when $n > 0$. Prove that the operation $\boxtimes$ is associative, hence $\Gamma_{m+n} = \Gamma_m \boxtimes \Gamma_n$.

▶ **86.** [*26*] Define an infinite Gray code that runs through all possible nonnegative integer n-tuples $(a_1, \ldots, a_n)$ in such a way that $\max(a_1, \ldots, a_n) \leq \max(a'_1, \ldots, a'_n)$ when $(a_1, \ldots, a_n)$ is followed by $(a'_1, \ldots, a'_n)$.

87. [*27*] Continuing the previous exercise, define an infinite Gray code that runs through *all* integer n-tuples $(a_1, \ldots, a_n)$, in such a way that $\max(|a_1|, \ldots, |a_n|) \leq \max(|a'_1|, \ldots, |a'_n|)$ when $(a_1, \ldots, a_n)$ is followed by $(a'_1, \ldots, a'_n)$.

▶ **88.** [*25*] After Algorithm K has terminated in step K4, what would happen if we immediately restarted it in step K2?

▶ **89.** [*25*] (*Gray code for Morse code.*) The Morse code words of length n (exercise 4.5.3–32) are strings of dots and dashes, where n is the number of dots plus twice the number of dashes.

    a) Show that it is possible to generate all Morse code words of length n by successively changing a dash to two dots or vice versa. For example, the path for $n = 3$ must be • —, • • •, — • or its reverse.

    b) What string follows • — — • • — — • — • in your sequence for $n = 15$?

90. [*26*] For what values of n can the Morse code words be arranged in a *cycle*, under the ground rules of exercise 89? [*Hint:* The number of code words is F_{n+1}.]

▶ **91.** [*34*] Design a loopless algorithm to visit all binary n-tuples $(a_1, \ldots, a_n)$ such that $a_1 \leq a_2 \geq a_3 \leq a_4 \geq \cdots$. [The number of such n-tuples is F_{n+2}.]

92. [*M30*] Is there an infinite sequence Φ_n whose first m^n elements form an m-ary de Bruijn cycle, for all m? [The case $n = 2$ is solved in (54).]

▶ **93.** [*M28*] Prove that Algorithm R outputs a de Bruijn cycle as advertised.

94. [*22*] What is the output of Algorithm D when $m = 5$, $n = 1$, and $r = 3$, if the coroutines $f()$ and $f'()$ generate the trivial cycles 01234 01234 01...?

▶ **95.** [*M23*] Suppose an infinite sequence $a_0 a_1 a_2 \ldots$ of period p is interleaved with an infinite sequence $b_0 b_1 b_2 \ldots$ of period q to form the infinite cyclic sequence

$$c_0 c_1 c_2 c_3 c_4 c_5 \ldots = a_0 b_0 a_1 b_1 a_2 b_2 \ldots.$$

    a) Under what circumstances does $c_0 c_1 c_2 \ldots$ have period pq? (The "period" of a sequence $a_0 a_1 a_2 \ldots$, for the purposes of this exercise, is the smallest integer $p > 0$ such that $a_k = a_{k+p}$ for all $k \geq 0$.)

    b) Which $2n$-tuples would occur as consecutive outputs of Algorithm D if step D6 were changed to say simply "If $t' = n$ and $x' < r$, go to D4"?

    c) Prove that Algorithm D outputs a de Bruijn cycle as advertised.

▶ **96.** [*M23*] Suppose a family of coroutines has been set up to generate a de Bruijn cycle of length m^n using Algorithms R and D, based recursively on simple coroutines for the base case $n = 2$.

    a) How many coroutines of each type will there be?

    b) What is the maximum number of coroutine activations needed to get one top-level digit of output?

97. [*M29*] The purpose of this exercise is to analyze the de Bruijn cycles constructed by Algorithms R and D in the important special case $m = 2$. Let $f_n(k)$ be the $(k+1)$st bit of the 2^n-cycle, so that $f_n(k) = 0$ for $0 \leq k < n$. Also let j_n be the index such that $0 \leq j_n < 2^n$ and $f_n(k) = 1$ for $j_n \leq k < j_n + n$.

    a) Write out the cycles $\big(f_n(0) \ldots f_n(2^n - 1)\big)$ for $n = 2, 3, 4$, and 5.

    b) Prove that, for all even values of n, there is a number $\delta_n = \pm 1$ such that we have

$$f_{n+1}(k) \equiv \begin{cases} \Sigma f_n(k), & \text{if } 0 < k \leq j_n \text{ or } 2^n + j_n < k \leq 2^{n+1}, \\ 1 + \Sigma f_n(k + \delta_n), & \text{if } j_n < k \leq 2^n + j_n, \end{cases}$$

    where the congruence is modulo 2. (In this formula Σf stands for the summation function $\Sigma f(k) = \sum_{j=0}^{k-1} f(j)$.) Hence $j_{n+1} = 2^n - \delta_n$ when n is even.

    c) Let $\big(c_n(0) c_n(1) \ldots c_n(2^{2n} - 5)\big)$ be the cycle produced when the simplified version of Algorithm D in exercise 95(b) is applied to $f_n()$. Where do the $(2n - 1)$-tuples 1^{2n-1} and $(01)^{n-1}0$ occur in this cycle?

    d) Use the results of (c) to express $f_{2n}(k)$ in terms of $f_n()$.

    e) Find a (somewhat) simple formula for j_n as a function of n.

98. [*M34*] Continuing the previous exercise, design an efficient algorithm to compute $f_n(k)$, given $n \geq 2$ and $k \geq 0$.

▶ **99.** [*M23*] Exploit the technology of the previous exercises to design an efficient algorithm that locates any given n-bit string in the cycle $\big(f_n(0) f_n(1) \ldots f_n(2^n - 1)\big)$.

100. [*40*] Do the de Bruijn cycles of exercise 97 provide a useful source of pseudo-random bits when n is large?

▶ **101.** [*M30*] (*Unique factorization of strings into nonincreasing primes.*)

    a) Prove that if λ and λ' are prime, then $\lambda\lambda'$ is prime if $\lambda < \lambda'$.

    b) Consequently every string α can be written in the form

$$\alpha = \lambda_1 \lambda_2 \ldots \lambda_t, \qquad \lambda_1 \geq \lambda_2 \geq \cdots \geq \lambda_t, \qquad \text{where each } \lambda_j \text{ is prime.}$$

    c) In fact, only one such factorization is possible. *Hint:* Show that λ_t must be the lexicographically smallest nonempty suffix of α.

    d) True or false: λ_1 is the longest prime prefix of α.

    e) What are the prime factors of 31415926535897932384626433832795028841197?

102. [*HM28*] Deduce the number of m-ary primes of length n from the unique factorization theorem in the previous exercise.

103. [*M20*] Use Eq. (59) to prove Fermat's theorem that $m^p \equiv m$ (modulo p).

104. [*17*] According to formula (60), about $1/n$ of all n-letter words are prime. How many of the 5757 five-letter GraphBase words are prime? Which of them is the smallest nonprime? The largest prime?

105. [*M31*] Let α be a preprime string of length n on an infinite alphabet.

  a) Show that if the final letter of α is increased, the resulting string is prime.
  b) If α has been factored as in exercise 101, show that it is the n-extension of λ_1.
  c) Furthermore α cannot be the n-extension of two different primes.

▸ **106.** [*M30*] By reverse-engineering Algorithm F, design an algorithm that visits all m-ary primes and preprimes in *decreasing* order.

107. [*HM30*] Analyze the running time of Algorithm F.

108. [*M35*] Let $\lambda_1 < \cdots < \lambda_t$ be the m-ary prime strings whose lengths divide n, and let $a_1 \ldots a_n$ be any m-ary string. The object of this exercise is to prove that $a_1 \ldots a_n$ appears in $\lambda_1 \ldots \lambda_t \lambda_1 \lambda_2$; hence $\lambda_1 \ldots \lambda_t$ is a de Bruijn cycle (since it has length m^n). For convenience we may assume that $m = 10$ and that strings correspond to decimal numbers; the same arguments will apply for arbitrary $m \geq 2$.

  a) Show that if $a_1 \ldots a_n = \alpha\beta$ is distinct from all its cyclic shifts, and if $\beta\alpha = \lambda_k$ is prime, then $\alpha\beta$ is a substring of $\lambda_k \lambda_{k+1}$, unless $\alpha = 9^j$ for some $j \geq 1$.
  b) Where does $\alpha\beta$ appear in $\lambda_1 \ldots \lambda_t$ if $\beta\alpha$ is prime and α consists of all 9s? *Hint:* Show that if $a_{n+1-l} \ldots a_n = 9^l$ in step F2 for some $l > 0$, and if j is not a divisor of n, the previous step F2 had $a_{n-l} \ldots a_n = 9^{l+1}$.
  c) Now consider n-tuples of the form $(\alpha\beta)^d$, where $d > 1$ is a divisor of n and $\beta\alpha = \lambda_k$ is prime.
  d) Where do 899135, 997879, 913131, 090909, 909090, and 911911 occur when $n=6$?
  e) Is $\lambda_1 \ldots \lambda_t$ the lexicographically least m-ary de Bruijn cycle of length m^n?

109. [*M22*] An m-ary de Bruijn torus of size $m^2 \times m^2$ for 2×2 windows is a matrix of m-ary digits d_{ij} such that each of the m^4 submatrices

$$\begin{pmatrix} d_{ij} & d_{i(j+1)} \\ d_{(i+1)j} & d_{(i+1)(j+1)} \end{pmatrix}, \qquad 0 \leq i,j < m^2$$

is different, where subscripts wrap around modulo m^2. Thus every possible m-ary 2×2 submatrix occurs exactly once; Ian Stewart [*Game, Set, and Math* (Oxford: Blackwell, 1989), Chapter 4] has therefore called it an m-ary *ourotorus*. For example,

$$\begin{pmatrix} 0 & 0 & 1 & 0 \\ 0 & 0 & 0 & 1 \\ 0 & 1 & 1 & 1 \\ 1 & 0 & 1 & 1 \end{pmatrix}$$

is a binary ourotorus; indeed, it is essentially the only such matrix when $m = 2$, except for shifting and/or transposition.

Consider the infinite matrix D whose entry in row $i = (\ldots a_2 a_1 a_0)_2$ and column $j = (\ldots b_2 b_1 b_0)_2$ is $d_{ij} = (\ldots c_2 c_1 c_0)_2$, where

$$c_0 = (a_0 \oplus b_0)(a_1 \oplus b_1) \oplus b_1;$$
$$c_k = (a_{2k} a_0 \oplus b_{2k}) b_0 \oplus (a_{2k+1} a_0 \oplus b_{2k+1})(b_0 \oplus 1), \quad \text{for } k > 0.$$

Show that the upper left $2^{2n} \times 2^{2n}$ submatrix of D is a 2^n-ary ourotorus for all $n \geq 0$.

110. [*M25*] Continuing the previous exercise, construct m-ary ourotoruses for all m.

111. [*20*] We can obtain the number 100 in twelve ways by inserting $+$ and $-$ signs into the sequence 123456789; for example, $100 = 1 + 23 - 4 + 5 + 6 + 78 - 9 = 123 - 45 - 67 + 89 = -1 + 2 - 3 + 4 + 5 + 6 + 78 + 9$.

a) What is the smallest positive integer that cannot be represented in such a way?

b) Consider also inserting signs into the 10-digit sequence 9876543210.

▸ **112.** [*25*] Continuing the previous exercise, how far can we go by inserting signs into 12345678987654321? For example, $100 = -1234 - 5 - 6 + 7898 - 7 - 6543 - 2 - 1$.

> *Tin tan din dan bim bam bom bo —*
> *tan tin din dan bam bim bo bom —*
> *tin tan dan din bim bam bom bo —*
> *tan tin dan din bam bim bo bom —*
> *tan dan tin bam din bo bim bom —*
> *.... Tin tan din dan bim bam bom bo.*
>
> — DOROTHY L. SAYERS, *The Nine Tailors* (1934)

> *A permutation on the ten decimal digits is simply a 10 digit decimal number*
> *in which all digits are distinct. Hence all we need to do is to produce*
> *all 10 digit numbers and select only those whose digits are distinct.*
> *Isn't it wonderful how high speed computing saves us from*
> *the drudgery of thinking! We simply program $k + 1 \to k$*
> *and examine the digits of k for undesirable equalities.*
> *This gives us the permutations in dictionary order too!*
> *On second sober thought ... we do need to think of something else.*
>
> — D. H. LEHMER (1957)

7.2.1.2. Generating all permutations. After n-tuples, the next most important item on nearly everybody's wish list for combinatorial generation is the task of visiting all *permutations* of some given set or multiset. Many different ways have been devised to solve this problem. In fact, almost as many different algorithms have been published for unsorting as for sorting! We will study the most important permutation generators in this section, beginning with a classical method that is both simple and flexible:

Algorithm L (*Lexicographic permutation generation*). Given a sequence of n elements $a_1 a_2 \ldots a_n$, initially sorted so that

$$a_1 \leq a_2 \leq \cdots \leq a_n, \tag{1}$$

this algorithm generates all permutations of $\{a_1, a_2, \ldots, a_n\}$, visiting them in lexicographic order. (For example, the permutations of $\{1, 2, 2, 3\}$ are

$$1223, \ 1232, \ 1322, \ 2123, \ 2132, \ 2213, \ 2231, \ 2312, \ 2321, \ 3122, \ 3212, \ 3221,$$

ordered lexicographically.) An auxiliary element a_0 is assumed to be present for convenience; a_0 must be strictly less than the largest element a_n.

L1. [Visit.] Visit the permutation $a_1 a_2 \ldots a_n$.

L2. [Find j.] Set $j \leftarrow n - 1$. If $a_j \geq a_{j+1}$, decrease j by 1 repeatedly until $a_j < a_{j+1}$. Terminate the algorithm if $j = 0$. (At this point j is the smallest subscript such that we have already visited all permutations beginning with $a_1 \ldots a_j$. Therefore the lexicographically next permutation will increase the value of a_j.)

L3. [Increase a_j.] Set $l \leftarrow n$. If $a_j \geq a_l$, decrease l by 1 repeatedly until $a_j < a_l$. Then interchange $a_j \leftrightarrow a_l$. (Since $a_{j+1} \geq \cdots \geq a_n$, element a_l is the smallest element greater than a_j that can legitimately follow $a_1 \ldots a_{j-1}$ in a permutation. Before the interchange we had $a_{j+1} \geq \cdots \geq a_{l-1} \geq a_l > a_j \geq a_{l+1} \geq \cdots \geq a_n$; after the interchange, we have $a_{j+1} \geq \cdots \geq a_{l-1} \geq a_j > a_l \geq a_{l+1} \geq \cdots \geq a_n$.)

L4. [Reverse $a_{j+1} \ldots a_n$.] Set $k \leftarrow j + 1$ and $l \leftarrow n$. Then, if $k < l$, interchange $a_k \leftrightarrow a_l$, set $k \leftarrow k + 1$, $l \leftarrow l - 1$, and repeat until $k \geq l$. Return to L1. ∎

This algorithm goes back to Nārāyaṇa Paṇḍita in 14th-century India (see Section 7.2.1.7); it also appeared in C. F. Hindenburg's preface to *Specimen Analyticum de Lineis Curvis Secundi Ordinis* by C. F. Rüdiger (Leipzig: 1784), xlvi–xlvii, and it has been frequently rediscovered ever since. The parenthetical remarks in steps L2 and L3 explain why it works.

In general, the lexicographic successor of any combinatorial pattern $a_1 \ldots a_n$ is obtainable by a three-step procedure:

1) Find the largest j such that a_j can be increased.
2) Increase a_j by the smallest feasible amount.
3) Find the lexicographically least way to extend the new $a_1 \ldots a_j$ to a complete pattern.

Algorithm L follows this general procedure in the case of permutation generation, just as Algorithm 7.2.1.1M followed it in the case of n-tuple generation; we will see numerous further instances later, as we consider other kinds of combinatorial patterns. Notice that we have $a_{j+1} \geq \cdots \geq a_n$ at the beginning of step L4. Therefore the first permutation beginning with the current prefix $a_1 \ldots a_j$ is $a_1 \ldots a_j a_n \ldots a_{j+1}$, and step L4 produces it by doing $\lfloor (n - j)/2 \rfloor$ interchanges.

In practice, step L2 finds $j = n - 1$ half of the time when the elements are distinct, because exactly $n!/2$ of the $n!$ permutations have $a_{n-1} < a_n$. Therefore Algorithm L can be speeded up by recognizing this special case, without making it significantly more complicated. (See exercise 1.) Similarly, the probability that $j \leq n - t$ is only $1/t!$ when the a's are distinct; hence the loops in steps L2–L4 usually go very fast. Exercise 6 analyzes the running time in general, showing that Algorithm L is reasonably efficient even when equal elements are present, unless some values appear much more often than others do in the multiset $\{a_1, a_2, \ldots, a_n\}$.

Adjacent interchanges. We saw in Section 7.2.1.1 that Gray codes are advantageous for generating n-tuples, and similar considerations apply when we want to generate permutations. The simplest possible change to a permutation is to interchange adjacent elements, and we know from Chapter 5 that any permutation can be sorted into order if we make a suitable sequence of such interchanges. (For example, Algorithm 5.2.2B works in this way.) Hence we can go backward and obtain any desired permutation, by starting with all elements in order and then exchanging appropriate pairs of adjacent elements.

A natural question now arises: Is it possible to run through *all* permutations of a given multiset in such a way that only two adjacent elements change places at every step? If so, the overall program that is examining all permutations will often be simpler and faster, because it will only need to calculate the effect of an exchange instead of to reprocess an entirely new array $a_1 \ldots a_n$ each time.

Alas, when the multiset has repeated elements, we can't always find such a Gray-like sequence. For example, the six permutations of $\{1, 1, 2, 2\}$ are connected to each other in the following way by adjacent interchanges:

$$1122 \; \underline{\quad} \; 1212 \; \overset{\displaystyle \diagup 2112 \diagdown}{\underset{\displaystyle \diagdown 1221 \diagup}{}} \; 2121 \; \underline{\quad} \; 2211; \tag{2}$$

this graph has no Hamiltonian path.

But most applications deal with permutations of *distinct* elements, and for this case there is good news: A simple algorithm makes it possible to generate all $n!$ permutations by making just $n! - 1$ adjacent interchanges. Furthermore, another such interchange returns to the starting point, so we have a Hamiltonian cycle analogous to Gray binary code.

The idea is to take such a sequence for $\{1, \ldots, n - 1\}$ and to insert the number n into each permutation in all ways. For example, if $n = 4$ the sequence $(123, 132, 312, 321, 231, 213)$ leads to the columns of the array

$$\begin{array}{cccccc} 1234 & 1324 & 3124 & 3214 & 2314 & 2134 \\ 1243 & 1342 & 3142 & 3241 & 2341 & 2143 \\ 1423 & 1432 & 3412 & 3421 & 2431 & 2413 \\ 4123 & 4132 & 4312 & 4321 & 4231 & 4213 \end{array} \tag{3}$$

when 4 is inserted in all four possible positions. Now we obtain the desired sequence by reading downwards in the first column, upwards in the second, downwards in the third, ..., upwards in the last: $(1234, 1243, 1423, 4123, 4132, 1432, 1342, 1324, 3124, 3142, \ldots, 2143, 2134)$.

In Section 5.1.1 we studied the inversions of a permutation, namely the pairs of elements (not necessarily adjacent) that are out of order. Every interchange of adjacent elements changes the total number of inversions by ± 1. In fact, when we consider the so-called inversion table $c_1 \ldots c_n$ of exercise 5.1.1–7, where c_j is the number of elements lying to the right of j that are less than j, we find that the permutations in (3) have the following inversion tables:

$$\begin{array}{cccccc} 0000 & 0010 & 0020 & 0120 & 0110 & 0100 \\ 0001 & 0011 & 0021 & 0121 & 0111 & 0101 \\ 0002 & 0012 & 0022 & 0122 & 0112 & 0102 \\ 0003 & 0013 & 0023 & 0123 & 0113 & 0103 \end{array} \tag{4}$$

And if we read these columns alternately down and up as before, we obtain precisely the reflected Gray code for mixed radices $(1, 2, 3, 4)$, as in Eqs. (46)–(51)

of Section 7.2.1.1. The same property holds for all n, as noticed by E. W. Dijkstra [*Acta Informatica* **6** (1976), 357–359], and it leads us to the following formulation:

Algorithm P (*Plain changes*). Given a sequence $a_1 a_2 \ldots a_n$ of n distinct elements, this algorithm generates all of their permutations by repeatedly interchanging adjacent pairs. It uses an auxiliary array $c_1 c_2 \ldots c_n$, which represents inversions as described above, running through all sequences of integers such that

$$0 \le c_j < j \qquad \text{for } 1 \le j \le n. \tag{5}$$

Another array $o_1 o_2 \ldots o_n$ governs the directions by which the entries c_j change.

P1. [Initialize.] Set $c_j \leftarrow 0$ and $o_j \leftarrow 1$ for $1 \le j \le n$.

P2. [Visit.] Visit the permutation $a_1 a_2 \ldots a_n$.

P3. [Prepare for change.] Set $j \leftarrow n$ and $s \leftarrow 0$. (The following steps determine the coordinate j for which c_j is about to change, preserving (5); variable s is the number of indices $k > j$ such that $c_k = k - 1$.)

P4. [Ready to change?] Set $q \leftarrow c_j + o_j$. If $q < 0$, go to P7; if $q = j$, go to P6.

P5. [Change.] Interchange $a_{j-c_j+s} \leftrightarrow a_{j-q+s}$. Then set $c_j \leftarrow q$ and return to P2.

P6. [Increase s.] Terminate if $j = 1$; otherwise set $s \leftarrow s + 1$.

P7. [Switch direction.] Set $o_j \leftarrow -o_j$, $j \leftarrow j - 1$, and go back to P4. ∎

This procedure, which clearly works for all $n \ge 1$, originated in 17th-century England, when bell ringers began the delightful custom of ringing a set of bells in all possible permutations. They called Algorithm P the method of *plain changes*. Figure 18(a) illustrates the "Cambridge Forty-Eight," an irregular and ad hoc sequence of 48 permutations on 5 bells that had been used in the early 1600s, before the plain-change principle revealed how to achieve all $5! = 120$ possibilities. The venerable history of Algorithm P has been traced to a manuscript by Peter Mundy now in the Bodleian Library, written about 1653 and transcribed by Ernest Morris in *The History and Art of Change Ringing* (1931), 29–30. Shortly afterwards, a famous book called *Tintinnalogia*, published anonymously in 1668 but now known to have been written by Richard Duckworth and Fabian Stedman, devoted its first 60 pages to a detailed description of plain changes, working up from $n = 3$ to the case of arbitrarily large n.

Cambridge Forty-eight, *for many years,*
was the greatest Peal *that was* Rang *or invented; but now,*
neither Forty-eight, *nor a* Hundred, *nor* Seven-hundred and twenty,
nor any Number can confine us; for we can Ring Changes, Ad infinitum.
... *On four Bells, there are* Twenty four several Changes,
in Ringing *of which, there is one Bell called the* Hunt,
and the other three are Extream *Bells;*
the Hunt *moves, and* hunts *up and down continually* ...;
two of the Extream *Bells makes a* Change
every time the Hunt *comes before or behind them.*

— DUCKWORTH and STEDMAN, *Tintinnalogia* (1668)

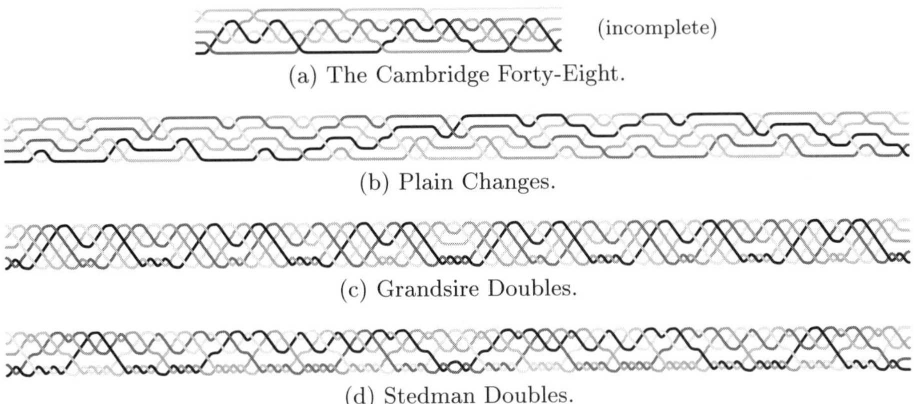

(a) The Cambridge Forty-Eight.

(b) Plain Changes.

(c) Grandsire Doubles.

(d) Stedman Doubles.

Fig. 18. Four patterns that were used in 17th-century
England to ring permutations of five different church-
bells. Pattern (b) corresponds to Algorithm P.

British bellringing enthusiasts soon went on to develop more complicated
schemes in which two or more pairs of bells change places simultaneously. For
example, they devised the pattern in Fig. 18(c) known as Grandsire Doubles,
"the best and most ingenious Peal that ever was composed, to be rang on five
bells" [*Tintinnalogia*, page 95]. Such fancier methods are more interesting than
Algorithm P from a musical or mathematical standpoint, but they are less useful
in computer applications, so we shall not dwell on them here. Interested readers
can learn more by reading W. G. Wilson's book, *Change Ringing* (1965); see
also A. T. White, *AMM* **103** (1996), 771–778.

H. F. Trotter published the first computer implementation of plain changes
in *CACM* **5** (1962), 434–435. The algorithm is quite efficient, especially when it
is streamlined as in exercise 16, because $n - 1$ out of every n permutations are
generated without using steps P6 and P7. By contrast, Algorithm L enjoys its
best case only about half of the time.

The fact that Algorithm P does exactly one interchange per visit means that
the permutations it generates are alternately even and odd (see exercise 5.1.1–
13). Therefore we can generate all the even permutations by simply bypassing
the odd ones. In fact, the c and o tables make it easy to keep track of the current
total number of inversions, $c_1 + \cdots + c_n$, as we go.

Many programs need to generate the same permutations repeatedly, and in
such cases we needn't run through the steps of Algorithm P each time. We can
simply prepare a list of suitable transitions, using the following method:

Algorithm T (*Plain change transitions*). This algorithm computes a table $t[1]$,
$t[2]$, ..., $t[n! - 1]$ such that the actions of Algorithm P are equivalent to the
successive interchanges $a_{t[k]} \leftrightarrow a_{t[k]+1}$ for $1 \leq k < n!$. We assume that $n \geq 2$.

T1. [Initialize.] Set $N \leftarrow n!$, $d \leftarrow N/2$, $t[d] \leftarrow 1$, and $m \leftarrow 2$.

T2. [Loop on m.] Terminate if $m = n$. Otherwise set $m \leftarrow m + 1$, $d \leftarrow d/m$, and $k \leftarrow 0$. (We maintain the condition $d = n!/m!$.)

T3. [Hunt down.] Set $k \leftarrow k + d$ and $j \leftarrow m - 1$. Then while $j > 0$, set $t[k] \leftarrow j$, $j \leftarrow j - 1$, and $k \leftarrow k + d$, until $j = 0$.

T4. [Offset.] Set $t[k] \leftarrow t[k] + 1$ and $k \leftarrow k + d$.

T5. [Hunt up.] While $j < m - 1$, set $j \leftarrow j + 1$, $t[k] \leftarrow j$, and $k \leftarrow k + d$. Return to T3 if $k < N$, otherwise return to T2. $\blacksquare$

For example, if $n = 4$ we get the table $(t[1], t[2], \ldots, t[23]) = (3, 2, 1, 3, 1, 2, 3, 1, 3, 2, 1, 3, 1, 2, 3, 1, 3, 2, 1, 3, 1, 2, 3)$.

Alphametics. Now let's consider a simple kind of puzzle in which permutations are useful: How can the pattern

$$
\begin{array}{r}
\texttt{SEND} \\
+\,\texttt{MORE} \\
\hline
\texttt{MONEY}
\end{array}
\tag{6}
$$

represent a correct sum, if every letter stands for a different decimal digit? [H. E. Dudeney, *Strand* **68** (1924), 97, 214.] Such puzzles are often called "alphametics," a word coined by J. A. H. Hunter [*Globe and Mail* (Toronto: 27 October 1955), 27]; another term, "cryptarithm," has also been suggested by S. Vatriquant [*Sphinx* **1** (May 1931), 50].

The classic alphametic (6) can easily be solved by hand (see exercise 21). But let's suppose we want to deal with a large set of complicated alphametics, some of which may be unsolvable while others may have dozens of solutions. Then we can save time by programming a computer to try out all permutations of digits that match a given pattern, seeing which permutations yield a correct sum. [A computer program for solving alphametics was published by John Beidler in *Creative Computing* **4**, 6 (November–December 1978), 110–113.]

We might as well raise our sights slightly and consider additive alphametics in general, dealing not only with simple sums like (6) but also with examples like

$$\texttt{VIOLIN} + \texttt{VIOLIN} + \texttt{VIOLA} \;=\; \texttt{TRIO} + \texttt{SONATA}.$$

Equivalently, we want to solve puzzles such as

$$2(\texttt{VIOLIN}) + \texttt{VIOLA} - \texttt{TRIO} - \texttt{SONATA} \;=\; 0, \tag{7}$$

where a sum of terms with integer coefficients is given and the goal is to obtain zero by substituting distinct decimal digits for the different letters. Each letter in such a problem has a "signature" obtained by substituting 1 for that letter and 0 for the others; for example, the signature for $\texttt{I}$ in (7) is

$$2(010010) + 01000 - 0010 - 000000,$$

namely 21010. If we arbitrarily assign the codes $(1, 2, \ldots, 10)$ to the letters $(\texttt{V}, \texttt{I}, \texttt{O}, \texttt{L}, \texttt{N}, \texttt{A}, \texttt{T}, \texttt{R}, \texttt{S}, \texttt{X})$, the respective signatures corresponding to (7) are

$$
\begin{aligned}
&s_1 = 210000, \quad s_2 = 21010, \quad s_3 = -7901, \quad s_4 = 210, \quad s_5 = -998, \\
&s_6 = -100, \quad s_7 = -1010, \quad s_8 = -100, \quad s_9 = -100000, \quad s_{10} = 0.
\end{aligned}
\tag{8}
$$

(An additional letter, X, has been added because we need ten of them.) The problem now is to find all permutations $a_1 \ldots a_{10}$ of $\{0, 1, \ldots, 9\}$ such that

$$a \cdot s = \sum_{j=1}^{10} a_j s_j = 0. \tag{9}$$

There also is a side condition, because the numbers in alphametics should not have zero as a leading digit. For example, the sums

7316		5731		6524		2817
$+\,0823$	and	$+\,0647$	and	$+\,0735$	and	$+\,0368$
08139		06378		07259		03185

and numerous others are *not* considered to be valid solutions of (6). In general there is a set F of first letters such that we must have

$$a_j \neq 0 \qquad \text{for all } j \in F; \tag{10}$$

the set F corresponding to (7) and (8) is $\{1, 7, 9\}$.

One way to tackle a family of additive alphametics is to start by using Algorithm T to prepare a table of $10! - 1$ transitions $t[k]$. Then, for each problem defined by a signature sequence $(s_1, \ldots, s_{10})$ and a first-letter set F, we can exhaustively look for solutions as follows:

A1. [Initialize.] Set $a_1 a_2 \ldots a_{10} \leftarrow 01 \ldots 9$, $v \leftarrow \sum_{j=1}^{10}(j-1)s_j$, $k \leftarrow 1$, and $\delta_j \leftarrow s_{j+1} - s_j$ for $1 \leq j < 10$.

A2. [Test.] If $v = 0$ and if (10) holds, output the solution $a_1 \ldots a_{10}$.

A3. [Swap.] Stop if $k = 10!$. Otherwise set $j \leftarrow t[k]$, $v \leftarrow v - (a_{j+1} - a_j)\delta_j$, $a_{j+1} \leftrightarrow a_j$, $k \leftarrow k + 1$, and return to A2. ∎

Step A3 is justified by the fact that swapping a_j with a_{j+1} simply decreases $a \cdot s$ by $(a_{j+1} - a_j)(s_{j+1} - s_j)$. Even though 10! is 3,628,800, a fairly large number, the operations in step A3 are so simple that the whole job takes only a fraction of a second on a modern computer.

An alphametic is said to be *pure* if it has a unique solution. Unfortunately (7) is not pure; the permutations 1764802539 and 3546281970 both solve (9) and (10), hence we have both

$$176478 + 176478 + 17640 = 2576 + 368020$$

and

$$354652 + 354652 + 35468 = 1954 + 742818.$$

Furthermore $s_6 = s_8$ in (8), so we can obtain two more solutions by interchanging the digits assigned to A and R.

On the other hand (6) *is* pure, yet the method we have described will find two different permutations that solve it. The reason is that (6) involves only eight distinct letters, hence we will set it up for solution by using two dummy signatures $s_9 = s_{10} = 0$. In general, an alphametic with m distinct letters will have $10 - m$ dummy signatures $s_{m+1} = \cdots = s_{10} = 0$, and each of its solutions will be found $(10 - m)!$ times unless we insist that, say, $a_{m+1} < \cdots < a_{10}$.

A general framework. A great many algorithms have been proposed for generating permutations of distinct objects, and the best way to understand them is to apply the multiplicative properties of permutations that we studied in Section 1.3.3. For this purpose we will change our notation slightly, by using 0-origin indexing and writing $a_0 a_1 \ldots a_{n-1}$ for permutations of $\{0, 1, \ldots, n-1\}$ instead of writing $a_1 a_2 \ldots a_n$ for permutations of $\{1, 2, \ldots, n\}$. More importantly, we will consider schemes for generating permutations in which most of the action takes place at the *left*, so that all permutations of $\{0, 1, \ldots, k-1\}$ will be generated during the first $k!$ steps, for $1 \le k \le n$. For example, one such scheme for $n = 4$ is

$$
\begin{array}{l}
0123, 1023, 0213, 2013, 1203, 2103, 0132, 1032, 0312, 3012, 1302, 3102, \\
0231, 2031, 0321, 3021, 2301, 3201, 1230, 2130, 1320, 3120, 2310, 3210;
\end{array} \qquad (11)
$$

this is called "reverse colex order," because if we reflect the strings from right to left we get 3210, 3201, 3120, ..., 0123, the reverse of lexicographic order. Another way to think of (11) is to view the entries as $(n-a_n) \ldots (n-a_2)(n-a_1)$, where $a_1 a_2 \ldots a_n$ runs lexicographically through the permutations of $\{1, 2, \ldots, n\}$.

Let's recall from Section 1.3.3 that a permutation like $\alpha = 250143$ can be written either in the two-line form

$$
\alpha = \begin{pmatrix} 012345 \\ 250143 \end{pmatrix}
$$

or in the more compact cycle form

$$
\alpha = (0\ 2)(1\ 5\ 3),
$$

with the meaning that α takes $0 \mapsto 2$, $1 \mapsto 5$, $2 \mapsto 0$, $3 \mapsto 1$, $4 \mapsto 4$, and $5 \mapsto 3$; a 1-cycle like '(4)' need not be indicated. Since 4 is a fixed point of this permutation we say that "α fixes 4." We also write $0\alpha = 2$, $1\alpha = 5$, and so on, saying that $j\alpha$ is "the image of j under α." Multiplication of permutations, like α times β where $\beta = 543210$, is readily carried out either in the two-line form

$$
\alpha\beta = \begin{pmatrix} 012345 \\ 250143 \end{pmatrix}\begin{pmatrix} 012345 \\ 543210 \end{pmatrix} = \begin{pmatrix} 012345 \\ 250143 \end{pmatrix}\begin{pmatrix} 250143 \\ 305412 \end{pmatrix} = \begin{pmatrix} 012345 \\ 305412 \end{pmatrix}
$$

or in the cycle form

$$
\alpha\beta = (0\ 2)(1\ 5\ 3) \cdot (0\ 5)(1\ 4)(2\ 3) = (0\ 3\ 4\ 1)(2\ 5).
$$

Notice that the image of 1 under $\alpha\beta$ is $1(\alpha\beta) = (1\alpha)\beta = 5\beta = 0$, etc. *Warning:* About half of all books that deal with permutations multiply them the other way (from right to left), imagining that $\alpha\beta$ means that β should be applied before α. The reason is that traditional functional notation, in which one writes $\alpha(1) = 5$, makes it natural to think that $\alpha\beta(1)$ should mean $\alpha(\beta(1)) = \alpha(4) = 4$. However, the present book subscribes to the other philosophy, and we shall always multiply permutations from left to right.

The order of multiplication needs to be understood carefully when permutations are represented by arrays of numbers. For example, if we "apply" the reflection $\beta = 543210$ to the permutation $\alpha = 250143$, the result 341052 is not $\alpha\beta$

but $\beta\alpha$. In general, the operation of replacing a permutation $\alpha = a_0 a_1 \ldots a_{n-1}$ by some rearrangement $a_{0\beta} a_{1\beta} \ldots a_{(n-1)\beta}$ takes $k \mapsto a_{k\beta} = k\beta\alpha$. Permuting the *positions* by β corresponds to *premultiplication* by β, changing α to $\beta\alpha$; permuting the *values* by β corresponds to *postmultiplication* by β, changing α to $\alpha\beta$. Thus, for example, a permutation generator that interchanges $a_1 \leftrightarrow a_2$ is premultiplying the current permutation by $(1\ 2)$, postmultiplying it by $(a_1\ a_2)$.

Following a proposal made by Évariste Galois in 1830, a nonempty set G of permutations is said to form a *group* if it is closed under multiplication, that is, if the product $\alpha\beta$ is in G whenever α and β are elements of G [see *Écrits et Mémoires Mathématiques d'Évariste Galois* (Paris: 1962), 47]. Consider, for example, the 4-cube represented as a 4×4 torus

$$
\begin{array}{|cccc|}
\hline
0 & 1 & 3 & 2 \\
4 & 5 & 7 & 6 \\
c & d & f & e \\
8 & 9 & b & a \\
\hline
\end{array}
\tag{12}
$$

as in exercise 7.2.1.1–17, and let G be the set of all permutations of the vertices $\{0, 1, \ldots, f\}$ that preserve adjacency: A permutation α is in G if and only if $u \,\text{---}\, v$ implies $u\alpha \,\text{---}\, v\alpha$ in the 4-cube. (Here we are using hexadecimal digits $(0, 1, \ldots, f)$ to stand for the integers $(0, 1, \ldots, 15)$. The labels in (12) are chosen so that $u \,\text{---}\, v$ if and only if u and v differ in only one bit position.) This set G is obviously a group, and its elements are called the symmetries or "automorphisms" of the 4-cube.

Groups of permutations G are conveniently represented inside a computer by means of a *Sims table*, introduced by Charles C. Sims [*Computational Methods in Abstract Algebra* (Oxford: Pergamon, 1970), 169–183], which is a family of subsets $S_1, S_2, \ldots$ of G having the following property: S_k contains exactly one permutation σ_{kj} that takes $k \mapsto j$ and fixes the values of all elements greater than k, whenever G contains such a permutation. We let σ_{kk} be the identity permutation, which is always present in G; but when $0 \le j < k$, any suitable permutation can be selected to play the role of σ_{kj}. The main advantage of a Sims table is that it provides a convenient representation of the entire group:

Lemma S. *Let $S_1, S_2, \ldots, S_{n-1}$ be a Sims table for a group G of permutations on $\{0, 1, \ldots, n-1\}$. Then every element α of G has a unique representation*

$$
\alpha = \sigma_1 \sigma_2 \ldots \sigma_{n-1}, \qquad \text{where } \sigma_k \in S_k \text{ for } 1 \le k < n. \tag{13}
$$

Proof. If α has such a representation and if σ_{n-1} is the permutation $\sigma_{(n-1)j} \in S_{n-1}$, then α takes $n - 1 \mapsto j$, because all elements of $S_1 \cup \cdots \cup S_{n-2}$ fix the value of $n - 1$. Conversely, if α takes $n - 1 \mapsto j$ we have $\alpha = \alpha'\sigma_{(n-1)j}$, where

$$
\alpha' = \alpha\, \sigma^-_{(n-1)j}
$$

is a permutation of G that fixes $n - 1$. (As in Section 1.3.3, σ^- denotes the inverse of σ.) The set G' of all such permutations is a group, and $S_1, \ldots, S_{n-2}$ is a Sims table for G'; therefore the result follows by induction on n. $\blacksquare$

For example, a bit of calculation shows that one possible Sims table for the automorphism group of the 4-cube is

$$S_{\mathsf{f}} = \{(),\ (01)(23)(45)(67)(89)(\mathsf{ab})(\mathsf{cd})(\mathsf{ef}),\ \ldots,$$
$$(\mathsf{0f})(\mathsf{1e})(\mathsf{2d})(\mathsf{3c})(\mathsf{4b})(\mathsf{5a})(69)(78)\};$$
$$S_{\mathsf{e}} = \{(),\ (12)(56)(\mathsf{9a})(\mathsf{de}),\ (14)(36)(\mathsf{9c})(\mathsf{be}),\ (18)(\mathsf{3a})(\mathsf{5c})(\mathsf{7e})\};$$
$$S_{\mathsf{d}} = \{(),\ (24)(35)(\mathsf{ac})(\mathsf{bd}),\ (28)(39)(\mathsf{6c})(\mathsf{7d})\};$$
$$S_{\mathsf{c}} = \{()\};$$
$$S_{\mathsf{b}} = \{(),\ (48)(59)(\mathsf{6a})(\mathsf{7b})\};$$
$$S_{\mathsf{a}} = S_{9} = \cdots = S_{1} = \{()\};$$

(14)

here S_{f} contains 16 permutations $\sigma_{\mathsf{f}j}$ for $0 \le j \le 15$, which respectively take $i \mapsto i \oplus (15 - j)$ for $0 \le i \le 15$. The set S_{e} contains only four permutations, because an automorphism that fixes f must take e into a neighbor of f; thus the image of e must be either e or d or b or 7. The set S_{c} contains only the identity permutation, because an automorphism that fixes f, e, and d must also fix c. Most groups have $S_k = \{()\}$ for all small values of k, as in this example; hence a Sims table usually needs to contain only a fairly small number of permutations although the group itself might be quite large.

The Sims representation (13) makes it easy to test if a given permutation α lies in G: First we determine $\sigma_{n-1} = \sigma_{(n-1)j}$, where α takes $n - 1 \mapsto j$, and we let $\alpha' = \alpha\sigma_{n-1}^{-}$; then we determine $\sigma_{n-2} = \sigma_{(n-2)j'}$, where α' takes $n - 2 \mapsto j'$, and we let $\alpha'' = \alpha'\sigma_{n-2}^{-}$; and so on. If at any stage the required σ_{kj} does not exist in S_k, the original permutation α does not belong to G. In the case of (14), this process must reduce α to the identity after finding σ_{f}, σ_{e}, σ_{d}, σ_{c}, and σ_{b}.

For example, let α be the permutation $(14)(28)(\mathsf{3c})(69)(\mathsf{7d})(\mathsf{be})$, which corresponds to transposing (12) about its main diagonal $\{0, 5, \mathsf{f}, \mathsf{a}\}$. Since α fixes f, σ_{f} will be the identity permutation (), and $\alpha' = \alpha$. Then σ_{e} is the member of S_{e} that takes $\mathsf{e} \mapsto \mathsf{b}$, namely $(14)(36)(\mathsf{9c})(\mathsf{be})$, and we find $\alpha'' = (28)(39)(\mathsf{6c})(\mathsf{7d})$. This permutation belongs to S_{d}, so α is indeed an automorphism of the 4-cube.

Conversely, (13) also makes it easy to generate all elements of the corresponding group. We simply run through all permutations of the form

$$\sigma(1, c_1)\sigma(2, c_2)\ldots\sigma(n - 1, c_{n-1}),$$

where $\sigma(k, c_k)$ is the $(c_k + 1)$st element of S_k for $0 \le c_k < s_k = |S_k|$ and $1 \le k < n$, using any algorithm of Section 7.2.1.1 that runs through all $(n - 1)$-tuples $(c_1, \ldots, c_{n-1})$ for the respective radices $(s_1, \ldots, s_{n-1})$.

Using the general framework. Our chief concern is the group of *all* permutations on $\{0, 1, \ldots, n-1\}$, and in this case every set S_k of a Sims table will contain $k+1$ elements $\{\sigma(k, 0), \sigma(k, 1), \ldots, \sigma(k, k)\}$, where $\sigma(k, 0)$ is the identity and the others take k to the values $\{0, \ldots, k-1\}$ in some order. (The permutation $\sigma(k, j)$ need not be the same as σ_{kj}, and it usually is different.) Every such Sims table leads to a permutation generator, according to the following outline:

Algorithm G (*General permutation generator*). Given a Sims table $(S_1, S_2, \ldots, S_{n-1})$ where each S_k has $k + 1$ elements $\sigma(k, j)$ as just described, this algorithm generates all permutations $a_0 a_1 \ldots a_{n-1}$ of $\{0, 1, \ldots, n - 1\}$, using an auxiliary control table $c_n \ldots c_2 c_1$.

G1. [Initialize.] Set $a_j \leftarrow j$ and $c_{j+1} \leftarrow 0$ for $0 \le j < n$.

G2. [Visit.] (At this point the mixed-radix number $\left[\begin{smallmatrix} c_{n-1}, & \ldots, & c_2, & c_1 \\ n, & \ldots, & 3, & 2 \end{smallmatrix}\right]$ is the number of permutations visited so far.) Visit the permutation $a_0 a_1 \ldots a_{n-1}$.

G3. [Add 1 to $c_n \ldots c_2 c_1$.] Set $k \leftarrow 1$. If $c_k = k$, set $c_k \leftarrow 0$, $k \leftarrow k + 1$, and repeat until $c_k < k$. Terminate the algorithm if $k = n$; otherwise set $c_k \leftarrow c_k + 1$.

G4. [Permute.] Apply the permutation $\tau(k, c_k)\omega(k - 1)^-$ to $a_0 a_1 \ldots a_{n-1}$, as explained below, and return to G2.　▌

Applying a permutation π to $a_0 a_1 \ldots a_{n-1}$ means replacing a_j by $a_{j\pi}$ for $0 \le j < n$; this corresponds to premultiplication by π as explained earlier. Let us define

$$\tau(k, j) = \sigma(k, j)\sigma(k, j - 1)^- \qquad \text{for } 1 \le j \le k; \tag{15}$$
$$\omega(k) = \sigma(1, 1) \ldots \sigma(k, k). \tag{16}$$

Then steps G3 and G4 maintain the property that

$$a_0 a_1 \ldots a_{n-1} \text{ is the permutation } \sigma(1, c_1)\sigma(2, c_2) \ldots \sigma(n - 1, c_{n-1}), \tag{17}$$

and Lemma S proves that every permutation is visited exactly once.

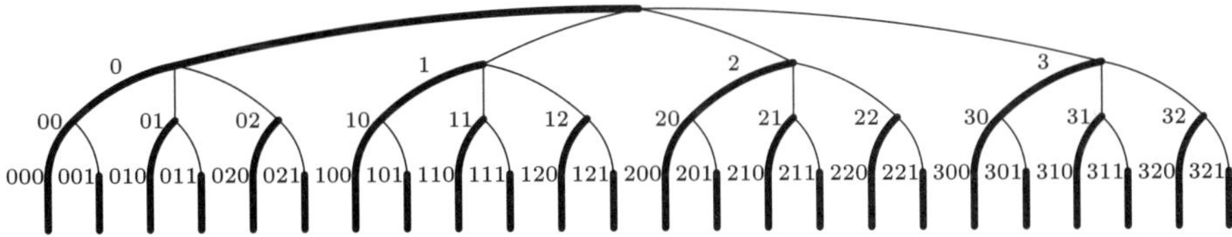

Fig. 19. Algorithm G implicitly traverses this tree when $n = 4$.

The tree in Fig. 19 illustrates Algorithm G in the case $n = 4$. According to (17), every permutation $a_0 a_1 a_2 a_3$ of $\{0, 1, 2, 3\}$ corresponds to a three-digit control string $c_3 c_2 c_1$, with $0 \le c_3 \le 3$, $0 \le c_2 \le 2$, and $0 \le c_1 \le 1$. Some nodes of the tree are labeled by a single digit c_3; these correspond to the permutations $\sigma(3, c_3)$ of the Sims table being used. Other nodes, labeled with two digits $c_3 c_2$, correspond to the permutations $\sigma(2, c_2)\sigma(3, c_3)$. A heavy line connects node c_3 to node $c_3 0$ and node $c_3 c_2$ to node $c_3 c_2 0$, because $\sigma(2, 0)$ and $\sigma(1, 0)$ are the identity permutation and these nodes are essentially equivalent. Adding 1 to the mixed-radix number $c_3 c_2 c_1$ in step G3 corresponds to moving from one node of Fig. 19 to its successor in preorder, and the transformation in step G4 changes the permutations accordingly. For example, when $c_3 c_2 c_1$ changes from 121 to 200, step G4 premultiplies the current permutation by

$$\tau(3, 2)\omega(2)^- = \tau(3, 2)\sigma(2, 2)^-\sigma(1, 1)^-;$$

premultiplying by $\sigma(1,1)^-$ takes us from node 121 to node 12, premultiplying by $\sigma(2,2)^-$ takes us from node 12 to node 1, and premultiplying by $\tau(3,2) = \sigma(3,2)\sigma(3,1)^-$ takes us from node 1 to node $2 \equiv 200$, which is the preorder successor of node 121. Stating this another way, premultiplication by $\tau(3,2)\omega(2)^-$ is exactly what is needed to change $\sigma(1,1)\sigma(2,2)\sigma(3,1)$ to $\sigma(1,0)\sigma(2,0)\sigma(3,2)$, preserving (17).

Algorithm G defines a huge number of permutation generators (see exercise 37), so it is no wonder that many of its special cases have appeared in the literature. Of course some of its variants are much more efficient than others, and we want to find examples where the operations are particularly well suited to the computer we are using.

We can, for instance, obtain permutations in reverse colex order as a special case of Algorithm G (see (11)), by letting $\sigma(k,j)$ be the $(j+1)$-cycle

$$\sigma(k,j) \;=\; (k{-}j \;\; k{-}j{+}1 \;\; \ldots \;\; k). \tag{18}$$

The reason is that $\sigma(k,j)$ should be the permutation that corresponds to $c_n \ldots c_1$ in reverse colex order when $c_k = j$ and $c_i = 0$ for $i \neq k$, and this permutation $a_0 a_1 \ldots a_{n-1}$ is $01 \ldots (k{-}j{-}1)(k{-}j{+}1) \ldots (k)(k{-}j)(k{+}1) \ldots (n{-}1)$. For example, when $n = 8$ and $c_n \ldots c_1 = 00030000$ the corresponding reverse colex permutation is 01345267, which is $(2\,3\,4\,5)$ in cycle form. When $\sigma(k,j)$ is given by (18), Eqs. (15) and (16) lead to the formulas

$$\tau(k,j) = (k{-}j \;\; k); \tag{19}$$

$$\omega(k) = (0\,1)(0\,1\,2)\ldots(0\,1 \ldots k) = (0\,k)(1\,k{-}1)(2\,k{-}2)\ldots = \phi(k); \tag{20}$$

here $\phi(k)$ is the "$(k{+}1)$-flip" that changes $a_0 \ldots a_k$ to $a_k \ldots a_0$. In this case $\omega(k)$ turns out to be the same as $\omega(k)^-$, because $\phi(k)^2 = (\,)$.

Equations (19) and (20) are implicitly present behind the scenes in Algorithm L and in its reverse colex equivalent (exercise 2), where step L3 essentially applies a transposition and step L4 does a flip. Step G4 actually does the flip first; but the identity

$$(k{-}j \;\; k)\phi(k-1) \;=\; \phi(k-1)(j{-}1 \;\; k) \tag{21}$$

shows that a flip followed by a transposition is the same as a (different) transposition followed by the flip.

In fact, equation (21) is a special case of the important identity

$$\pi^- (j_1 \;\; j_2 \;\; \ldots \;\; j_t)\,\pi \;=\; (j_1\pi \;\; j_2\pi \;\; \ldots \;\; j_t\pi), \tag{22}$$

which is valid for *any* permutation π and any t-cycle $(j_1 \;\; j_2 \;\; \ldots \;\; j_t)$. On the left of (22) we have, for example, $j_1\pi \mapsto j_1 \mapsto j_2 \mapsto j_2\pi$, in agreement with the cycle on the right. Therefore if α and π are any permutations whatsoever, the permutation $\pi^-\alpha\pi$ (called the *conjugate* of α by π) has exactly the same cycle structure as α; we simply replace each element j in each cycle by $j\pi$.

Another significant special case of Algorithm G was introduced by R. J. Ord-Smith [*CACM* **10** (1967), 452; **12** (1969), 638; see also *Comp. J.* **14** (1971),

136–139], whose algorithm is obtained by setting

$$\sigma(k, j) = (k \;\ldots\; 1\; 0)^j. \tag{23}$$

Now it is clear from (15) that

$$\tau(k, j) = (k \;\ldots\; 1\; 0); \tag{24}$$

and once again we have

$$\omega(k) = (0\; k)(1\; k{-}1)(2\; k{-}2) \ldots = \phi(k), \tag{25}$$

because $\sigma(k, k) = (0\; 1\; \ldots\; k)$ is the same as before. The nice thing about this method is that the permutation needed in step G4, namely $\tau(k, c_k)\omega(k-1)^-$, does not depend on c_k:

$$\tau(k, j)\omega(k-1)^- = (k \;\ldots\; 1\; 0)\phi(k-1)^- = \phi(k). \tag{26}$$

Thus, Ord-Smith's algorithm is the special case of Algorithm G in which step G4 simply interchanges $a_0 \leftrightarrow a_k$, $a_1 \leftrightarrow a_{k-1}$, $\ldots$; this operation is usually quick, because k is small, and it saves some of the work of Algorithm L. (See exercise 38 and the reference to G. S. Klügel in Section 7.2.1.7.)

We can do even better by rigging things so that step G4 needs to do only a single transposition each time, somewhat as in Algorithm P but not necessarily on adjacent elements. Many such schemes are possible. The best is probably to let

$$\tau(k, j)\omega(k-1)^- = \begin{cases} (k\; 0), & \text{if } k \text{ is even,} \\ (k\; j{-}1), & \text{if } k \text{ is odd,} \end{cases} \tag{27}$$

as suggested by B. R. Heap [*Comp. J.* **6** (1963), 293–294]. Notice that Heap's method always transposes $a_k \leftrightarrow a_0$ except when $k = 3, 5, \ldots$; and the value of k, in 5 of every 6 steps, is either 1 or 2. Exercise 40 proves that Heap's method does indeed generate all permutations.

Bypassing unwanted blocks. One noteworthy advantage of Algorithm G is that it runs through all permutations of $a_0 \ldots a_{k-1}$ before touching a_k; then it performs another $k!$ cycles before changing a_k again, and so on. Therefore if at any time we reach a setting of the final elements $a_k \ldots a_{n-1}$ that is unimportant to the problem we're working on, we can skip quickly over all permutations that end with the undesirable suffix. More precisely, we could replace step G2 by the following substeps:

G2.0. [Acceptable?] If $a_k \ldots a_{n-1}$ is not an acceptable suffix, go to G2.1. Otherwise set $k \leftarrow k - 1$. Then if $k > 0$, repeat this step; if $k = 0$, proceed to step G2.2.

G2.1. [Skip this suffix.] If $c_k = k$, apply $\sigma(k, k)^-$ to $a_0 \ldots a_{n-1}$, set $c_k \leftarrow 0$, $k \leftarrow k + 1$, and repeat until $c_k < k$. Terminate if $k = n$; otherwise set $c_k \leftarrow c_k + 1$, apply $\tau(k, c_k)$ to $a_0 \ldots a_{n-1}$, and return to G2.0.

G2.2. [Visit.] Visit the permutation $a_0 \ldots a_{n-1}$. ■

Step G1 should also set $k \leftarrow n - 1$. Notice that the new steps are careful to preserve condition (17). The algorithm has become more complicated, because we need to know the permutations $\tau(k,j)$ and $\sigma(k,k)$ in addition to the permutations $\tau(k,j)\omega(k-1)^-$ that appear in G4. But the additional complications are often worth the effort, because the resulting program might run significantly faster.

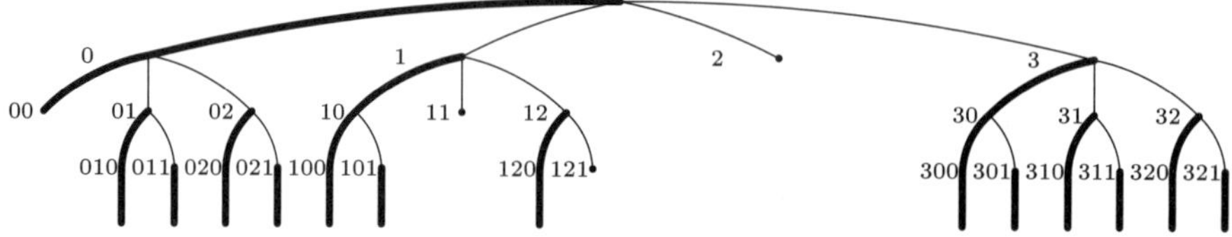

Fig. 20. Unwanted branches can be pruned from the tree of Fig. 19, if Algorithm G is suitably extended.

For example, Fig. 20 shows what happens to the tree of Fig. 19 when the suffixes of $a_0 a_1 a_2 a_3$ that correspond to nodes 00, 11, 121, and 2 are not acceptable. (Each suffix $a_k \ldots a_{n-1}$ of the permutation $a_0 \ldots a_{n-1}$ corresponds to a *prefix* $c_n \ldots c_k$ of the control string $c_n \ldots c_1$, because the permutations $\sigma(1, c_1) \ldots \sigma(k-1, c_{k-1})$ do not affect $a_k \ldots a_{n-1}$.) Step G2.1 premultiplies by $\tau(k,j)$ to move from node $c_{n-1} \ldots c_{k+1} j$ to its right sibling $c_{n-1} \ldots c_{k+1}(j+1)$, and it premultiplies by $\sigma(k,k)^-$ to move up from node $c_{n-1} \ldots c_{k+1} k$ to its parent $c_{n-1} \ldots c_{k+1}$. Thus, to get from the rejected prefix 121 to its preorder successor, the algorithm premultiplies by $\sigma(1,1)^-$, $\sigma(2,2)^-$, and $\tau(3,2)$, thereby moving from node 121 to 12 to 1 to 2. (This is a somewhat exceptional case, because a prefix with $k=1$ is rejected only if we don't want to visit the unique permutation $a_0 a_1 \ldots a_{n-1}$ that has suffix $a_1 \ldots a_{n-1}$.) After node 2 is rejected, $\tau(3,3)$ takes us to node 3, etc.

Notice, incidentally, that bypassing a suffix $a_k \ldots a_{n-1}$ in this extension of Algorithm G is essentially the same as bypassing a prefix $a_1 \ldots a_j$ in our original notation, if we go back to the idea of generating permutations $a_1 \ldots a_n$ of $\{1, \ldots, n\}$ and doing most of the work at the right-hand end. Our original notation corresponds to choosing a_1 first, then a_2, ..., then a_n; the notation in Algorithm G essentially chooses a_{n-1} first, then a_{n-2}, ..., then a_0. Algorithm G's conventions may seem backward, but they make the formulas for Sims table manipulation a lot simpler. A good programmer soon learns to switch without difficulty from one viewpoint to another.

We can apply these ideas to alphametics, because it is clear for example that most choices of the values for the letters D, E, and Y will make it impossible for SEND plus MORE to equal MONEY: We need to have $(D + E - Y) \bmod 10 = 0$ in that problem. Therefore many permutations can be eliminated from consideration.

In general, if r_k is the maximum power of 10 that divides the signature value s_k, we can sort the letters and assign codes $\{0, 1, \ldots, 9\}$ so that $r_0 \geq r_1 \geq \cdots \geq r_9$. For example, to solve the trio sonata problem (7), we could use $(0, 1, \ldots, 9)$ respectively for $(X, S, V, A, R, I, L, T, O, N)$, obtaining the signatures

$$s_0 = 0, \quad s_1 = -100000, \quad s_2 = 210000, \quad s_3 = -100, \quad s_4 = -100,$$
$$s_5 = 21010, \quad s_6 = 210, \quad s_7 = -1010, \quad s_8 = -7901, \quad s_9 = -998;$$

hence $(r_0, \ldots, r_9) = (\infty, 5, 4, 2, 2, 1, 1, 1, 0, 0)$. Now if we get to step G2.0 for a value of k with $r_{k-1} \neq r_k$, we can say that the suffix $a_k \ldots a_9$ is unacceptable unless $a_k s_k + \cdots + a_9 s_9$ is a multiple of $10^{r_{k-1}}$. Also, (10) tells us that $a_k \ldots a_9$ is unacceptable if $a_k = 0$ and $k \in F$; the first-letter set F is now $\{1, 2, 7\}$.

Our previous approach to alphametics with steps A1–A3 above used brute force to run through 10! possibilities. It operated rather fast under the circumstances, since the adjacent-transposition method allowed it to get by with only 6 memory references per permutation; but still, 10! is 3,628,800, so the entire process cost almost 22 megamems, regardless of the alphametic being solved. By contrast, the extended Algorithm G with Heap's method and the cutoffs just described will find all four solutions to (7) with fewer than 128 *kilo*mems! Thus the suffix-skipping technique runs more than 170 times faster than the previous method, which simply blasted away blindly.

Most of the 128 kilomems in the new approach are spent applying $\tau(k, c_k)$ in step G2.1. The other memory references come primarily from applications of $\sigma(k, k)^-$ in that step, but τ is needed 7812 times while σ^- is needed only 2162 times. The reason is easy to understand from Fig. 20, because the "shortcut move" $\tau(k, c_k)\omega(k - 1)^-$ in step G4 hardly ever applies; in this case it is used only four times, once for each solution. Thus, preorder traversal of the tree is accomplished almost entirely by τ steps that move to the right and σ^- steps that move upward. The τ steps dominate in a problem like this, where very few complete permutations are actually visited, because each step $\sigma(k, k)^-$ is preceded by k steps $\tau(k, 1)$, $\tau(k, 2)$, $\ldots$, $\tau(k, k)$.

This analysis reveals that Heap's method — which goes to great lengths to optimize the permutations $\tau(k, j)\omega(k - 1)^-$ so that each transition in step G4 is a simple transposition — is *not* especially good for the extended Algorithm G unless comparatively few suffixes are rejected in step G2.0. The simpler reverse colex order, for which $\tau(k, j)$ itself is always a simple transposition, is now much more attractive (see (19)). Indeed, Algorithm G with reverse colex order solves the alphametic (7) with only 97 kilomems.

Similar results occur with respect to other alphametic problems. For example, if we apply the extended Algorithm G to the alphametics in exercise 24, parts (a) through (h), the computations involve respectively

$$\begin{matrix} (551, 110, 14, 8, 350, 84, 153, 1598) \text{ kilomems with Heap's method;} \\ (429, 84, 10, 5, 256, 63, 117, 1189) \text{ kilomems with reverse colex.} \end{matrix} \qquad (28)$$

The speedup factor for reverse colex in these examples, compared to brute force with Algorithm T, ranges from 18 in case (h) to 4200 in case (d), and it is about 80 on the average; Heap's method gives an average speedup of about 60.

We know from Algorithm L, however, that lexicographic order is easily handled *without* the complication of the control table $c_n \ldots c_1$ used by Algorithm G. And a closer look at Algorithm L shows that we can improve its behavior when permutations are frequently being skipped, by using a linked list instead of a sequential array. The improved algorithm is well-suited to a wide variety of algorithms that wish to generate restricted classes of permutations:

Algorithm X (*Lexicographic permutations with restricted prefixes*). This algorithm generates all permutations $a_1 a_2 \ldots a_n$ of $\{1, 2, \ldots, n\}$ that pass a given sequence of tests

$$t_1(a_1), \quad t_2(a_1, a_2), \quad \ldots, \quad t_n(a_1, a_2, \ldots, a_n),$$

visiting them in lexicographic order. It uses an auxiliary table of links l_0, l_1, $\ldots$, l_n to maintain a cyclic list of unused elements, so that if the currently available elements are

$$\{1, \ldots, n\} \setminus \{a_1, \ldots, a_k\} = \{b_1, \ldots, b_{n-k}\}, \qquad \text{where } b_1 < \cdots < b_{n-k}, \quad (29)$$

then we have

$$l_0 = b_1, \quad l_{b_j} = b_{j+1} \quad \text{for } 1 \leq j < n - k, \quad \text{and} \quad l_{b_{n-k}} = 0. \qquad (30)$$

It also uses an auxiliary table $u_1 \ldots u_n$ to undo operations that have been performed on the l array.

X1. [Initialize.] Set $l_k \leftarrow k + 1$ for $0 \leq k < n$, and $l_n \leftarrow 0$. Then set $k \leftarrow 1$.

X2. [Enter level k.] Set $p \leftarrow 0$, $q \leftarrow l_0$.

X3. [Test $a_1 \ldots a_k$.] Set $a_k \leftarrow q$. If $t_k(a_1, \ldots, a_k)$ is false, go to X5. Otherwise, if $k = n$, visit $a_1 \ldots a_n$ and go to X6.

X4. [Increase k.] Set $u_k \leftarrow p$, $l_p \leftarrow l_q$, $k \leftarrow k + 1$, and return to X2.

X5. [Increase a_k.] Set $p \leftarrow q$, $q \leftarrow l_p$. If $q \neq 0$ return to X3.

X6. [Decrease k.] Set $k \leftarrow k - 1$, and terminate if $k = 0$. Otherwise set $p \leftarrow u_k$, $q \leftarrow a_k$, $l_p \leftarrow q$, and go to X5. ∎

The basic idea of this elegant algorithm is due to M. C. Er [*Comp. J.* **30** (1987), 282]. We can apply it to alphametics by changing notation slightly, obtaining permutations $a_0 \ldots a_9$ of $\{0, \ldots, 9\}$ and letting l_{10} play the former role of l_0. The resulting algorithm needs only 49 kilomems to solve the trio-sonata problem (7), and it solves the alphametics of exercise 24(a)–(h) in

$$(248, 38, 4, 3, 122, 30, 55, 553) \text{ kilomems}, \qquad (31)$$

respectively. Thus it runs about 165 times faster than the brute-force approach.

Another way to apply Algorithm X to alphametics is often faster yet (see exercise 49).

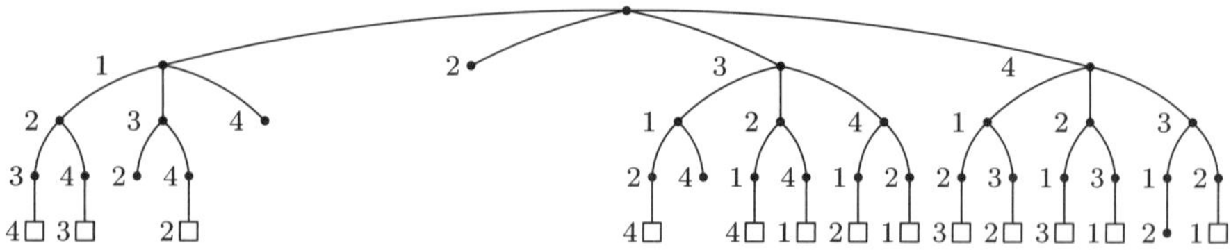

Fig. 21. The tree implicitly traversed by Algorithm X when $n = 4$, if all permutations are visited except those beginning with 132, 14, 2, 314, or 4312.

***Dual methods.** If S_1, $\ldots$, S_{n-1} is a Sims table for a permutation group G, we learned in Lemma S that every element of G can be expressed uniquely as a product $\sigma_1 \ldots \sigma_{n-1}$, where $\sigma_k \in S_k$; see (13). Exercise 50 shows that every element α can also be expressed uniquely in the dual form

$$\alpha = \sigma_{n-1}^- \ldots \sigma_2^- \sigma_1^-, \qquad \text{where } \sigma_k \in S_k \text{ for } 1 \le k < n, \tag{32}$$

and this fact leads to another large family of permutation generators. In particular, when G is the group of all $n!$ permutations, every permutation can be written

$$\sigma(n-1, c_{n-1})^- \ldots \sigma(2, c_2)^- \sigma(1, c_1)^-, \tag{33}$$

where $0 \le c_k \le k$ for $1 \le k < n$ and the permutations $\sigma(k, j)$ are the same as in Algorithm G. Now, however, we want to vary c_{n-1} most rapidly and c_1 least rapidly, so we arrive at an algorithm of a different kind:

Algorithm H (*Dual permutation generator*). Given a Sims table as in Algorithm G, this algorithm generates all permutations $a_0 \ldots a_{n-1}$ of $\{0, \ldots, n-1\}$, using an auxiliary table $c_0 \ldots c_{n-1}$.

H1. [Initialize.] Set $a_j \leftarrow j$ and $c_j \leftarrow 0$ for $0 \le j < n$.

H2. [Visit.] (At this point the mixed-radix number $\begin{bmatrix} c_1, & c_2, & \ldots, & c_{n-1} \\ 2, & 3, & \ldots, & n \end{bmatrix}$ is the number of permutations visited so far.) Visit the permutation $a_0 a_1 \ldots a_{n-1}$.

H3. [Add 1 to $c_0 c_1 \ldots c_{n-1}$.] Set $k \leftarrow n-1$. If $c_k = k$, set $c_k \leftarrow 0$, $k \leftarrow k-1$, and repeat until $k = 0$ or $c_k < k$. Terminate the algorithm if $k = 0$; otherwise set $c_k \leftarrow c_k + 1$.

H4. [Permute.] Apply the permutation $\tau(k, c_k) \omega(k+1)^-$ to $a_0 a_1 \ldots a_{n-1}$, as explained below, and return to H2. ∎

Although this algorithm looks almost identical to Algorithm G, the permutations τ and ω that it needs in step H4 are quite different from those needed in step G4. The new rules, which replace (15) and (16), are

$$\tau(k, j) = \sigma(k, j)^- \sigma(k, j-1), \qquad \text{for } 1 \le j \le k, \tag{34}$$

$$\omega(k) = \sigma(n-1, n-1)^- \sigma(n-2, n-2)^- \ldots \sigma(k, k)^-. \tag{35}$$

The number of possibilities is just as vast as it was for Algorithm G, so we will confine our attention to a few cases that have special merit. One natural case to try is, of course, the Sims table that makes Algorithm G produce reverse colex order, namely

$$\sigma(k, j) \;=\; (k{-}j \quad k{-}j{+}1 \quad \ldots \quad k) \tag{36}$$

as in (18). The resulting permutation generator turns out to be very nearly the same as the method of plain changes; so we can say that Algorithms L and P are essentially dual to each other. (See exercise 52.)

Another natural idea is to construct a Sims table for which step H4 always makes a single transposition of two elements, by analogy with the construction of (27) that achieves maximum efficiency in step G4. But such a mission now turns out to be impossible: We cannot achieve it even when $n = 4$. For if we start with the identity permutation $a_0 a_1 a_2 a_3 = 0123$, the transitions that take us from control table $c_0 c_1 c_2 c_3 = 0000$ to 0001 to 0002 to 0003 must move the 3; so, if they are transpositions, they must be $(3\,a)$, $(a\,b)$, and $(b\,c)$ for some permutation abc of $\{0, 1, 2\}$. The permutation corresponding to $c_0 c_1 c_2 c_3 = 0003$ is now $\sigma(3,3)^- = (b\,c)(a\,b)(3\,a) = (3\,a\,b\,c)$; and the next permutation, which corresponds to $c_0 c_1 c_2 c_3 = 0010$, will be $\sigma(2,1)^-$, which must fix the element 3. The only suitable transposition is $(3\,c)$, hence $\sigma(2,1)^-$ must be $(3\,c)(3\,a\,b\,c) = (a\,b\,c)$. Similarly we find that $\sigma(2,2)^-$ must be $(a\,c\,b)$, and the permutation corresponding to $c_0 c_1 c_2 c_3 = 0023$ will be $(3\,a\,b\,c)(a\,c\,b) = (3\,c)$. Step H4 is now supposed to convert this to the permutation $\sigma(1,1)^-$, which corresponds to the control table 0100 that follows 0023. But the only transposition that will convert $(3\,c)$ into a permutation that fixes 2 and 3 is $(3\,c)$; and the resulting permutation also fixes 1, so it cannot be $\sigma(1,1)^-$.

The proof in the preceding paragraph shows that we cannot use Algorithm H to generate all permutations with the minimum number of transpositions. But it also suggests a simple generation scheme that comes very close to the minimum, and the resulting algorithm is quite attractive because it needs to do extra work only once per $n(n-1)$ steps. (See exercise 53.)

Finally, let's consider the dual of Ord-Smith's method, when

$$\sigma(k, j) = (k \ \ldots \ 1 \ 0)^j \tag{37}$$

as in (23). Once again the value of $\tau(k, j)$ is independent of j,

$$\tau(k, j) = (0 \ 1 \ \ldots \ k), \tag{38}$$

and this fact is particularly advantageous in Algorithm H because it allows us to dispense with the control table $c_0 c_1 \ldots c_{n-1}$. The reason is that $c_{n-1} = 0$ in step H3 if and only if $a_{n-1} = n - 1$, because of (32); and indeed, when $c_j = 0$ for $k < j < n$ in step H3 we have $c_k = 0$ if and only if $a_k = k$. Therefore we can reformulate this variant of Algorithm H as follows.

Algorithm C (*Permutation generation by cyclic shifts*). This algorithm visits all permutations $a_1 \ldots a_n$ of the distinct elements $\{x_1, \ldots, x_n\}$.

C1. [Initialize.] Set $a_j \leftarrow x_j$ for $1 \le j \le n$.

C2. [Visit.] Visit the permutation $a_1 \ldots a_n$, and set $k \leftarrow n$.

C3. [Shift.] Replace $a_1 a_2 \ldots a_k$ by the cyclic shift $a_2 \ldots a_k a_1$, and return to C2 if $a_k \ne x_k$.

C4. [Decrease k.] Set $k \leftarrow k - 1$, and go back to C3 if $k > 1$. ∎

For example, the successive permutations of $\{1, 2, 3, 4\}$ generated when $n = 4$ are

$$
\begin{array}{l}
1234, \ 2341, \ 3412, \ 4123, \ (1234), \\
2314, \ 3142, \ 1423, \ 4231, \ (2314), \\
3124, \ 1243, \ 2431, \ 4312, \ (3124), \ (1234), \\
2134, \ 1342, \ 3421, \ 4213, \ (2134), \\
1324, \ 3241, \ 2413, \ 4132, \ (1324), \\
3214, \ 2143, \ 1432, \ 4321, \ (3214), \ (2134), \ (1234),
\end{array}
$$

with unvisited intermediate permutations shown in parentheses. This algorithm
may well be the simplest permutation generator of all, in terms of minimum
program length. It is due to G. G. Langdon, Jr. [*CACM* **10** (1967), 298–299;
11 (1968), 392]; similar methods had been published previously by C. Tompkins
[*Proc. Symp. Applied Math.* **6** (1956), 202–205] and, more explicitly, by R. Seitz
[*Unternehmensforschung* **6** (1962), 2–15]. The procedure is particularly well
suited to applications in which cyclic shifting is efficient, for example when successive permutations are being kept in a machine register instead of in an array.

The main disadvantage of dual methods is that they usually do not adapt
well to situations where large blocks of permutations need to be skipped, because the set of all permutations with a given value of the first control entries
$c_0 c_1 \ldots c_{k-1}$ is usually not of importance. The special case (36) is, however,
sometimes an exception, because the $n!/k!$ permutations with $c_0 c_1 \ldots c_{k-1} =
00 \ldots 0$ in that case are precisely those $a_0 a_1 \ldots a_{n-1}$ in which 0 precedes 1,
1 precedes 2, $\ldots$, and $k - 2$ precedes $k - 1$.

***Ehrlich's swap method.** Gideon Ehrlich has discovered a completely different
approach to permutation generation, based on yet another way to use a control
table $c_1 \ldots c_{n-1}$. His method obtains each permutation from its predecessor by
interchanging the leftmost element with another:

Algorithm E (*Ehrlich swaps*). This algorithm generates all permutations of the
distinct elements $a_0 \ldots a_{n-1}$ by using auxiliary tables $b_0 \ldots b_{n-1}$ and $c_1 \ldots c_n$.

E1. [Initialize.] Set $b_j \leftarrow j$ and $c_{j+1} \leftarrow 0$ for $0 \le j < n$.

E2. [Visit.] Visit the permutation $a_0 \ldots a_{n-1}$.

E3. [Find k.] Set $k \leftarrow 1$. Then if $c_k = k$, set $c_k \leftarrow 0$, $k \leftarrow k + 1$, and repeat until
$c_k < k$. Terminate if $k = n$, otherwise set $c_k \leftarrow c_k + 1$.

E4. [Swap.] Interchange $a_0 \leftrightarrow a_{b_k}$.

E5. [Flip.] Set $j \leftarrow 1$, $k \leftarrow k - 1$. If $j < k$, interchange $b_j \leftrightarrow b_k$, set $j \leftarrow j + 1$,
$k \leftarrow k - 1$, and repeat until $j \ge k$. Return to E2. ∎

Notice that steps E2 and E3 are identical to steps G2 and G3 of Algorithm G.
The most amazing thing about this algorithm, which Ehrlich communicated to
Martin Gardner in 1987, is that it works; exercise 55 contains a proof. A similar
method, which simplifies the operations of step E5, can be validated in the same
way (see exercise 56). The average number of interchanges performed in step E5
is less than 0.18 (see exercise 57).

As it stands, Algorithm E isn't faster than other methods we have seen. But
it has the nice property that it changes each permutation in a minimal way, using
only $n - 1$ different kinds of transpositions. Whereas Algorithm P used adjacent
interchanges, $a_{t-1} \leftrightarrow a_t$, Algorithm E uses first-element swaps, $a_0 \leftrightarrow a_t$, also
called *star transpositions*, for some well-chosen sequence of indices $t[1]$, $t[2]$, $\ldots$,
$t[n! - 1]$. And if we are generating permutations repeatedly for the same fairly
small value of n, we can precompute this sequence, as we did in Algorithm T

for the index sequence of Algorithm P. Notice that star transpositions have an advantage over adjacent interchanges, because we always know the value of a_0 from the previous swap; we need not read it from memory.

Let E_n be the sequence of $n! - 1$ indices t such that Algorithm E swaps a_0 with a_t in step E4. Since E_{n+1} begins with E_n, we can regard E_n as the first $n! - 1$ elements of an infinite sequence

$$E_\infty = 121213212123121213212124313132131312\ldots. \qquad (39)$$

For example, if $n = 4$ and $a_0 a_1 a_2 a_3 = 1234$, the permutations visited by Algorithm E are

$$\begin{array}{llllll}
1234, & 2134, & 3124, & 1324, & 2314, & 3214, \\
4213, & 1243, & 2143, & 4123, & 1423, & 2413, \\
3412, & 4312, & 1342, & 3142, & 4132, & 1432, \\
2431, & 3421, & 4321, & 2341, & 3241, & 4231.
\end{array} \qquad (40)$$

***Using fewer generators.** After seeing Algorithms P and E, we might naturally ask whether all permutations can be obtained by using just *two* basic operations, instead of $n - 1$. For example, Nijenhuis and Wilf [*Combinatorial Algorithms* (1975), Exercise 6] noticed that all permutations can be generated for $n = 4$ if we replace $a_1 a_2 a_3 \ldots a_n$ at each step by either $a_2 a_3 \ldots a_n a_1$ or $a_2 a_1 a_3 \ldots a_n$, and they wondered whether such a method exists for all n.

In general, if G is any group of permutations and if α_1, ..., α_k are elements of G, the *Cayley graph* for G with generators $(\alpha_1, \ldots, \alpha_k)$ is the directed graph whose vertices are the permutations π of G and whose arcs go from π to $\alpha_1 \pi$, ..., $\alpha_k \pi$. [Arthur Cayley, *American J. Math.* **1** (1878), 174–176.] The question of Nijenhuis and Wilf is equivalent to asking whether the Cayley graph for all permutations of $\{1, 2, \ldots, n\}$, with generators σ and τ where σ is the cyclic permutation $(1\ 2\ \ldots\ n)$ and τ is the transposition $(1\ 2)$, has a Hamiltonian path.

A basic theorem due to R. A. Rankin [*Proc. Cambridge Philos. Soc.* **44** (1948), 17–25] allows us to conclude in many cases that Cayley graphs with two generators do not have a Hamiltonian cycle:

Theorem R. *Let G be a group consisting of g permutations. If the Cayley graph for G with generators (α, β) has a Hamiltonian cycle, and if the permutations $(\alpha, \beta, \alpha\beta^-)$ are respectively of order (a, b, c), then either c is even or g/a and g/b are odd.*

(The *order* of a permutation α is the least positive integer a such that α^a is the identity.)

Proof. See exercise 73. ∎

In particular, when $\alpha = \sigma$ and $\beta = \tau$ as above, we have $g = n!$, $a = n$, $b = 2$, and $c = n - 1$, because $\sigma\tau^- = (2\ \ldots\ n)$. Therefore we conclude that no Hamiltonian cycle is possible when $n \geq 4$ is even. However, a Hamiltonian *path* is easy to construct when $n = 4$, because we can join up the 12-cycles

$$\begin{aligned}
1234 &\to 2341 \to 3412 \to 4312 \to 3124 \to 1243 \to 2431 \\
&\to 4231 \to 2314 \to 3142 \to 1423 \to 4123 \to 1234, \\
2134 &\to 1342 \to 3421 \to 4321 \to 3214 \to 2143 \to 1432 \\
&\to 4132 \to 1324 \to 3241 \to 2413 \to 4213 \to 2134,
\end{aligned} \tag{41}$$

by starting at 2341 and jumping from 1234 to 2134, ending at 4213.

Ruskey, Jiang, and Weston [*Discrete Applied Math.* **57** (1995), 75–83] undertook an exhaustive search in the σ–τ graph for $n = 5$ and discovered that it has five essentially distinct Hamiltonian cycles, one of which (the "most beautiful") is illustrated in Fig. 22(a). They also found a Hamiltonian path for $n = 6$; this was a difficult feat, because it is the outcome of a 720-stage binary decision tree. Unfortunately the solution they discovered has no apparent logical structure. A somewhat less complex path is described in exercise 70, but even that path cannot be called simple. Therefore a σ–τ approach will probably not be of practical interest for larger values of n unless a new construction is discovered. R. C. Compton and S. G. Williamson [*Linear and Multilinear Algebra* **35** (1993), 237–293] have proved that Hamiltonian cycles exist for all n if the three generators σ, σ^-, and τ are allowed instead of just σ and τ; their cycles have the interesting property that every nth transformation is τ, and the intervening $n - 1$ transformations are either all σ or all σ^-. But their method is too complicated to explain in a short space.

Exercise 69 describes a general permutation algorithm that is reasonably simple and needs only three generators, each of order 2. Figure 22(b) illustrates the case $n = 5$ of this method, which was motivated by examples of bell-ringing.

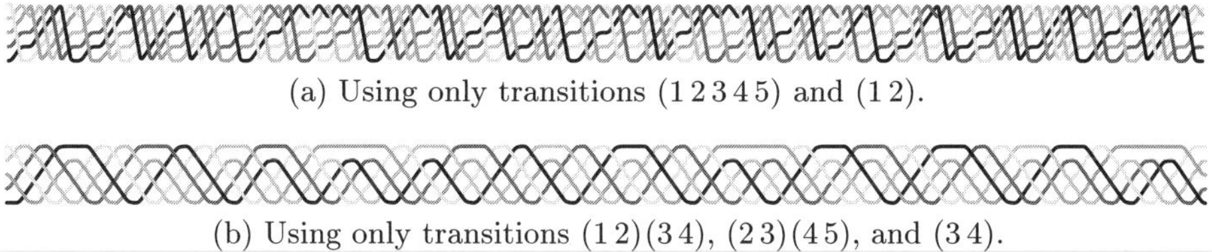

(a) Using only transitions $(1\,2\,3\,4\,5)$ and $(1\,2)$.

(b) Using only transitions $(1\,2)(3\,4)$, $(2\,3)(4\,5)$, and $(3\,4)$.

Fig. 22. Hamiltonian cycles for 5! permutations.

Faster, faster. What is the fastest way to generate permutations? This question has often been raised in computer publications, because people who examine $n!$ possibilities want to keep the running time as small as possible. But the answers have generally been contradictory, because there are many different ways to formulate the question. Let's try to understand the related issues by studying how permutations might be generated most rapidly on the **MMIX** computer.

Suppose first that our goal is to produce permutations in an array of n consecutive memory words (octabytes). The fastest way to do this, of all those we've seen in this section, is to streamline Heap's method (27), as suggested by R. Sedgewick [*Computing Surveys* **9** (1977), 157–160].

The key idea is to optimize the code for the most common cases of steps G2 and G3, namely the cases in which all activity occurs at the beginning of the array. If registers u, v, and w contain the contents of the first three words, and if the next six permutations to be generated involve permuting those words in all six possible ways, we can clearly do the job as follows:

$$
\begin{array}{llll}
\texttt{PUSHJ 0,Visit} \\
\texttt{STO v,A0;} & \texttt{STO u,A1;} & \texttt{PUSHJ 0,Visit} \\
\texttt{STO w,A0;} & \texttt{STO v,A2;} & \texttt{PUSHJ 0,Visit} \\
\texttt{STO u,A0;} & \texttt{STO w,A1;} & \texttt{PUSHJ 0,Visit} \\
\texttt{STO v,A0;} & \texttt{STO u,A2;} & \texttt{PUSHJ 0,Visit} \\
\texttt{STO w,A0;} & \texttt{STO v,A1;} & \texttt{PUSHJ 0,Visit}
\end{array}
\tag{42}
$$

(Here $\texttt{A0}$ is the address of octabyte a_0, etc.) A complete permutation program, which takes care of getting the right things into u, v, and w, appears in exercise 77, but the other instructions are less important because they need to be performed only $\frac{1}{6}$ of the time. The total cost per permutation, not counting the $4v$ needed for $\texttt{PUSHJ}$ and $\texttt{POP}$ on each call to $\texttt{Visit}$, comes to approximately $2.77\mu + 5.69v$ with this approach. If we use four registers u, v, w, x, and if we expand (42) to 24 calls on $\texttt{Visit}$, the running time per permutation drops to about $2.19\mu + 3.07v$. And with r registers and $r!$ $\texttt{Visit}$s, exercise 78 shows that the cost is $(2 + O(1/r!))(\mu + v)$, which is very nearly the cost of two $\texttt{STO}$ instructions.

The latter is, of course, the minimum possible time for any method that generates all permutations in a sequential array. ... Or is it? We have assumed that the visiting routine wants to see permutations in consecutive locations, but perhaps that routine is able to read the permutations from different starting points. Then we can arrange to keep a_{n-1} fixed and to keep two copies of the other elements in its vicinity:

$$
a_0 a_1 \ldots a_{n-2} a_{n-1} a_0 a_1 \ldots a_{n-2}.
\tag{43}
$$

If we now let $a_0 a_1 \ldots a_{n-2}$ run through $(n-1)!$ permutations, always changing both copies simultaneously by doing two $\texttt{STO}$ commands instead of one, we can let every call to $\texttt{Visit}$ look at the n permutations

$$
a_0 a_1 \ldots a_{n-1}, \quad a_1 \ldots a_{n-1} a_0, \quad \ldots, \quad a_{n-1} a_0 \ldots a_{n-2},
\tag{44}
$$

which all appear consecutively. The cost per permutation is now reduced to the cost of three simple instructions like $\texttt{ADD}$, $\texttt{CMP}$, $\texttt{PBNZ}$, plus $O(1/n)$. [See Varol and Rotem, *Comp. J.* **24** (1981), 173–176.]

Furthermore, we might not want to waste time storing permutations into memory at all. Suppose, for example, that our goal is to generate all permutations of $\{0, 1, \ldots, n-1\}$. The value of n will probably be at most 16, because $16! = 20{,}922{,}789{,}888{,}000$ and $17! = 355{,}687{,}428{,}096{,}000$. Therefore an entire permutation will fit in the 16 nybbles of an octabyte, and we can keep it in a single register. This will be advantageous only if the visiting routine doesn't need to unpack the individual nybbles; but let's suppose that it doesn't. How fast can we generate permutations in the nybbles of a 64-bit register?

One idea, suggested by a technique due to A. J. Goldstein [*U. S. Patent 3383661* (14 May 1968)], is to precompute the table $(t[1], \ldots, t[5039])$ of plain-change transitions for seven elements, using Algorithm T. These numbers $t[k]$ lie between 1 and 6, so we can pack 20 of them into a 64-bit word. It is convenient to put the number $\sum_{k=1}^{20} 2^{3k-1} t[20j+k]$ into word j of an auxiliary table, for $0 \le j < 252$, with $t[5040] = 1$; for example, the table begins with the codeword

$$00|001|010|011|100|101|110|100|110|101|100|011|010|001|110|001|010|011|100|101|110|00.$$

The following program reads such codes efficiently:

```
Perm        ⟨Set register a to the first permutation⟩
0H      LDA   p,T        p ← address of first codeword.
        JMP   3F
1H          ⟨Visit the permutation in register a⟩
            ⟨Swap the nybbles of a that lie t bits from the right⟩
        SRU   c,c,3      c ← c ≫ 3.
2H      AND   t,c,#1c    t ← c ∧ (11100)₂.
        PBNZ  t,1B       Branch if t ≠ 0.
        ADD   p,p,8
3H      LDO   c,p,0      c ← next codeword.
        PBNZ  c,2B       (The final codeword is followed by 0.)
            ⟨If not done, advance the leading n − 7 nybbles and return to 0B⟩
```

$$(45)$$

Exercise 79 shows how to ⟨Swap the nybbles ...⟩ with seven instructions, using bit manipulation operations that are found on most computers. Therefore the cost per permutation is just a bit more than $10v$. (The instructions that fetch new codewords cost only $(\mu + 5v)/20$; and the instructions that advance the leading $n-7$ nybbles are even more negligible since their cost is divided by 5040.) Notice that there is now no need for PUSHJ and POP as there was with (42); we ignored those instructions before, but they did cost $4v$.

We can, however, do even better by adapting Langdon's cyclic-shift method, Algorithm C. Suppose we start with the lexicographically largest permutation and operate as follows:

```
        GREG  @
0H      OCTA  #fedcba9876543210&(1<<(4*N)-1)
Perm    LDOU  a,0B                            Set a ← # ...3210.
        JMP   2F
1H      SRU   a,a,4*(16-N)                    a ← ⌊a/16^{16-n}⌋.
        OR    a,a,t                           a ← a ∨ t.
2H          ⟨Visit the permutation in register a⟩
        SRU   t,a,4*(N-1)                     t ← ⌊a/16^{n-1}⌋.
        SLU   a,a,4*(17-N)                    a ← 16^{17-n}a mod 16^{16}.
        PBNZ  t,1B                            To 1B if t ≠ 0.
            ⟨Continue with Langdon's method⟩
```

$$(46)$$

The running time per permutation is now only $5v + O(1/n)$, again without the need for PUSHJ and POP. See exercise 81 for an interesting way to extend (46) to a complete program, obtaining a remarkably short and fast routine.

Fast permutation generators are amusing, but in practice we can usually save more time by streamlining the visiting routine than by speeding up the generator.

Topological sorting. Instead of working with all $n!$ permutations of $\{1, \ldots, n\}$, we often want to look only at permutations that obey certain restrictions. For example, we might be interested only in permutations for which 1 precedes 3, 2 precedes 3, and 2 precedes 4; there are five such permutations of $\{1, 2, 3, 4\}$, namely

$$1234, \ 1243, \ 2134, \ 2143, \ 2413. \tag{47}$$

The problem of *topological sorting*, which we studied in Section 2.2.3 as a first example of nontrivial data structures, is the general problem of finding a permutation that satisfies m such conditions $x_1 \prec y_1, \ldots, x_m \prec y_m$, where $x \prec y$ means that x should precede y in the permutation. This problem arises frequently in practice, so it has several different names; for example, it is often called the *linear embedding* problem, because we want to arrange objects in a line while preserving certain order relationships. It is also the problem of extending a partial ordering to a total ordering (see exercise 2.2.3–14).

Our goal in Section 2.2.3 was to find a *single* permutation that satisfies all the relations. But now we want rather to find *all* such permutations, all topological sorts. Indeed, we will assume in the present section that the elements x and y on which the relations are defined are integers between 1 and n, and that we have $x < y$ whenever $x \prec y$. Consequently the permutation $12 \ldots n$ will always be topologically correct. (If this simplifying assumption is not met, we can preprocess the data by using Algorithm 2.2.3T to rename the objects appropriately.)

Many important classes of permutations are special cases of this topological ordering problem. For example, the permutations of $\{1, \ldots, 8\}$ such that

$$1 \prec 2, \quad 2 \prec 3, \quad 3 \prec 4, \quad 6 \prec 7, \quad 7 \prec 8$$

are equivalent to permutations of the multiset $\{1, 1, 1, 1, 2, 3, 3, 3\}$, because we can map $\{1, 2, 3, 4\} \mapsto 1$, $5 \mapsto 2$, and $\{6, 7, 8\} \mapsto 3$. We know how to generate permutations of a multiset using Algorithm L, but now we will learn another way.

Notice that x precedes y in a permutation $a_1 \ldots a_n$ if and only if $a'_x < a'_y$ in the inverse permutation $a'_1 \ldots a'_n$. Therefore the algorithm we are about to study will also find all permutations $a'_1 \ldots a'_n$ such that $a'_j < a'_k$ whenever $j \prec k$. For example, we learned in Section 5.1.4 that a Young tableau is an arrangement of $\{1, \ldots, n\}$ in rows and columns so that each row is increasing from left to right and each column is increasing from top to bottom. The problem of generating all 3×3 Young tableaux is therefore equivalent to generating all $a'_1 \ldots a'_9$ such that

$$\begin{aligned}
a'_1 < a'_2 < a'_3, \quad a'_4 < a'_5 < a'_6, \quad a'_7 < a'_8 < a'_9, \\
a'_1 < a'_4 < a'_7, \quad a'_2 < a'_5 < a'_8, \quad a'_3 < a'_6 < a'_9,
\end{aligned} \tag{48}$$

and this is a special kind of topological sorting.

We might also want to find all *matchings* of $2n$ elements, namely all ways to partition $\{1, \ldots, 2n\}$ into n pairs. There are $(2n-1)(2n-3)\ldots(1) = (2n)!/(2^n n!)$ ways to do this, and they correspond to permutations that satisfy

$$a_1' < a_2', \quad a_3' < a_4', \quad \ldots, \quad a_{2n-1}' < a_{2n}', \qquad a_1' < a_3' < \cdots < a_{2n-1}'. \qquad (49)$$

An elegant algorithm for exhaustive topological sorting was discovered by Y. L. Varol and D. Rotem [*Comp. J.* **24** (1981), 83–84], who realized that a method analogous to plain changes (Algorithm P) can be used. Suppose we have found a way to arrange $\{1, \ldots, n - 1\}$ topologically, so that $a_1 \ldots a_{n-1}$ satisfies all the conditions that do not involve n. Then we can easily write down all the allowable ways to insert the final element n without changing the relative order of $a_1 \ldots a_{n-1}$: We simply start with $a_1 \ldots a_{n-1} n$, then shift n left one step at a time, until it cannot move further. Applying this idea recursively yields the following straightforward procedure.

Algorithm V (*All topological sorts*). Given a relation $\prec$ on $\{1, \ldots, n\}$ with the property that $x \prec y$ implies $x < y$, this algorithm generates all permutations $a_1 \ldots a_n$ and their inverses $a_1' \ldots a_n'$ with the property that $a_j' < a_k'$ whenever $j \prec k$. We assume for convenience that $a_0 = 0$ and that $0 \prec k$ for $1 \le k \le n$.

V1. [Initialize.] Set $a_j \leftarrow j$ and $a_j' \leftarrow j$ for $0 \le j \le n$.

V2. [Visit.] Visit the permutation $a_1 \ldots a_n$ and its inverse $a_1' \ldots a_n'$. Then set $k \leftarrow n$.

V3. [Can k move left?] Set $j \leftarrow a_k'$ and $l \leftarrow a_{j-1}$. If $l \prec k$, go to V5.

V4. [Yes, move it.] Set $a_{j-1} \leftarrow k$, $a_j \leftarrow l$, $a_k' \leftarrow j - 1$, and $a_l' \leftarrow j$. Go to V2.

V5. [No, put k back.] While $j < k$, set $l \leftarrow a_{j+1}$, $a_j \leftarrow l$, $a_l' \leftarrow j$, and $j \leftarrow j+1$. Then set $a_k \leftarrow a_k' \leftarrow k$. Decrease k by 1 and return to V3 if $k > 0$. ∎

For example, Theorem 5.1.4H tells us that there are exactly 42 Young tableaux of size 3×3. If we apply Algorithm V to the relations (48) and write the inverse permutation in array form

$$\begin{array}{|l|}\hline a_1' \, a_2' \, a_3' \\ a_4' \, a_5' \, a_6' \\ a_7' \, a_8' \, a_9' \\ \hline \end{array}, \qquad (50)$$

we get the following 42 results:

123	123	123	123	123	124	124	124	124	124	125	125	125	125
456	457	458	467	468	356	357	358	367	368	367	368	346	347
789	689	679	589	579	789	689	679	589	579	489	479	789	689

125	126	126	127	126	126	127	134	134	134	134	134	135	135
348	347	348	348	357	358	358	256	257	258	267	268	267	268
679	589	579	569	489	479	469	789	689	679	589	579	489	479

145	145	135	135	135	136	136	137	136	136	137	146	146	147
267	268	246	247	248	247	248	248	257	258	258	257	258	258
389	379	789	689	679	589	579	569	489	479	469	389	379	369

Let t_r be the number of topological sorts for which the final $n - r$ elements are in their initial position $a_j = j$ for $r < j \le n$. Equivalently, t_r is the number of topological sorts $a_1 \ldots a_r$ of $\{1, \ldots, r\}$, when we ignore the relations involving elements greater than r. Then the recursive mechanism underlying Algorithm V shows that step V2 is performed N times and step V3 is performed M times, where

$$M = t_n + \cdots + t_1 \qquad \text{and} \qquad N = t_n. \tag{51}$$

Also, step V4 and the loop operations of V5 are performed $N - 1$ times; the rest of step V5 is done $M - N + 1$ times. Therefore the total running time of the algorithm is a linear combination of M, N, and n.

If the element labels are chosen poorly, M might be much larger than N. For example, if the constraints input to Algorithm V are

$$2 \prec 3, \quad 3 \prec 4, \quad \ldots, \quad n - 1 \prec n, \tag{52}$$

then $t_j = j$ for $1 \le j \le n$ and we have $M = \frac{1}{2}(n^2 + n)$, $N = n$. But those constraints are also equivalent to

$$1 \prec 2, \quad 2 \prec 3, \quad \ldots, \quad n - 2 \prec n - 1, \tag{53}$$

under renaming of the elements; then M is reduced to $2n - 1 = 2N - 1$.

Exercise 89 shows that a simple preprocessing step will find element labels so that a slight modification of Algorithm V is able to generate all topological sorts in $O(N + n)$ steps. Thus topological sorting can always be done efficiently.

Think twice before you permute. We have seen several attractive algorithms for permutation generation in this section, but many algorithms are known by which permutations that are optimum for particular purposes can be found *without* running through all possibilities. For example, Theorem 6.1S showed that we can find the best way to arrange records on a sequential storage simply by sorting them with respect to a certain cost criterion, and this process takes only $O(n \log n)$ steps. In Section 7.5.2 we will study the *assignment problem,* which asks how to permute the columns of a square matrix so that the sum of the diagonal elements is maximized. That problem can be solved in at most $O(n^3)$ operations, so it would be foolish to use a method of order $n!$ unless n is extremely small. Even in cases like the traveling salesrep problem, when no efficient algorithm is known, we can usually find a much better approach than to examine every possible solution. Permutation generation is best used when there is good reason to look at each permutation individually.

EXERCISES

▶ **1.** [*20*] Explain how to make Algorithm L run faster, by streamlining its operations when the value of j is near n.

2. [*20*] Rewrite Algorithm L so that it produces all permutations of $a_1 \ldots a_n$ in reverse colex order. (In other words, the values of the reflections $a_n \ldots a_1$ should be lexicographically decreasing, as in (11). This form of the algorithm is often simpler and faster than the original, because fewer calculations depend on the value of n.)

▶ **3.** [*M21*] The *rank* of a combinatorial arrangement X with respect to a generation algorithm is the number of other arrangements that the algorithm visits prior to X. Explain how to compute the rank of a given permutation $a_1 \ldots a_n$ with respect to Algorithm L, if $\{a_1, \ldots, a_n\} = \{1, \ldots, n\}$. What is the rank of 314592687?

4. [*M23*] Generalizing exercise 3, explain how to compute the rank of $a_1 \ldots a_n$ with respect to Algorithm L when $\{a_1, \ldots, a_n\}$ is the multiset $\{n_1 \cdot x_1, \ldots, n_t \cdot x_t\}$; here $n_1 + \cdots + n_t = n$ and $x_1 < \cdots < x_t$. (The total number of permutations is, of course, the multinomial coefficient

$$\binom{n}{n_1, \ldots, n_t} = \frac{n!}{n_1! \ldots n_t!};$$

see Eq. 5.1.2–(3).) What is the rank of 314159265?

5. [*HM25*] Compute the mean and variance of the number of comparisons made by Algorithm L in (a) step L2, (b) step L3, when the elements $\{a_1, \ldots, a_n\}$ are distinct.

6. [*HM34*] Derive generating functions for the mean number of comparisons made by Algorithm L in (a) step L2, (b) step L3, when $\{a_1, \ldots, a_n\}$ is a general multiset as in exercise 4. Also give the results in closed form when $\{a_1, \ldots, a_n\}$ is the binary multiset $\{s \cdot 0, (n - s) \cdot 1\}$.

7. [*HM35*] What is the limit as $t \to \infty$ of the average number of comparisons made per permutation in step L2 when Algorithm L is being applied to the multiset (a) $\{2 \cdot 1, 2 \cdot 2, \ldots, 2 \cdot t\}$? (b) $\{1 \cdot 1, 2 \cdot 2, \ldots, t \cdot t\}$? (c) $\{2 \cdot 1, 4 \cdot 2, \ldots, 2^t \cdot t\}$?

▶ **8.** [*21*] The *variations* of a multiset are the permutations of all its submultisets. For example, the variations of $\{1, 2, 2, 3\}$ are

> ϵ, 1, 12, 122, 1223, 123, 1232, 13, 132, 1322,
>
> > 2, 21, 212, 2123, 213, 2132, 22, 221, 2213, 223, 2231, 23, 231, 2312, 232, 2321,
> >
> > 3, 31, 312, 3122, 32, 321, 3212, 322, 3221.

Show that simple changes to Algorithm L will generate all variations of a given multiset $\{a_1, a_2, \ldots, a_n\}$.

9. [*22*] Continuing the previous exercise, design an algorithm to generate all r-variations of a given multiset $\{a_1, a_2, \ldots, a_n\}$, also called its r-permutations, namely all permutations of its r-element submultisets. (For example, the solution to an alphametic with r distinct letters is an r-variation of $\{0, 1, \ldots, 9\}$.)

10. [*20*] What are the values of $a_1 a_2 \ldots a_n$, $c_1 c_2 \ldots c_n$, and $o_1 o_2 \ldots o_n$ at the end of Algorithm P, if $a_1 a_2 \ldots a_n = 12 \ldots n$ at the beginning?

11. [*M22*] How many times is each step of Algorithm P performed? (Assume that $n \geq 2$.)

▶ **12.** [*M23*] What is the 1000000th permutation visited by (a) Algorithm L, (b) Algorithm P, (c) Algorithm C, if $\{a_1, \ldots, a_n\} = \{0, \ldots, 9\}$? *Hint:* In mixed-radix notation we have $1000000 = \begin{bmatrix} 2, & 6, & 6, & 2, & 5, & 1, & 2, & 2, & 0, & 0 \\ 10, & 9, & 8, & 7, & 6, & 5, & 4, & 3, & 2, & 1 \end{bmatrix} = \begin{bmatrix} 0, & 0, & 1, & 2, & 3, & 0, & 2, & 7, & 1, & 0 \\ 1, & 2, & 3, & 4, & 5, & 6, & 7, & 8, & 9, & 10 \end{bmatrix}$.

13. [*M21*] (Martin Gardner, 1974.) True or false: If $a_1 a_2 \ldots a_n$ is initially $12 \ldots n$, Algorithm P begins by visiting all $n!/2$ permutations in which 1 precedes 2; then the next permutation is $n \ldots 21$.

14. [*M22*] True or false: If $a_1 a_2 \ldots a_n$ is initially $x_1 x_2 \ldots x_n$ in Algorithm P, we always have $a_{j - c_j + s} = x_j$ at the beginning of step P5.

15. [*M23*] (Selmer Johnson, 1963.) Show that the offset variable s never exceeds 2 in Algorithm P.

16. [*21*] Explain how to make Algorithm P run faster, by streamlining its operations when the value of j is near n. (This problem is analogous to exercise 1.)

▸ **17.** [*20*] Extend Algorithm P so that the *inverse permutation* $a_1' \ldots a_n'$ is available for processing when $a_1 \ldots a_n$ is visited in step P2. (The inverse satisfies $a_k' = j$ if and only if $a_j = k$.)

18. [*21*] (*Rosary permutations.*) Devise an efficient way to generate $(n-1)!/2$ permutations that represent all possible undirected cycles on the vertices $\{1, \ldots, n\}$; that is, no cyclic shift of $a_1 \ldots a_n$ or $a_n \ldots a_1$ will be generated if $a_1 \ldots a_n$ is generated. The permutations (1234, 1324, 3124) could, for example, be used when $n = 4$.

19. [*25*] Construct an algorithm that generates all permutations of n distinct elements *looplessly* in the spirit of Algorithm 7.2.1.1L.

▸ **20.** [*20*] The n-cube has $2^n n!$ symmetries, one for each way to permute and/or complement the coordinates. Such a symmetry is conveniently represented as a *signed permutation*, namely a permutation with optional signs attached to the elements. For example, $23\bar{1}$ is a signed permutation that transforms the vertices of the 3-cube by changing $x_1 x_2 x_3$ to $x_2 x_3 \bar{x}_1$, so that $000 \mapsto 001$, $001 \mapsto 011$, $\ldots$, $111 \mapsto 110$. Design a simple algorithm that generates all signed permutations of $\{1, 2, \ldots, n\}$, where each step either interchanges two adjacent elements or negates the first element.

21. [*M21*] (E. P. McCravy, 1971.) How many solutions does the alphametic (6) have in radix b?

22. [*M15*] True or false: If an alphametic has a solution in radix b, it has a solution in radix $b + 1$.

23. [*M20*] True or false: A pure alphametic cannot have two identical signatures $s_j = s_k \neq 0$ when $j \neq k$.

24. [*25*] Solve the following alphametics by hand or by computer:

a) `SEND + A + TAD + MORE = MONEY`.
b) `ZEROES + ONES = BINARY`.   (Peter MacDonald, 1977)
c) `DCLIX + DLXVI = MCCXXV`.   (Willy Enggren, 1972)
d) `COUPLE + COUPLE = QUARTET`.   (Michael R. W. Buckley, 1977)
e) `FISH + N + CHIPS = SUPPER`.   (Bob Vinnicombe, 1978)
f) `SATURN + URANUS + NEPTUNE + PLUTO = PLANETS`.   (Willy Enggren, 1968)
g) `EARTH + AIR + FIRE + WATER = NATURE`.   (Herman Nijon, 1977)
h) `AN + ACCELERATING + INFERENTIAL + ENGINEERING + TALE + ELITE + GRANT + FEE + ET + CETERA = ARTIFICIAL + INTELLIGENCE`.
i) `HARDY + NESTS = NASTY + HERDS`.

▸ **25.** [*M21*] Devise a fast way to compute $\min(a \cdot s)$ and $\max(a \cdot s)$ over all valid permutations $a_1 \ldots a_{10}$ of $\{0, \ldots, 9\}$, given the signature vector $s = (s_1, \ldots, s_{10})$ and the first-letter set F of an alphametic problem. (Such a procedure makes it possible to rule out many cases quickly when a large family of alphametics is being considered, as in several of the exercises that follow, because a solution can exist only when $\min(a \cdot s) \leq 0 \leq \max(a \cdot s)$.)

26. [*25*] What is the unique alphametic solution to

$$\texttt{NIIHAU} \pm \texttt{KAUAI} \pm \texttt{OAHU} \pm \texttt{MOLOKAI} \pm \texttt{LANAI} \pm \texttt{MAUI} \pm \texttt{HAWAII} = 0?$$

27. [*30*] Construct pure additive alphametics in which all words have five letters.

28. [*M25*] A *partition* of the integer n is an expression of the form $n = n_1 + \cdots + n_t$ with $n_1 \geq \cdots \geq n_t > 0$. Such a partition is called *doubly true* if $\alpha(n) = \alpha(n_1) + \cdots + \alpha(n_t)$ is also a pure alphametic, where $\alpha(n)$ is the "name" of n in some language. Doubly true partitions were introduced by Alan Wayne in *AMM* **54** (1947), 38, 412–414, where he suggested solving TWENTY = SEVEN + SEVEN + SIX and a few others.

   a) Find all partitions that are doubly true in English when $1 \leq n \leq 20$.

   b) Wayne also gave the example EIGHTY = FIFTY + TWENTY + NINE + ONE. Find all doubly true partitions for $1 \leq n \leq 100$ in which the parts are *distinct*, using the names ONE, TWO, ..., NINETYNINE, ONEHUNDRED.

▶ **29.** [*M25*] Continuing the previous exercise, find all equations of the form $n_1 + \cdots + n_t = n_1' + \cdots + n_{t'}'$ that are both mathematically and alphametically true in English, when $\{n_1, \ldots, n_t, n_1', \ldots, n_{t'}'\}$ are distinct positive integers less than 20. For example,

$$\text{TWELVE} + \text{NINE} + \text{TWO} = \text{ELEVEN} + \text{SEVEN} + \text{FIVE};$$

the alphametics should all be pure.

30. [*25*] Solve these multiplicative alphametics by hand or by computer:

   a) TWO × TWO = SQUARE.   (H. E. Dudeney, 1929)

   b) HIP × HIP = HURRAY.   (Willy Enggren, 1970)

   c) PI × R × R = AREA.   (Brian Barwell, 1981)

   d) NORTH/SOUTH = EAST/WEST.   (Nob Yoshigahara, 1995)

   e) NAUGHT × NAUGHT = ZERO × ZERO × ZERO.   (Alan Wayne, 2003)

31. [*M22*] (Nob Yoshigahara.) What is the unique solution to A/BC+D/EF+G/HI = 1, when $\{A, \ldots, I\} = \{1, \ldots, 9\}$?

32. [*M25*] (H. E. Dudeney, 1901.) Find all ways to represent 100 by inserting a plus sign and a slash into a permutation of the digits $\{1, \ldots, 9\}$. For example, $100 = 91 + 5742/638$. The plus sign should precede the slash.

33. [*25*] Continuing the previous exercise, find all positive integers less than 150 that (a) cannot be represented in such a fashion; (b) have a unique representation.

34. [*M26*] Make the equation EVEN + ODD + PRIME = x doubly true when (a) x is a perfect 5th power; (b) x is a perfect 7th power.

▶ **35.** [*M20*] The automorphisms of a 4-cube have many different Sims tables, only one of which is shown in (14). How many different Sims tables are possible for that group, when the vertices are numbered as in (12)?

36. [*M23*] Find a Sims table for the group of all automorphisms of the 4×4 tic-tac-toe board

$$\begin{array}{|cccc|} \hline 0 & 1 & 2 & 3 \\ 4 & 5 & 6 & 7 \\ 8 & 9 & \text{a} & \text{b} \\ \text{c} & \text{d} & \text{e} & \text{f} \\ \hline \end{array},$$

namely the permutations that take lines into lines, where a "line" is a set of four elements that belong to a row, column, or diagonal.

▶ **37.** [*HM22*] How many Sims tables can be used with Algorithms G or H? Estimate the logarithm of this number as $n \to \infty$.

38. [*HM21*] Prove that the average number of transpositions per permutation when using Ord-Smith's algorithm (26) is approximately $\sinh 1 \approx 1.175$.

39. [*16*] Write down the 24 permutations generated for $n = 4$ by (a) Ord-Smith's method (26); (b) Heap's method (27).

40. [*M23*] Show that Heap's method (27) corresponds to a valid Sims table.

▶ **41.** [*M33*] Design an algorithm that generates all r-variations of $\{0, 1, \ldots, n - 1\}$ by interchanging just two elements when going from one variation to the next. (See exercise 9.) *Hint:* Generalize Heap's method (27), obtaining the results in positions $a_{n-r} \ldots a_{n-1}$ of an array $a_0 \ldots a_{n-1}$. For example, one solution when $n = 5$ and $r = 2$ uses the final two elements of the respective permutations 01234, 31204, 30214, 30124, 40123, 20143, 24103, 24013, 34012, 14032, 13042, 13402, 23401, 03421, 02431, 02341, 12340, 42310, 41320, 41230.

42. [*M20*] Construct a Sims table for all permutations in which every $\sigma(k, j)$ and every $\tau(k, j)$ for $1 \le j \le k$ is a cycle of length ≤ 3.

43. [*M24*] Construct a Sims table for all permutations in which every $\sigma(k, k)$, $\omega(k)$, and $\tau(k, j)\omega(k - 1)^-$ for $1 \le j \le k$ is a cycle of length ≤ 3.

44. [*20*] When blocks of unwanted permutations are being skipped by the extended Algorithm G, is the Sims table of Ord-Smith's method (23) superior to the Sims table of the reverse colex method (18)?

45. [*20*] (a) What are the indices $u_1 \ldots u_9$ when Algorithm X visits the permutation 314592687? (b) What permutation is visited when $u_1 \ldots u_9 = 314157700$?

46. [*20*] True or false: When Algorithm X visits $a_1 \ldots a_n$, we have $u_k > u_{k+1}$ if and only if $a_k > a_{k+1}$, for $1 \le k < n$.

▶ **47.** [*M21*] Express the number of times that each step of Algorithm X is performed in terms of the numbers N_0, N_1, $\ldots$, N_n, where N_k is the number of prefixes $a_1 \ldots a_k$ that satisfy $t_j(a_1, \ldots, a_j)$ for $1 \le j \le k$.

▶ **48.** [*M25*] Compare the running times of Algorithm X and Algorithm L, in the case when the tests $t_1(a_1)$, $t_2(a_1, a_2)$, $\ldots$, $t_n(a_1, a_2, \ldots, a_n)$ always are true.

▶ **49.** [*28*] The text's suggested method for solving additive alphametics with Algorithm X essentially chooses digits from right to left; in other words, it assigns tentative values to the least significant digits before considering digits that correspond to higher powers of 10.

Explore an alternative approach that chooses digits from left to right. For example, such a method will deduce immediately that $M = 1$ when $SEND + MORE = MONEY$. *Hint:* See exercise 25.

50. [*M15*] Explain why the dual formula (32) follows from (13).

51. [*M16*] True or false: If the sets $S_k = \{\sigma(k, 0), \ldots, \sigma(k, k)\}$ form a Sims table for the group of all permutations, so also do the sets $S_k^- = \{\sigma(k, 0)^-, \ldots, \sigma(k, k)^-\}$.

▶ **52.** [*M22*] What permutations $\tau(k, j)$ and $\omega(k)$ arise when Algorithm H is used with the Sims table (36)? Compare the resulting generator with Algorithm P.

▶ **53.** [*M26*] (F. M. Ives.) Construct a Sims table for which Algorithm H will generate all permutations by making only $n! + O((n - 2)!)$ transpositions.

54. [*20*] Would Algorithm C work properly if step C3 did a right-cyclic shift, setting $a_1 \ldots a_{k-1}a_k \leftarrow a_k a_1 \ldots a_{k-1}$, instead of a left-cyclic shift?

55. [*M27*] Consider the *factorial ruler function*

$$\rho_!(m) = \max\{k \mid m \bmod k! = 0\}.$$

Let σ_k and τ_k be permutations of the nonnegative integers such that $\sigma_j \tau_k = \tau_k \sigma_j$ whenever $j \le k$. Let α_0 and β_0 be the identity permutation, and for $m > 0$ define

$$\alpha_m = \beta_{m-1}^{-} \tau_{\rho!(m)} \beta_{m-1} \alpha_{m-1}, \qquad \beta_m = \sigma_{\rho!(m)} \beta_{m-1}.$$

For example, if σ_k is the flip operation $(1\ k{-}1)(2\ k{-}2)\ldots = (0\ k)\phi(k)$ and if $\tau_k = (0\ k)$, and if Algorithm E is started with $a_j = j$ for $0 \le j < n$, then α_m and β_m are the contents of $a_0 \ldots a_{n-1}$ and $b_0 \ldots b_{n-1}$ after step E5 has been performed m times.

   a) Prove that $\beta_{(n+1)!}\alpha_{(n+1)!} = \sigma_{n+1}\sigma_n^{-}\tau_{n+1}\tau_n^{-}(\beta_{n!}\alpha_{n!})^{n+1}$.

   b) Use the result of (a) to establish the validity of Algorithm E.

56. [*M22*] Prove that Algorithm E remains valid if step E5 is replaced by

   E5′. [Transpose pairs.] If $k > 2$, interchange $b_{j+1} \leftrightarrow b_j$ for $j = k-2,\ k-4,\ \ldots,$ (2 or 1). Return to E2. ∎

57. [*HM22*] What is the average number of interchanges made in step E5?

58. [*M21*] True or false: If Algorithm E begins with $a_0 \ldots a_{n-1} = x_1 \ldots x_n$ then the final permutation visited begins with $a_0 = x_n$.

59. [*M20*] Some authors define the arcs of a Cayley graph as running from π to $\pi\alpha_j$ instead of from π to $\alpha_j\pi$. Are the two definitions essentially different?

▶ **60.** [*21*] A *Gray cycle for permutations* is a cycle $(\pi_0, \pi_1, \ldots, \pi_{n!-1})$ that includes every permutation of $\{1, 2, \ldots, n\}$ and has the property that π_k differs from $\pi_{(k+1) \bmod n!}$ by an adjacent transposition. It can also be described as a Hamiltonian cycle on the Cayley graph for the group of all permutations on $\{1, 2, \ldots, n\}$, with the $n-1$ generators $((1\ 2), (2\ 3), \ldots, (n{-}1\ n))$. The *delta sequence* of such a Gray cycle is the sequence of integers $\delta_0 \delta_1 \ldots \delta_{n!-1}$ such that

$$\pi_{(k+1) \bmod n!} = (\delta_k\ \delta_k{+}1)\,\pi_k.$$

(See 7.2.1.1–(24), which describes the analogous situation for binary n-tuples.) For example, Fig. 23 illustrates the Gray cycle defined by plain changes when $n = 4$; its delta sequence is $(32131231)^3$.

   a) Find all Gray cycles for permutations of $\{1, 2, 3, 4\}$.

   b) Two Gray cycles are considered to be equivalent if their delta sequences can be obtained from each other by cyclic shifting $(\delta_k \ldots \delta_{n!-1}\delta_0 \ldots \delta_{k-1})$ and/or reversal $(\delta_{n!-1} \ldots \delta_1\delta_0)$ and/or complementation $((n{-}\delta_0)(n{-}\delta_1)\ldots(n{-}\delta_{n!-1}))$. Which of the Gray cycles in (a) are equivalent?

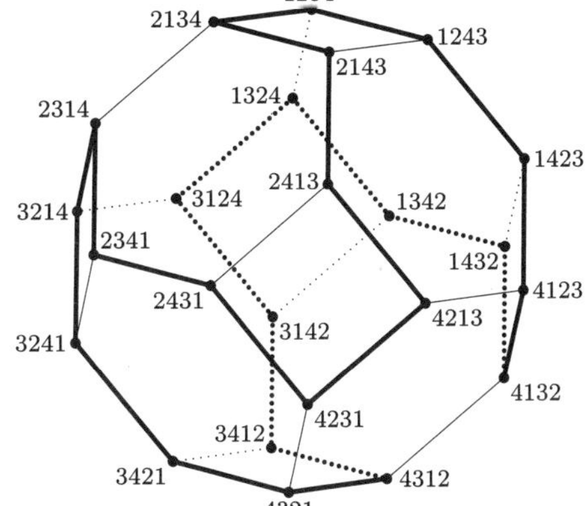

Fig. 23. Algorithm P traces out this Hamiltonian cycle on the truncated octahedron of Fig. 5–1.

61. [*21*] Continuing the previous exercise, a *Gray code for permutations* is like a Gray cycle except that the final permutation $\pi_{n!-1}$ is not required to be adjacent to the initial permutation π_0. Study the set of all Gray codes for $n = 4$ that start with 1234.

▶ **62.** [*M23*] What permutations can be reached as the final element of a Gray code that starts at $12\ldots n$?

63. [*M25*] Estimate the total number of Gray cycles for permutations of $\{1, 2, 3, 4, 5\}$.

64. [*23*] A "doubly Gray" code for permutations is a Gray cycle with the additional property that $\delta_{k+1} = \delta_k \pm 1$ for all k. Compton and Williamson have proved that such codes exist for all $n \geq 3$. How many doubly Gray codes exist for $n = 5$?

65. [*M25*] For which integers N is there a Gray path through the N lexicographically smallest permutations of $\{1, \ldots, n\}$? (Exercise 7.2.1.1–26 solves the analogous problem for binary n-tuples.)

66. [*22*] Ehrlich's swap method suggests another type of Gray cycle for permutations, in which the $n - 1$ generators are the star transpositions $(1\ 2)$, $(1\ 3)$, $\ldots$, $(1\ n)$. For example, Fig. 24 shows the relevant graph when $n = 4$. Analyze the Hamiltonian cycles of this graph.

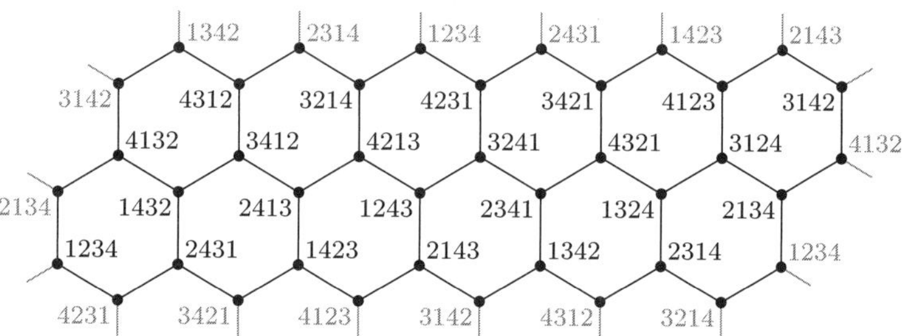

Fig. 24. The Cayley graph for permutations of $\{1, 2, 3, 4\}$, generated by the star transpositions $(1\,2)$, $(1\,3)$, and $(1\,4)$, drawn as a twisted torus.

67. [*26*] Continuing the previous exercise, find a first-element-swap Gray cycle for $n = 5$ in which each star transposition $(1\ j)$ occurs 30 times, for $2 \leq j \leq 5$.

68. [*M30*] (Kompel'makher and Liskovets, 1975.) Let G be the Cayley graph for all permutations of $\{1, \ldots, n\}$, with generators $(\alpha_1, \ldots, \alpha_k)$ where each α_j is a transposition $(u_j\ v_j)$; also let A be the graph with vertices $\{1, \ldots, n\}$ and edges $u_j \!-\! v_j$ for $1 \leq j \leq k$. Prove that G has a Hamiltonian cycle if and only if A is connected. (Figure 23 is the special case when A is a path; Figure 24 is the special case when A is a "star.")

▶ **69.** [*28*] If $n \geq 4$, the following algorithm generates all permutations $A_1 A_2 A_3 \ldots A_n$ of $\{1, 2, 3, \ldots, n\}$ using only three transformations,

$$\rho = (1\,2)(3\,4)(5\,6)\ldots, \qquad \sigma = (2\,3)(4\,5)(6\,7)\ldots, \qquad \tau = (3\,4)(5\,6)(7\,8)\ldots,$$

never applying ρ and τ next to each other. Explain why it works.

> **Z1.** [Initialize.] Set $A_j \leftarrow j$ for $1 \leq j \leq n$. Also set $a_j \leftarrow 2j$ for $j \leq n/2$ and $a_{n-j} \leftarrow 2j + 1$ for $j < n/2$. Then invoke Algorithm P, but with parameter $n - 1$ instead of n. We will treat that algorithm as a coroutine, which should

return control to us whenever it "visits" $a_1 \ldots a_{n-1}$ in step P2. We will also share its variables (except n).

Z2. [Set x and y.]   Invoke Algorithm P again, obtaining a new permutation $a_1 \ldots a_{n-1}$ and a new value of j. If $j = 2$, interchange $a_{1+s} \leftrightarrow a_{2+s}$ (thereby undoing the effect of step P5) and repeat this step; in such a case we are at the halfway point of Algorithm P. If $j = 1$ (so that Algorithm P has terminated), set $x \leftarrow y \leftarrow 0$ and go to Z3. Otherwise set

$$x \leftarrow a_{j-c_j+s+[o_j=-1]}, \qquad y \leftarrow a_{j-c_j+s-[o_j=+1]};$$

these are the two elements most recently interchanged in step P5.

Z3. [Visit.] Visit the permutation $A_1 \ldots A_n$. Then go to Z5 if $A_1 = x$ and $A_2 = y$.

Z4. [Apply ρ, then σ.] Interchange $A_1 \leftrightarrow A_2$, $A_3 \leftrightarrow A_4$, $A_5 \leftrightarrow A_6$, ... Visit $A_1 \ldots A_n$. Then interchange $A_2 \leftrightarrow A_3$, $A_4 \leftrightarrow A_5$, $A_6 \leftrightarrow A_7$, ... Terminate if $A_1 \ldots A_n = 1 \ldots n$, otherwise return to Z3.

Z5. [Apply τ, then σ.] Interchange $A_3 \leftrightarrow A_4$, $A_5 \leftrightarrow A_6$, $A_7 \leftrightarrow A_8$, ... Visit $A_1 \ldots A_n$. Then interchange $A_2 \leftrightarrow A_3$, $A_4 \leftrightarrow A_5$, $A_6 \leftrightarrow A_7$, ..., and return to Z2.   ▮

Hint: Show first that the algorithm works if modified so that $A_j \leftarrow n + 1 - j$ and $a_j \leftarrow j$ in step Z1, and if the "flip" permutations

$$\rho' = (1 \ n)(2 \ n{-}1)\ldots, \qquad \sigma' = (2 \ n)(3 \ n{-}1)\ldots, \qquad \tau' = (2 \ n{-}1)(3 \ n{-}2)\ldots$$

are used instead of ρ, σ, τ in steps Z4 and Z5. In this modification, step Z3 should go to Z5 if $A_1 = x$ and $A_n = y$.

▶ **70.** [*M33*] The two 12-cycles (41) can be regarded as σ–τ cycles for the twelve permutations of $\{1, 1, 3, 4\}$:

$$1134 \to 1341 \to 3411 \to 4311 \to 3114 \to 1143 \to 1431$$
$$\to 4131 \to 1314 \to 3141 \to 1413 \to 4113 \to 1134.$$

Replacing $\{1, 1\}$ by $\{1, 2\}$ yields disjoint cycles, and we obtained a Hamiltonian path by jumping from one to the other. Can a σ–τ path for all permutations of 6 elements be formed in a similar way, based on a 360-cycle for the permutations of $\{1, 1, 3, 4, 5, 6\}$?

71. [*48*] Does the Cayley graph with generators $\sigma = (1\,2\,\ldots\,n)$ and $\tau = (1\,2)$ have a Hamiltonian cycle whenever $n \geq 3$ is odd?

72. [*M21*] Given a Cayley graph with generators $(\alpha_1, \ldots, \alpha_k)$, assume that each α_j takes $x \mapsto y$. (For example, both σ and τ in exercise 71 take $1 \mapsto 2$.) Prove that any Hamiltonian path starting at $12 \ldots n$ in G must end at a permutation that takes $y \mapsto x$.

▶ **73.** [*M30*] Let α, β, and σ be permutations of a set X, where $X = A \cup B$. Assume that $x\sigma = x\alpha$ when $x \in A$ and $x\sigma = x\beta$ when $x \in B$, and that the order of $\alpha\beta^-$ is odd.

  a) Prove that all three permutations α, β, σ have the same sign; that is, they are all even or all odd. *Hint:* A permutation has odd order if and only if its cycles all have odd length.

  b) Derive Theorem R from part (a).

74. [*M30*] (R. A. Rankin.) Assuming that $\alpha\beta = \beta\alpha$ in Theorem R, prove that a Hamiltonian cycle exists if and only if there is a number k such that $0 \leq k \leq g/c$ and $t + k \perp c$, where $\beta^{g/c} = \gamma^t$, $\gamma = \alpha\beta^-$. *Hint:* Represent elements of the group in the form $\beta^j \gamma^k$.

75. [*M25*] The directed torus $C_m \times C_n$ has mn vertices (x, y) for $0 \le x < m$, $0 \le y < n$, and arcs $(x, y) \to (x, y)\alpha = ((x+1) \bmod m, y)$, $(x, y) \to (x, y)\beta = (x, (y+1) \bmod n)$. Prove that, if $m > 1$ and $n > 1$, the number of Hamiltonian cycles of this digraph is

$$\sum_{k=1}^{d-1} \binom{d}{k} [\gcd((d-k)m, kn) = d], \qquad d = \gcd(m, n).$$

76. [*M31*] The cells numbered $0, 1, \ldots, 63$ in Fig. 25 illustrate a *northeasterly knight's tour* on an 8×8 torus: If k appears in cell (x_k, y_k), then $(x_{k+1}, y_{k+1}) = (x_k + 2, y_k + 1)$ or $(x_k + 1, y_k + 2)$, modulo 8, and $(x_{64}, y_{64}) = (x_0, y_0)$. How many such tours are possible on an $m \times n$ torus, when $m, n \ge 3$?

29	24	19	14	49	44	39	34
58	53	48	43	38	9	4	63
23	18	13	8	3	62	33	28
52	47	42	37	32	27	22	57
17	12	7	2	61	56	51	46
6	41	36	31	26	21	16	11
35	30	1	60	55	50	45	40
0	59	54	25	20	15	10	5

Fig. 25. A northeasterly knight's tour.

▸ **77.** [*22*] Complete the MMIX program whose inner loop appears in (42), using Heap's method (27).

78. [*M23*] Analyze the running time of the program in exercise 77, generalizing it so that the inner loop does $r!$ visits (with $a_0 \ldots a_{r-1}$ in global registers).

79. [*20*] What seven MMIX instructions will ⟨ Swap the nybbles … ⟩ as (45) requires? For example, if register t contains the value 4 and register a contains the nybbles #12345678, register a should change to #12345687.

80. [*21*] Solve the previous exercise with only five MMIX instructions. *Hint:* Use MXOR.

▸ **81.** [*22*] Complete the MMIX program (46) by specifying how to ⟨ Continue with Langdon's method ⟩.

82. [*M21*] Analyze the running time of the program in exercise 81.

83. [*22*] Use the σ–τ path of exercise 70 to design an MMIX routine analogous to (42) that generates all permutations of #123456 in register a.

84. [*20*] Suggest a good way to generate all $n!$ permutations of $\{1, \ldots, n\}$ on p processors that are running in parallel.

▸ **85.** [*25*] Assume that n is small enough that $n!$ fits in a computer word. What's a good way to convert a given permutation $\alpha = a_1 \ldots a_n$ of $\{1, \ldots, n\}$ into an integer $k = r(\alpha)$ in the range $0 \le k < n!$? Both functions $k = r(\alpha)$ and $\alpha = r^{[-1]}(k)$ should be computable in only $O(n)$ steps.

86. [*20*] A partial order relation is supposed to be transitive; that is, $x \prec y$ and $y \prec z$ should imply $x \prec z$. But Algorithm V does not require its input relation to satisfy this condition.

Show that if $x \prec y$ and $y \prec z$, Algorithm V will produce identical results whether or not $x \prec z$.

87. [*20*] (F. Ruskey.) Consider the inversion tables $c_1 \ldots c_n$ of the permutations visited by Algorithm V. What noteworthy property do they have? (Compare with the inversion tables (4) in Algorithm P.)

88. [*21*] Show that Algorithm V can be used to generate all ways to partition the digits $\{0, 1, \ldots, 9\}$ into two 3-element sets and two 2-element sets.

▶ **89.** [*M30*] Consider the numbers t_0, t_1, $\ldots$, t_n in (51). Clearly $t_0 = t_1 = 1$.

a) Say that index j is "trivial" if $t_j = t_{j-1}$. For example, 9 is trivial with respect to the Young tableau relations (48). Explain how to modify Algorithm V so that the variable k takes on only nontrivial values.

b) Analyze the running time of the modified algorithm. What formulas replace (51)?

c) Say that the interval $[j \mathinner{.\,.} k]$ is not a chain if we do not have $l \prec l+1$ for $j \leq l < k$. Prove that in such a case $t_k \geq 2t_{j-1}$.

d) Every inverse topological sort $a'_1 \ldots a'_n$ defines a labeling that corresponds to relations $a'_{j_1} \prec a'_{k_1}$, $\ldots$, $a'_{j_m} \prec a'_{k_m}$, which are equivalent to the original relations $j_1 \prec k_1$, $\ldots$, $j_m \prec k_m$. Explain how to find a labeling such that $[j \mathinner{.\,.} k]$ is not a chain when j and k are consecutive nontrivial indices.

e) Prove that with such a labeling, $M < 4N$ in the formulas of part (b).

90. [*M21*] Algorithm V can be used to produce all permutations that are h-ordered for all h in a given set, namely all $a'_1 \ldots a'_n$ such that $a'_j < a'_{j+h}$ for $1 \leq j \leq n - h$ (see Section 5.2.1). Analyze the running time of Algorithm V when it generates all permutations that are both 2-ordered and 3-ordered.

91. [*HM21*] Analyze the running time of Algorithm V when it is used with the relations (49) to find matchings.

92. [*M18*] How many permutations is Algorithm V likely to visit, in a "random" case? Let P_n be the number of partial orderings on $\{1, \ldots, n\}$, namely the number of relations that are reflexive, antisymmetric, and transitive. Let Q_n be the number of such relations with the additional property that $j < k$ whenever $j \prec k$. Express the expected number of ways to sort n elements topologically, averaged over all partial orderings, in terms of P_n and Q_n.

93. [*35*] Prove that all topological sorts can be generated in such a way that only one or two adjacent transpositions are made at each step. (The example $1 \prec 2$, $3 \prec 4$ shows that a single transposition per step cannot always be achieved, even if we allow nonadjacent swaps, because only two of the six relevant permutations are odd.)

▶ **94.** [*25*] Show that in the case of matchings, using the relations in (49), all topological sorts can be generated with just one transposition per step.

95. [*21*] Discuss how to generate all *up-down permutations* of $\{1, \ldots, n\}$, namely those $a_1 \ldots a_n$ such that $a_1 < a_2 > a_3 < a_4 > \cdots$.

96. [*21*] Discuss how to generate all *cyclic permutations* of $\{1, \ldots, n\}$, namely those $a_1 \ldots a_n$ whose cycle representation consists of a single n-cycle.

97. [*21*] Discuss how to generate all *derangements* of $\{1, \ldots, n\}$, namely those $a_1 \ldots a_n$ such that $a_1 \neq 1$, $a_2 \neq 2$, $a_3 \neq 3$, $\ldots$.

98. [*HM23*] Analyze the asymptotic running time of the method in the previous exercise.

99. [*M30*] Given $n \geq 3$, show that all derangements of $\{1, \ldots, n\}$ can be generated by making at most two transpositions between visits.

100. [*21*] Discuss how to generate all *indecomposable* permutations of $\{1, \ldots, n\}$, namely those $a_1 \ldots a_n$ such that $\{a_1, \ldots, a_j\} \neq \{1, \ldots, j\}$ for $1 \leq j < n$.

101. [*21*] Discuss how to generate all *involutions* of $\{1, \ldots, n\}$, namely those permutations $a_1 \ldots a_n$ with $a_{a_1} \ldots a_{a_n} = 1 \ldots n$.

102. [*M30*] Show that all involutions of $\{1, \ldots, n\}$ can be generated by making at most two transpositions between visits.

103. [*M32*] Show that all even permutations of $\{1, \ldots, n\}$ can be generated by successive *rotations of three consecutive elements*.

▶ **104.** [*M22*] A permutation $a_1 \ldots a_n$ of $\{1, \ldots, n\}$ is *well-balanced* if

$$\sum_{k=1}^{n} k a_k = \sum_{k=1}^{n} (n + 1 - k) a_k.$$

For example, 3142 is well-balanced when $n = 4$.

a) Prove that no permutation is well-balanced when $n \bmod 4 = 2$.
b) Prove that if $a_1 \ldots a_n$ is well-balanced, so are its reversal $a_n \ldots a_1$, its complement $(n+1-a_1) \ldots (n+1-a_n)$, and its inverse $a_1' \ldots a_n'$.
c) Determine the number of well-balanced permutations for small values of n.

▶ **105.** [*26*] A *weak order* is a relation $\preceq$ that is transitive ($x \preceq y$ and $y \preceq z$ implies $x \preceq z$) and complete ($x \preceq y$ or $y \preceq x$ always holds). We can write $x \equiv y$ if $x \preceq y$ and $y \preceq x$; $x \prec y$ if $x \preceq y$ and $y \npreceq x$. There are thirteen weak orders on three elements $\{1, 2, 3\}$, namely

$$1 \equiv 2 \equiv 3, \quad 1 \equiv 2 \prec 3, \quad 1 \prec 2 \equiv 3, \quad 1 \prec 2 \prec 3, \quad 1 \equiv 3 \prec 2, \quad 1 \prec 3 \prec 2,$$

$$2 \prec 1 \equiv 3, \quad 2 \prec 1 \prec 3, \quad 2 \equiv 3 \prec 1, \quad 2 \prec 3 \prec 1, \quad 3 \prec 1 \equiv 2, \quad 3 \prec 1 \prec 2, \quad 3 \prec 2 \prec 1.$$

a) Explain how to generate all weak orders of $\{1, \ldots, n\}$ systematically, as sequences of digits separated by the symbols $\equiv$ or $\prec$.
b) A weak order can also be represented as a sequence $a_1 \ldots a_n$ where $a_j = k$ if j is preceded by $k \prec$ signs. For example, the thirteen weak orders on $\{1, 2, 3\}$ are respectively 000, 001, 011, 012, 010, 021, 101, 102, 100, 201, 110, 120, 210 in this form. Find a simple way to generate all such sequences of length n.

106. [*M40*] Can exercise 105(b) be solved with a Gray-like code?

▶ **107.** [*30*] (John H. Conway, 1973.) To play the solitaire game of "topswops," start by shuffling a pack of n cards labeled $\{1, \ldots, n\}$ and place them face up in a pile. Then if the top card is $k > 1$, deal out the top k cards and put them back on top of the pile, thereby changing the permutation from $a_1 \ldots a_n$ to $a_k \ldots a_1 a_{k+1} \ldots a_n$. Continue until the top card is 1. For example, the 7-step sequence

$$31452 \to 41352 \to 53142 \to 24135 \to 42135 \to 31245 \to 21345 \to 12345$$

might occur when $n = 5$. What is the longest sequence possible when $n = 13$?

108. [*M27*] If the longest n-card game of topswops has length $f(n)$, prove that $f(n) \leq F_{n+1} - 1$.

109. [*M47*] Find good upper and lower bounds on the topswops function $f(n)$.

▶ **110.** [*25*] Find all permutations $a_0 \ldots a_9$ of $\{0, \ldots, 9\}$ such that

$$\{a_0, a_2, a_3, a_7\} = \{2, 5, 7, 8\},$$
$$\{a_1, a_4, a_5\} = \{0, 3, 6\},$$
$$\{a_1, a_3, a_7, a_8\} = \{3, 4, 5, 7\},$$
$$\{a_0, a_3, a_4\} = \{0, 7, 8\}.$$

Also suggest an algorithm for solving large problems of this type.

▶ **111.** [*M25*] Several permutation-oriented analogs of de Bruijn cycles have been proposed. The simplest and nicest of these is the notion of a *universal cycle of permutations*, introduced by B. W. Jackson in *Discrete Math.* **117** (1993), 141–150, namely a cycle of $n!$ digits such that each permutation of $\{1,\ldots,n\}$ occurs exactly once as a block of $n-1$ consecutive digits (with its redundant final element suppressed). For example, (121323) is a universal cycle of permutations for $n = 3$, and it is essentially the only such cycle.

Find a universal cycle of permutations for $n = 4$, and prove that such cycles exist for all $n \geq 2$.

▶ **112.** [*HM43*] Exactly how many universal cycles exist, for permutations of ≤ 9 objects?

ANSWERS TO EXERCISES

SECTION 7.2.1.1

1. Let $m_j = u_j - l_j + 1$, and visit $(a_1 + l_1, \ldots, a_n + l_n)$ instead of visiting $(a_1, \ldots, a_n)$ in Algorithm M. Or, change '$a_j \leftarrow 0$' to '$a_j \leftarrow l_j$' and '$a_j = m_j - 1$' to '$a_j = u_j$' in that algorithm, and set $l_0 \leftarrow 0$, $u_0 \leftarrow 1$ in step M1.

2. $(0, 0, 1, 2, 3, 0, 2, 7, 0, 9)$.

3. Step M4 is performed $m_1 m_2 \ldots m_k$ times when $j = k$; therefore the total is $\sum_{k=0}^{n} \prod_{j=1}^{k} m_j = m_1 \ldots m_n (1 + 1/m_n + 1/m_n m_{n-1} + \cdots + 1/m_n \ldots m_1)$. If all m_j are 2 or more, this is less than $2m_1 \ldots m_n$. [Thus, we should keep in mind that fancy Gray-code methods, which change only one digit per visit, actually reduce the total number of digit changes by at most a factor of 2.]

4. **N1.** [Initialize.] Set $a_j \leftarrow m_j - 1$ for $0 \le j \le n$, where $m_0 = 2$.

N2. [Visit.] Visit the n-tuple $(a_1, \ldots, a_n)$.

N3. [Prepare to subtract one.] Set $j \leftarrow n$.

N4. [Borrow if necessary.] If $a_j = 0$, set $a_j \leftarrow m_j - 1$, $j \leftarrow j - 1$, and repeat this step.

N5. [Decrease, unless done.] If $j = 0$, terminate the algorithm. Otherwise set $a_j \leftarrow a_j - 1$ and go back to step N2. ∎

5. Bit reflection is easy on a machine like MMIX, but on other computers we can proceed as follows:

R1. [Initialize.] Set $j \leftarrow k \leftarrow 0$.

R2. [Swap.] Interchange $A[j + 1] \leftrightarrow A[k + 2^{n-1}]$. Also, if $j > k$, interchange $A[j] \leftrightarrow A[k]$ and $A[j + 2^{n-1} + 1] \leftrightarrow A[k + 2^{n-1} + 1]$.

R3. [Advance k.] Set $k \leftarrow k + 2$, and terminate if $k \ge 2^{n-1}$.

R4. [Advance j.] Set $h \leftarrow 2^{n-2}$. If $j \ge h$, repeatedly set $j \leftarrow j - h$ and $h \leftarrow h/2$ until $j < h$. Then set $j \leftarrow j + h$. (Now $j = (b_0 \ldots b_{n-1})_2$ if $k = (b_{n-1} \ldots b_0)_2$.) Return to R2. ∎

6. If $g\big((0 b_{n-1} \ldots b_1 b_0)_2\big) = \big(0(b_{n-1}) \ldots (b_2 \oplus b_1)(b_1 \oplus b_0)\big)_2$ then $g\big((1 b_{n-1} \ldots b_1 b_0)_2\big) = 2^n + g\big((0 \overline{b}_{n-1} \ldots \overline{b}_1 \overline{b}_0)_2\big) = \big(1(\overline{b}_{n-1}) \ldots (\overline{b}_2 \oplus \overline{b}_1)(\overline{b}_1 \oplus \overline{b}_0)\big)_2$, where $\overline{b} = b \oplus 1$.

7. To accommodate $2r$ sectors one can use $g(k)$ for $2^n - r \le k < 2^n + r$, where $n = \lceil \lg r \rceil$, because $g(2^n - r) \oplus g(2^n + r - 1) = 2^n$ by (5). [G. C. Tootill, *Proc. IEE* **103**, Part B Supplement (1956), 434.] See also exercise 26.

8. Use Algorithm G with $n \leftarrow n - 1$ and include the parity bit a_∞ at the right. (This yields $g(0)$, $g(2)$, $g(4)$, ...)

9. Replace the rightmost ring, since $\nu(1011000)$ is odd.

10. $A_n + B_n = g^{[-1]}(2^n - 1) = \lfloor 2^{n+1}/3 \rfloor$ and $A_n = B_n + n$. Hence $A_n = \lfloor 2^n/3 + n/2 \rfloor$ and $B_n = \lfloor 2^n/3 - n/2 \rfloor$.

Historical notes: The early Japanese mathematician Yoriyuki Arima (1714–1783) treated this problem in his *Shūki Sanpō* (1769), Problem 44, observing that the n-ring puzzle reduces to an $(n - 1)$-ring puzzle after a certain number of steps. Let $C_n = A_n - A_{n-1} = B_n - B_{n-1} + 1$ be the number of rings removed during this reduction. Arima noticed that $C_n = 2C_{n-1} - [n \text{ even}]$; thus he could compute $A_n = C_1 + C_2 + \cdots + C_n$ for $n = 9$ without actually knowing the formula $C_n = \lceil 2^{n-1}/3 \rceil$.

More than two centuries earlier, Cardano had already mentioned the "complicati annuli" in his *De Subtilitate Libri XXI* (Nuremberg: 1550), Book 15. He wrote that they are "useless yet admirably subtle," stating erroneously that 95 moves are needed to remove seven rings and 95 more to put them back. John Wallis devoted seven pages to this puzzle in the Latin edition of his *Algebra* **2** (Oxford: 1693), Chapter 111, presenting detailed but nonoptimum methods for the nine-ring case. He included the operation of sliding a ring through the bar as well as putting it on or off, and he hinted that shortcuts were available, but he did not attempt to find a shortest solution.

11. The solution to $S_n = S_{n-2} + 1 + S_{n-2} + S_{n-1}$ when $S_1 = S_2 = 1$ is $S_n = 2^{n-1} - [n \text{ even}]$. [*Math. Quest. Educational Times* **3** (1865), 66–67.]

12. (a) The theory of $n - 1$ Chinese rings proves that Gray binary code yields the compositions in a convenient order $(4, 31, 211, 22, 112, 1111, 121, 13)$:

    A1. [Initialize.] Set $t \leftarrow 0$, $j \leftarrow 1$, $s_1 \leftarrow n$. (We assume that $n > 1$.)

    A2. [Visit.] Visit $s_1 \ldots s_j$. Then set $t \leftarrow 1 - t$, and go to A4 if $t = 0$.

    A3. [Odd step.] If $s_j > 1$, set $s_j \leftarrow s_j - 1$, $s_{j+1} \leftarrow 1$, $j \leftarrow j + 1$; otherwise set $j \leftarrow j - 1$ and $s_j \leftarrow s_j + 1$. Return to A2.

    A4. [Even step.] If $s_{j-1} > 1$, set $s_{j-1} \leftarrow s_{j-1} - 1$, $s_{j+1} \leftarrow s_j$, $s_j \leftarrow 1$, $j \leftarrow j + 1$; otherwise set $j \leftarrow j - 1$, $s_j \leftarrow s_{j+1}$, $s_{j-1} \leftarrow s_{j-1} + 1$ (but terminate if $j - 1 = 0$). Return to A2.   ▌

(b) Now $q_1, \ldots, q_{t-1}$ represent rings on the bar:

    B1. [Initialize.] Set $t \leftarrow 1$, $q_0 \leftarrow n$. (We assume that $n > 1$.)

    B2. [Visit.] Set $q_t \leftarrow 0$ and visit $(q_0 - q_1) \ldots (q_{t-1} - q_t)$. Go to B4 if t is even.

    B3. [Odd step.] If $q_{t-1} = 1$, set $t \leftarrow t - 1$; otherwise set $q_t \leftarrow 1$ and $t \leftarrow t + 1$. Return to step B2.

    B4. [Even step.] If $q_{t-2} = q_{t-1} + 1$, set $q_{t-2} \leftarrow q_{t-1}$ and $t \leftarrow t - 1$ (but terminate if $t = 2$); otherwise set $q_t \leftarrow q_{t-1}$, $q_{t-1} \leftarrow q_t + 1$, $t \leftarrow t + 1$. Return to B2.   ▌

These algorithms [see J. Misra, *ACM Trans. Math. Software* **1** (1975), 285] are loopless even in their initialization steps.

13. In step A1, also set $C \leftarrow 1$. In step A3, set $C \leftarrow s_j C$ if $s_j > 1$, otherwise $C \leftarrow C/(s_{j-1}+1)$. In step A4, set $C \leftarrow s_{j-1}C$ if $s_{j-1} > 1$, otherwise $C \leftarrow C/(s_{j-2}+1)$.

Similar modifications apply to steps B1, B3, B4. Sufficient precision is needed to accommodate the value $C = n!$ for the composition $1 \ldots 1$; we are stretching the definition of looplessness by assuming that arithmetic operations take unit time.

14. S1. [Initialize.] Set $j \leftarrow 0$.

   S2. [Visit.] Visit the string $a_1 \ldots a_j$.

   S3. [Lengthen.] If $j < n$, set $j \leftarrow j+1$, $a_j \leftarrow 0$, and return to S2.

   S4. [Increase.] If $a_j < m_j - 1$, set $a_j \leftarrow a_j + 1$ and return to S2.

   S5. [Shorten.] Set $j \leftarrow j - 1$, and return to S4 if $j > 0$. ∎

15. T1. [Initialize.] Set $j \leftarrow 0$.

   T2. [Even visit.] If j is even, visit the string $a_1 \ldots a_j$.

   T3. [Lengthen.] If $j < n$, set $j \leftarrow j+1$, $a_j \leftarrow 0$, and return to T2.

   T4. [Odd visit.] If j is odd, visit the string $a_1 \ldots a_j$.

   T5. [Increase.] If $a_j < m_j - 1$, set $a_j \leftarrow a_j + 1$ and return to T2.

   T6. [Shorten.] Set $j \leftarrow j - 1$, and return to T4 if $j > 0$. ∎

This algorithm is loopless, although it may appear at first glance to contain loops; at most four steps separate consecutive visits. The basic idea is related to exercise 2.3.1–5 and to "prepostorder" traversal (Algorithm 7.2.1.6Q).

16. Suppose $\text{LINK}(j - 1) = j + nb_j$ for $1 \leq j \leq n$ and $\text{LINK}(j - 1 + n) = j + n(1 - b_j)$ for $1 < j \leq n$. These links represent $(a_1, \ldots, a_n)$ if and only if $g(b_1 \ldots b_n) = a_1 \ldots a_n$, so we can use a loopless Gray binary generator to achieve the desired result.

17. Put the concatenation of 3-bit codes $(g(j), g(k))$ in row j and column k, for $0 \leq j, k < 8$. [It is not difficult to prove that this is essentially the *only* solution, except for permuting and/or complementing coordinates and/or rotating rows, because the coordinate that changes when moving north or south depends only on the row, and a similar statement applies to columns. Karnaugh's isomorphism between the 4-cube and the 4×4 torus can be traced back to *The Design of Switching Circuits* by W. Keister, A. E. Ritchie, and S. H. Washburn (1951), page 174. Incidentally, Keister went on to design an ingenious variant of Chinese rings called SpinOut, and a generalization called The Hexadecimal Puzzle, *U.S. Patents 3637215–3637216* (1972).]

18. Use 2-bit Gray code to represent the digits $u_j = (0, 1, 2, 3)$ respectively as the bit pairs $u'_{2j-1} u'_{2j} = (00, 01, 11, 10)$. [C. Y. Lee introduced his metric in *IEEE Trans.* **IT-4** (1958), 77–82. A similar $m/2$-bit encoding works for even values of m; for example, when $m = 8$ we can represent $(0, 1, 2, 3, 4, 5, 6, 7)$ by $(0000, 0001, 0011, 0111, 1111, 1110,$ $1100, 1000)$. But such a scheme leaves out some of the binary patterns when $m > 4$.]

19. (a) A modular Gray quaternary algorithm needs slightly less computation than Algorithm M, but it doesn't matter because 256 is so small. The result is $z_0^8 + z_1^8 +$ $z_2^8 + z_3^8 + 14(z_0^4 z_2^4 + z_1^4 z_3^4) + 56 z_0 z_1 z_2 z_3 (z_0^2 + z_2^2)(z_1^2 + z_3^2)$.

   (b) Replacing (z_0, z_1, z_2, z_3) by $(1, z, z^2, z)$ gives $1 + 112 z^6 + 30 z^8 + 112 z^{10} + z^{16}$; thus all of the nonzero Lee weights are ≥ 6. Now use the construction in the previous exercise to convert each $(u_0, u_1, u_2, u_3, u_4, u_5, u_6, u_\infty)$ into a 16-bit number.

20. Recover the quaternary vector $(u_0, u_1, u_2, u_3, u_4, u_5, u_6, u_\infty)$ from u', and use Algorithm 4.6.1D to find the remainder of $u_0 + u_1 x + \cdots + u_6 x^6$ divided by $g(x)$, mod 4; that algorithm can be used in spite of the fact that the coefficients do not belong to a field, because $g(x)$ is monic. Express the remainder as $x^j + 2x^k$ (modulo $g(x)$ and 4), and let $d = (k - j) \bmod 7$, $s = (u_0 + \cdots + u_6 + u_\infty) \bmod 4$.

Case 1, $s = 1$: If $k = \infty$, the error was x^j (in other words, the correct vector has $u_j \leftarrow (u_j - 1) \bmod 4$); otherwise there were three or more errors.

Case 2, $s = 3$: If $j = k$ the error was $-x^j$; otherwise ≥ 3 errors occurred.

Case 3, $s = 0$: If $j = k = \infty$, no errors were made; if $j = \infty$ and $k < \infty$, at least four errors were made. Otherwise the errors were $x^a - x^b$, where $a = (j + (\infty, 6, 5, 2, 3, 1, 4, 0)) \bmod 7$ according as $d = (0, 1, 2, 3, 4, 5, 6, \infty)$, and $b = (j+2d) \bmod 7$.

Case 4, $s = 2$: If $j = \infty$ the errors were $2x^k$. Otherwise the errors were

$$x^j + x^\infty, \text{ if } k = \infty;$$
$$-x^j - x^\infty, \text{ if } d = 0;$$
$$x^a + x^b, \text{ if } d \in \{1, 2, 4\}, \ a = (j - 3d) \bmod 7, \ b = (j - 2d) \bmod 7;$$
$$-x^a - x^b, \text{ if } d \in \{3, 5, 6\}, \ a = (j - 3d) \bmod 7, \ b = (j - d) \bmod 7.$$

Given $u' = (1100100100001111)_2$, we have $u = (2, 0, 3, 1, 0, 0, 2, 2)$ and $2 + 3x^2 + x^3 + 2x^6 \equiv 1 + 3x + 3x^2 \equiv x^5 + 2x^6$; also $s = 2$. Thus the errors are $x^2 + x^3$, and the nearest errorfree codeword is $(2, 0, 2, 0, 0, 0, 2, 2)$. Algorithm 4.6.1D tells us that $2 + 2x^2 + 2x^6 \equiv (2 + 2x + 2x^3)g(x)$ (modulo 4); so the eight information bits correspond to $(v_0, v_1, v_2, v_3) = (2, 2, 0, 2)$. [A more intelligent algorithm would also say, "Aha: The first 16 bits of π."]

For generalizations to other efficient coding schemes based on quaternary vectors, see the classic paper by Hammons, Kumar, Calderbank, Sloane, and Solé, *IEEE Trans.* **IT-40** (1994), 301–319.

21. (a) $C(\epsilon) = 1$, $C(0\alpha) = C(1\alpha) = C(\alpha)$, and $C(*\alpha) = 2C(\alpha) - [10\ldots0 \in \alpha]$. Iterating this recurrence gives $C(\alpha) = 2^t - 2^{t-1}e_t - 2^{t-2}e_{t-1} - \cdots - 2^0 e_1$, where $e_j = [10\ldots0 \in \alpha_j]$ and α_j is the suffix of α following the jth asterisk. In the example we have $\alpha_1 = *10**0*$, $\alpha_2 = 10**0*$, $\ldots$, $\alpha_5 = \epsilon$; thus $e_1 = 0$, $e_2 = 1$, $e_3 = 1$, $e_4 = 0$, and $e_5 = 1$ (by convention), hence $C(**10**0*) = 2^5 - 2^4 - 2^2 - 2^1 = 10$.

(b) We may remove trailing asterisks so that $t = t'$. Then $e_t = 1$ implies $e_{t-1} = \cdots = e_1 = 0$. [The case $C(\alpha) = 2^{t'-1}$ occurs if and only if α ends in $10^j *^k$.]

(c) To compute the sum of $C(\alpha)$ over all t-subcubes, note that $\binom{n}{t}$ clusters begin at the n-tuple $0\ldots0$, and $\binom{n-1}{t}$ begin at each succeeding n-tuple (namely one cluster for each t-subcube containing that n-tuple and specifying the bit that changed). Thus the average is $(\binom{n}{t} + (2^n - 1)\binom{n-1}{t})/2^{n-t}\binom{n}{t} = 2^t(1 - t/n) + 2^{t-n}(t/n)$. [The formula in (c) holds for *any* n-bit Gray path, but (a) and (b) are specific to the reflected Gray binary code. These results are due to C. Faloutsos, *IEEE Trans.* **SE-14** (1988), 1381–1393.]

22. Let $\alpha*^j$ and $\beta*^k$ be consecutive lieves of a Gray binary trie, where α and β are binary strings and $j \leq k$. Then the last $k - j$ bits of α are a string α' such that α and $\beta\alpha'$ are consecutive elements of Gray binary code, hence adjacent. [Interesting applications of this property to cube-connected message-passing concurrent computers are discussed in *A VLSI Architecture for Concurrent Data Structures* by William J. Dally (Kluwer, 1987), Chapter 3.]

23. $2^j = g(k) \oplus g(l) = g(k \oplus l)$ implies that $l = k \oplus g^{[-1]}(2^j) = k \oplus (2^{j+1} - 1)$. In other words, if $k = (b_{n-1}\ldots b_0)_2$ we have $l = (b_{n-1}\ldots b_{j+1}\bar{b}_j\ldots\bar{b}_0)_2$.

24. Defining $g(k) = k \oplus \lfloor k/2 \rfloor$ as usual, we find $g(k) = g(-1 - k)$; hence there are *two* 2-adic integers k such that $g(k)$ has a given 2-adic value l. One of them is even, the other is odd. We can conveniently define $g^{[-1]}$ to be the solution that is even; then (8) is replaced by $b_j = a_{j-1} \oplus \cdots \oplus a_0$, for $j \geq 0$. For example, $g^{[-1]}(1) = -2$ by this definition; when l is a normal integer, the "sign" of $g^{[-1]}(l)$ is the parity of l.

25. Let $p = k \oplus l$; exercise 7.1–00 tells us that $2^{\lfloor \lg p \rfloor + 1} - p \le |k - l| \le p$. We have $\nu(g(p)) = \nu(g(k) \oplus g(l)) = t$ if and only if there are positive integers $j_1, \ldots, j_t$ such that $p = (1^{j_1} 0^{j_2} 1^{j_3} \ldots (0 \text{ or } 1)^{j_t})_2$. The largest possible $p < 2^n$ occurs when $j_1 = n + 1 - t$ and $j_2 = \cdots = j_t = 1$, yielding $p = 2^n - \lceil 2^t/3 \rceil$. The smallest possible $2^{\lfloor \lg p \rfloor + 1} - p = (1^{j_2} 0^{j_3} \ldots (1 \text{ or } 0)^{j_t})_2 + 1$ occurs when $j_2 = \cdots = j_t = 1$, yielding $p = \lceil 2^t/3 \rceil$. [C. K. Yuen, *IEEE Trans.* **IT-20** (1974), 668; S. R. Cavior, *IEEE Trans.* **IT-21** (1975), 596.]

26. Let $N = 2^{n_t} + \cdots + 2^{n_1}$ where $n_t > \cdots > n_1 \ge 0$; also, let Γ_n be any Gray code for $\{0, 1, \ldots, 2^n - 1\}$ that begins at 0 and ends at 1, except that Γ_0 is simply 0. Use

$$\Gamma_{n_t}^R, \; 2^{n_t} + \Gamma_{n_{t-1}}, \; \ldots, \; 2^{n_t} + \cdots + 2^{n_3} + \Gamma_{n_2}^R, \; 2^{n_t} + \cdots + 2^{n_2} + \Gamma_{n_1}, \; \text{if } t \text{ is even};$$

$$\Gamma_{n_t}, \; 2^{n_t} + \Gamma_{n_{t-1}}^R, \; \ldots, \; 2^{n_t} + \cdots + 2^{n_3} + \Gamma_{n_2}^R, \; 2^{n_t} + \cdots + 2^{n_2} + \Gamma_{n_1}, \; \text{if } t \text{ is odd}.$$

27. In general, if $k = (b_{n-1} \ldots b_0)_2$, the $(k+1)$st largest element of S_n is equal to

$$1/(2 - (-1)^{a_{n-1}}/(2 - \cdots /(2 - (-1)^{a_1}/(2 - (-1)^{a_0})) \ldots)),$$

corresponding to the sign pattern $g(k) = (a_{n-1} \ldots a_0)_2$. Thus we can compute any element of S_n in $O(n)$ steps, given its rank. Setting $k = 2^{100} - 10^{10}$ and $n = 100$ yields the answer $373065177/1113604409$. [Whenever $f(x)$ is a positive and monotonic function, the 2^n elements $f(\pm f(\ldots \pm f(\pm x) \ldots))$ are ordered according to Gray binary code, as observed by H. E. Salzer, *CACM* **16** (1973), 180. In this particular case there is, however, another way to get the answer, because we also have $S_n = /\!/2, \pm 2, \ldots, \pm 2, \pm 1/\!/$ using the notation of Section 4.5.3; continued fractions in this form are ordered by complementing alternate bits of k.]

28. (a) As $t = 1, 2, \ldots$, bit a_j of median(G_t) runs through the periodic sequence

$$0, \ldots, 0, *, 1, \ldots, 1, *, 0, \ldots, 0, *, \ldots$$

with asterisks at every 2^{1+j}th step. Thus the strings that correspond to the binary representations of $\lfloor (t-1)/2 \rfloor$ and $\lfloor t/2 \rfloor$ are medians. And those strings are in fact "extreme" cases, in the sense that all medians agree with the common bits of $\lfloor (t-1)/2 \rfloor$ and $\lfloor t/2 \rfloor$, hence asterisks appear where they disagree. For example, when $t = 100 = (01100100)_2$ and $n = 8$, we have median$(G_{100}) = 001100**$.

(b) Since $G_{2t} = 2G_t \cup (2G_t + 1)$, we may assume that $t = (a_{n-2} \ldots a_1 a_0 1)_2$ is odd. If α is $g(p)$ and β is $g(q)$ in Gray binary, we have $p = (p_{n-1} \ldots p_0)_2$ and $q = (p_{n-1} \ldots p_{j+1} \bar{p}_j \ldots \bar{p}_0)_2$; and $a_{n-1} a_{n-2} = 01 = p_{n-1} p_{n-2}$. We cannot have $p < t \le q$, because this would imply that $j = n - 1$ and $p_{n-3} = p_{n-4} = \cdots = p_0 = 1$. [See A. J. Bernstein, K. Steiglitz, and J. E. Hopcroft, *IEEE Trans.* **IT-12** (1966), 425–430.]

29. Assuming that $p \ne 0$, let $l = \lfloor \lg p \rfloor$ and $S_a = \{s \mid 2^l a \le s < 2^l (a + 1)\}$ for $0 \le a < 2^{n-l}$. Then $(k \oplus p) - k$ has a constant sign for all $k \in S_a$, and

$$\sum_{k \in S_a} \left| (k \oplus p) - k \right| = 2^l |S_a| = 2^{2l}.$$

Also $g^{[-1]}(g(k) \oplus p) = k \oplus g^{[-1]}(p)$, and $\lfloor \lg g^{[-1]}(p) \rfloor = \lfloor \lg p \rfloor$. Therefore

$$\frac{1}{2^n} \sum_{k=0}^{2^n - 1} \left| g^{[-1]}(g(k) \oplus p) - k \right| = \frac{1}{2^n} \sum_{a=0}^{2^{n-l}-1} \sum_{k \in S_a} \left| (k \oplus g^{[-1]}(p)) - k \right| = \frac{1}{2^n} \sum_{a=0}^{2^{n-l}-1} 2^{2l} = 2^l.$$

[See Morgan M. Buchner, Jr., *Bell System Tech. J.* **48** (1969), 3113–3130.]

30. The cycle containing $k > 1$ has length $2^{\lfloor \lg \lg k \rfloor + 1}$, because it is easy to show from Eq. (7) that if $k = (b_{n-1} \ldots b_0)_2$ we have

$$g^{[2^l]}(k) = (c_{n-1} \ldots c_0)_2, \qquad \text{where } c_j = b_j \oplus b_{j+l+1}.$$

To permute all elements k such that $\lfloor \lg k \rfloor = t$, there are two cases: If t is a power of 2, the cycle containing $2\lfloor k/2 \rfloor$ also contains $2\lfloor k/2 \rfloor + 1$, so we must double the cycle leaders for $t - 1$. Otherwise the cycle containing $2\lfloor k/2 \rfloor$ is disjoint from the cycle containing $2\lfloor k/2 \rfloor + 1$, so $L_t = (2L_{t-1}) \cup (2L_{t-1} + 1) = (L_{t-1}*)_2$. This argument, discovered by Jörg Arndt in 2001, establishes the hint and yields the following algorithm:

> **P1.** [Initialize.] Set $t \leftarrow 1$, $m \leftarrow 0$. (We may assume that $n \geq 2$.)

> **P2.** [Loop through leaders.] Set $r \leftarrow m$. Perform Algorithm Q with $k = 2^t + r$; then if $r > 0$, set $r \leftarrow (r-1) \wedge m$ and repeat until $r = 0$. [See exercise 7.1–00.]

> **P3.** [Increase $\lg k$.] Set $t \leftarrow t + 1$. Terminate if t is now equal to n; otherwise set $m \leftarrow 2m + [t \wedge (t - 1) \neq 0]$ and return to P2. ∎

> **Q1.** [Begin a cycle.] Set $s \leftarrow X_k$, $l \leftarrow k$, $j \leftarrow l \oplus \lfloor l/2 \rfloor$.

> **Q2.** [Follow the cycle.] If $j \neq k$ set $X_l \leftarrow X_j$, $l \leftarrow j$, $j \leftarrow l \oplus \lfloor l/2 \rfloor$, and repeat until $j = k$. Then set $X_l \leftarrow s$. ∎

31. We get a field from f_n if and only if we get one from $f_n^{[2]}$, which takes $(a_{n-1} \ldots a_0)_2$ to $((a_{n-1} \oplus a_{n-2})(a_{n-1} \oplus a_{n-3})(a_{n-2} \oplus a_{n-4}) \ldots (a_2 \oplus a_0)(a_1))_2$. Let $c_n(x)$ be the characteristic polynomial of the matrix A defining this transformation, mod 2; then $c_1(x) = x + 1$, $c_2(x) = x^2 + x + 1$, and $c_{j+1}(x) = xc_j(x) + c_{j-1}(x)$. Since $c_n(A)$ is the zero matrix, by the Cayley–Hamilton theorem, a field is obtained if and only if $c_n(x)$ is a primitive polynomial, and this condition can be tested as in Section 3.2.2. The first such values of n are 1, 2, 3, 5, 6, 9, 11, 14, 23, 26, 29, 30, 33, 35, 39, 41, 51, 53, 65, 69, 74, 81, 83, 86, 89, 90, 95.

[Running the recurrence backwards shows that $c_{-j-1}(x) = c_j(x)$, hence $c_j(x)$ divides $c_{(2j+1)k+j}(x)$; for example, $c_{3k+1}(x)$ is always a multiple of $x+1$. All numbers n of the form $2jk + j + k$ are therefore excluded when $j > 0$ and $k > 0$. The polynomials $c_{18}(x)$, $c_{50}(x)$, $c_{98}(x)$, and $c_{99}(x)$ are irreducible but not primitive.]

32. Mostly true, but false at the points where $w_k(x)$ changes sign. (Walsh originally suggested that $w_k(x)$ should be zero at such points; but the convention adopted here is better, because it makes simple formulas like (15)–(19) valid for all x.)

33. By induction on k, we have

$$w_k(x) = w_{\lfloor k/2 \rfloor}(2x) = r_1(2x)^{b_1+b_2} r_2(2x)^{b_2+b_3} \ldots = r_1(x)^{b_0+b_1} r_2(x)^{b_1+b_2} r_3(x)^{b_2+b_3} \ldots$$

for $0 \leq x < \frac{1}{2}$, because $r_j(2x) = r_{j+1}(x)$ and $r_1(x) = 1$ in this range. And when $\frac{1}{2} \leq x < 1$,

$$w_k(x) = (-1)^{\lceil k/2 \rceil} w_{\lfloor k/2 \rfloor}(2x - 1) = r_1(x)^{b_0+b_1} r_1(2x - 1)^{b_1+b_2} r_2(2x - 1)^{b_2+b_3} \ldots$$
$$= r_1(x)^{b_0+b_1} r_2(x)^{b_1+b_2} r_3(x)^{b_2+b_3} \ldots$$

because $\lceil k/2 \rceil \equiv b_0 + b_1$ (modulo 2) and $r_j(2x - 1) = r_{j+1}(x - \frac{1}{2}) = r_{j+1}(x)$ for $j \geq 1$.

34. $p_k(x) = \prod_{j \geq 0} r_{j+1}^{b_j}$; hence $w_k(x) = p_k(x)p_{\lfloor k/2 \rfloor}(x) = p_{g(k)}(x)$. [R. E. A. C. Paley, *Proc. London Math. Soc.* (2) **34** (1932), 241–279.]

35. If $j = (a_{n-1} \ldots a_0)_2$ and $k = (b_{n-1} \ldots b_0)_2$, the element in row j and column k is $(-1)^{f(j,k)}$, where $f(j,k)$ is the sum of all $a_r b_s$ such that: $r = s$ (Hadamard); $r+s = n-1$ (Paley); $r + s = n$ or $n - 1$ (Walsh).

Let R_n, F_n, and G_n be permutation matrices for the permutations that take $j = (a_{n-1} \ldots a_0)_2$ to $k = (a_0 \ldots a_{n-1})_2$, $k = 2^n - 1 - j = (\bar{a}_{n-1} \ldots \bar{a}_0)_2$, and $k = g^{[-1]}(j) = ((a_{n-1}) \ldots (a_{n-1} \oplus \cdots \oplus a_0))_2$, respectively. Then, using the Kronecker product of matrices, we have the recursive formulas

$$R_{n+1} = \begin{pmatrix} R_n \otimes (1\ 0) \\ R_n \otimes (0\ 1) \end{pmatrix}, \qquad F_{n+1} = F_n \otimes \begin{pmatrix} 0 & 1 \\ 1 & 0 \end{pmatrix}, \qquad G_{n+1} = \begin{pmatrix} G_n & 0 \\ 0 & G_n F_n \end{pmatrix},$$

$$H_{n+1} = H_n \otimes \begin{pmatrix} 1 & 1 \\ 1 & \bar{1} \end{pmatrix}, \qquad P_{n+1} = \begin{pmatrix} P_n \otimes (1\ 1) \\ P_n \otimes (1\ \bar{1}) \end{pmatrix}, \qquad W_{n+1} = \begin{pmatrix} W_n \otimes (1\ 1) \\ F_n W_n \otimes (1\ \bar{1}) \end{pmatrix}.$$

Thus $W_n = G_n^T P_n = P_n G_n$; $H_n = P_n R_n = R_n P_n$; and $P_n = W_n G_n^T = G_n W_n = H_n R_n = R_n H_n$.

36. W1. [Hadamard transform.] For $k = 0, 1, \ldots, n - 1$, replace the pair (X_j, X_{j+2^k}) by $(X_j + X_{j+2^k}, X_j - X_{j+2^k})$ for all j with $\lfloor j/2^k \rfloor$ even, $0 \le j < 2^n$. (These operations effectively set $X^T \leftarrow H_n X^T$.)

W2. [Bit reversal.] Apply the algorithm of exercise 5 to the vector X. (These operations effectively set $X^T \leftarrow R_n X^T$, in the notation of exercise 35.)

W3. [Gray binary permutation.] Apply the algorithm of exercise 30 to the vector X. (These operations effectively set $X^T \leftarrow G_n^T X^T$.) $\blacksquare$

If n has one of the special values in exercise 31, it may be faster to combine steps W2 and W3 into a single permutation step.

37. If $k = 2^{e_1} + \cdots + 2^{e_t}$ with $e_1 > \cdots > e_t \ge 0$, the sign changes occur at $S_{e_1} \cup \cdots \cup S_{e_t}$, where

$$S_0 = \left\{ \frac{1}{2} \right\}, \qquad S_1 = \left\{ \frac{1}{4}, \frac{3}{4} \right\}, \qquad \ldots, \qquad S_e = \left\{ \frac{2j+1}{2^e} \,\middle|\, 0 \le j < 2^e \right\}.$$

Therefore the number of sign changes in $(0 \mathrel{..} x)$ is $\sum_{j=1}^t \lfloor 2^{e_j} x + \frac{1}{2} \rfloor$. Setting $x = l/(k+1)$ gives $l + O(t)$ changes; so the lth is at a distance of at most $O(\nu(k))/2^{\lfloor \lg k \rfloor}$ from $l/(k+1)$.

[This argument makes it plausible that infinitely many pairs (k, l) exist with $|z_{kl} - l/(k + 1)| = \Omega((\log k)/k)$. But no explicit construction of such "bad" pairs is immediately apparent.]

38. Let $t_0(x) = 1$ and $t_k(x) = \omega^{\lfloor 3x \rfloor \lceil 2k/3 \rceil} t_{\lfloor k/3 \rfloor}(3x)$, where $\omega = e^{2\pi i/3}$. Then $t_k(x)$ winds around the origin $\frac{2}{3}k$ times as x increases from 0 to 1. If $s_k(x) = \omega^{\lfloor 3^k x \rfloor}$ is the ternary analog of the Rademacher function $r_k(x)$, we have $t_k(x) = \prod_{j \ge 0} s_{j+1}(x)^{b_j - b_{j+1}}$ when $k = (b_{n-1} \ldots b_0)_3$, as in the modular ternary Gray code.

39. Let's call the symbols $\{x_0, x_1, \ldots, x_7\}$ instead of $\{a, b, c, d, e, f, g, h\}$. We want to find a permutation p of $\{0, 1, \ldots, 7\}$ such that the matrix with $(-1)^{j \cdot k} x_{p(j) \oplus k}$ in row j and column k has orthogonal rows; this condition is equivalent to requiring that

$$(j + j') \cdot (p(j) + p(j')) \equiv 1 \pmod{2}, \qquad \text{for } 0 \le j < j' < 8.$$

One solution is $p(0) \ldots p(7) = 0\,1\,7\,2\,5\,6\,3\,4$, yielding the identity $(a^2 + b^2 + c^2 + d^2 + e^2 + f^2 + g^2 + h^2)(A^2 + B^2 + C^2 + D^2 + E^2 + F^2 + G^2 + H^2) = \mathcal{A}^2 + \mathcal{B}^2 + \mathcal{C}^2 + \mathcal{D}^2 +$

$\mathcal{E}^2 + \mathcal{F}^2 + \mathcal{G}^2 + \mathcal{H}^2$, where

$$
\begin{pmatrix} \mathcal{A} \\ \mathcal{B} \\ \mathcal{C} \\ \mathcal{D} \\ \mathcal{E} \\ \mathcal{F} \\ \mathcal{G} \\ \mathcal{H} \end{pmatrix}
=
\begin{pmatrix}
a & b & c & d & e & f & g & h \\
b & -a & d & -c & f & -e & h & -g \\
h & g & -f & -e & d & c & -b & -a \\
c & -d & -a & b & g & -h & -e & f \\
f & e & h & g & -b & -a & -d & -c \\
g & -h & e & -f & -c & d & -a & b \\
d & c & -b & -a & -h & -g & f & e \\
e & -f & -g & h & -a & b & c & -d
\end{pmatrix}
\begin{pmatrix} A \\ B \\ C \\ D \\ E \\ F \\ G \\ H \end{pmatrix} .
$$

[This identity was discovered by C. F. Degen, *Mémoires de l'Acad. Sci. St. Petersbourg* (5) **8** (1818), 207–219. The related octonions are discussed in an interesting survey by J. C. Baez, *Bull. Amer. Math. Soc.* **39** (2002), 145–205.]

(b) There *is* no 16×16 solution. The closest one can come is

$$p(0) \dots p(15) \;=\; 0\ 1\ 11\ 2\ 14\ 15\ 13\ 4\ 9\ 10\ 7\ 12\ 5\ 6\ 3\ 8,$$

which fails if and only if $j \oplus j' = 5$. (See *Philos. Mag.* **34** (1867), 461–475. In §9, §10, §11, and §13 of this paper, Sylvester stated and proved the basic results about what has somehow come to be known as the Hadamard transform — although Hadamard himself gave credit to Sylvester [*Bull. des Sciences Mathématiques* (2) **17** (1893), 240–246]. Moreover, Sylvester introduced transforms of m^n elements in §14, using mth roots of unity.)

40. Yes; this change would in fact run through the swapped subsets in lexicographic binary order rather than in Gray binary order. (Any 5×5 matrix of 0s and 1s that is nonsingular mod 2 will generate all 32 possibilities when we run through all linear combinations of its rows.) The most important thing is the appearance of the ruler function, or some other Gray code delta sequence, not the fact that only one a_j changes per step, in cases like this where any number of the a_j can be changed simultaneously at the same cost.

41. At most 16; for example, `fired`, `fires`, `finds`, `fines`, `fined`, `fares`, `fared`, `wares`, `wards`, `wands`, `wanes`, `waned`, `wines`, `winds`, `wires`, `wired`. We also get 16 from `paced`/`links` and `paled`/`mints`; perhaps also from a word mixed with an antipodal nonword.

42. Suppose $n \le 2^{2^r} + r + 1$, and let $s = 2^r$. We use an auxiliary table of 2^{r+s} bits f_{jk} for $0 \le j < 2^s$ and $0 \le k < s$, representing focus pointers as in Algorithm L, together with an auxiliary s-bit "register" $j = (j_{s-1} \dots j_0)_2$ and an $(r+2)$-bit "program counter" $p = (p_{r+1} \dots p_0)_2$. At each step we examine the program counter and possibly the j register and one of the f bits; then, based on the bits seen, we complement a bit of the Gray code, complement a bit of the program counter, and possibly change a j or f bit, thereby emulating step L3 with respect to the most significant $n - r - 2$ bits.

For example, here is the construction when $r = 1$:

$p_2p_1p_0$	Change	Set		$p_2p_1p_0$	Change	Set	
0 0 0	a_0, p_0	$j_0 \leftarrow f_{00}$	$\Big\} \; j \leftarrow f_0$	1 1 0	a_0, p_0	$f_{j0} \leftarrow f_{(j+1)0}$	$\Big\} \; f_j \leftarrow f_{j+1}$
0 0 1	a_1, p_1	$j_1 \leftarrow f_{01}$		1 1 1	a_1, p_1	$f_{j1} \leftarrow f_{(j+1)1}$	
0 1 1	a_0, p_0	$f_{00} \leftarrow 0$	$\Big\} \; f_0 \leftarrow 0$	1 0 1	a_0, p_0	$f_{(j+1)0} \leftarrow (j+1)_0$	$\Big\} \; f_{j+1} \leftarrow j+1$
0 1 0	a_2, p_2	$f_{01} \leftarrow 0$		1 0 0	a_{j+3}, p_2	$f_{(j+1)1} \leftarrow (j+1)_1$	

The process stops when it attempts to change bit a_n.

[In fact, we need change only *one* auxiliary bit per step if we allow ourselves to examine some Gray binary bits as well as the auxiliary bits, because $p_r \dots p_0 = a_r \dots a_0$, and we can set $f_0 \leftarrow 0$ in a more clever way when j doesn't have its final value $2^s - 1$. This construction, suggested by Fredman in 2001, improves on another that he had published in *SICOMP* **7** (1978), 134–146. With a more elaborate construction it is possible to reduce the number of auxiliary bits to $O(n)$.]

43. This number was estimated by Silverman, Vickers, and Sampson [*IEEE Trans.* **IT-29** (1983), 894–901] to be about 7×10^{22}. Exact calculation might be feasible because every 6-bit Gray cycle has only five or fewer segments that lie in a 5-cube corresponding to at least one of the six coordinates. (In unpublished work, Steve Winker had used a similar idea to evaluate $d(5)$ in less than 15 minutes on a "generic" computer in 1972.)

44. All $(n+1)$-bit delta sequences with just two occurrences of the coordinate j are produced by the following construction: Let $\delta_1 \dots \delta_{2^n-1}$ and $\varepsilon_1 \dots \varepsilon_{2^n-1}$ be n-bit delta sequences for Gray *paths*, with $2^{\delta_1} \oplus \cdots \oplus 2^{\delta_{2^n-1}} = 2^{\varepsilon_1} \oplus \cdots \oplus 2^{\varepsilon_{2^n-1}}$. Form the cycle

$$\delta_{k+1} \dots \delta_{2^n-1}\, n\, \varepsilon_1 \dots \varepsilon_{2^n-1}\, n\, \delta_1 \dots \delta_k$$

for some k with $0 \le k < 2^n$, then interchange $n \leftrightarrow j$.

All $(n+2)$-bit delta sequences with just two occurrences of coordinates h and j (with h before j) are, similarly, produced from four n-bit sequences $\delta_1 \dots \delta_{2^n-1}$, $\dots$, $\eta_1 \dots \eta_{2^n-1}$ where $2^{\delta_1} \oplus \cdots \oplus 2^{\eta_{2^n-1}} = 0$, by interchanging $n \leftrightarrow h$ and $n+1 \leftrightarrow j$ in

$$\delta_{k+1} \dots \delta_{2^n-1}\, n\, \varepsilon_1 \dots \varepsilon_{2^n-1}\, (n{+}1)\, \zeta_1 \dots \zeta_{2^n-1}\, n\, \eta_1 \dots \eta_{2^n-1}\, (n{+}1)\, \delta_1 \dots \delta_k.$$

Let $a(n)$ and $b(n)$ be the number of n-bit cycles defined in parts (a) and (b); then $(a(1), \dots, a(5)) = (1, 0, 0, 1920, 318996480)$ and $(b(1), \dots, b(5)) = (0, 2, 12, 384, 4200960)$. The constructions above prove that $a(n{+}1) + 2b(n{+}1) = 2^n(n{+}1)A(n)$ and $b(n{+}2) = 2^n(n{+}2)(n{+}1)B(n)$, if there are $A(n)$ and $B(n)$ ways to choose the respective sequences δ, ε, ζ, and η. If we restrict ourselves to cases where the Gray paths are extendible to Gray cycles, with $\delta_0 = \varepsilon_0 = \zeta_0 = \eta_0$, we get $a'(n+1)$ and $b'(n+2)$ sequences where $a'(n+1) + 2b'(n+1) = 2^n(n+1)d(n)^2/n$ and $b'(n+2) = 2^n(n+2)(n+1)d(n)^4/n^3$.

45. We have $d(n{+}1) \ge 2^n d(n)^2/n$, because $2^n d(n)^2/n$ is a lower bound on the number of $(n{+}1)$-bit delta sequences with exactly two appearances of 0. Hence $d(n{+}1)^{1/2^{n+1}} > d(n)^{1/2^n}$; and $d(n) \ge \frac{5}{32}\alpha^{2^n}$ for $n \ge 5$, where $\alpha = (\frac{32}{5}d(5))^{1/32} \approx 2.06$.

Indeed, we can establish even faster growth by using the previous exercise, because $d(n+1) \ge a'(n+1) + b'(n+1)$ and $b'(n+1) \le \frac{25}{64}(n+1)d(n)^2/n$ for $n \ge 5$. Hence $d(n+1) \ge (2^n - \frac{25}{64})(n+1)d(n)^2/n$ for $n \ge 5$, and iteration of this relation shows that

$$\lim_{n \to \infty} d(n)^{1/2^n} \ge d(5)^{1/32} \prod_{n=5}^{\infty} \left(2^n - \frac{25}{64}\right)^{1/2^{n+1}} \left(\frac{n+1}{n}\right)^{1/2^{n+1}} \approx 2.3606.$$

[See R. J. Douglas, *Disc. Math.* **17** (1977), 143–146; M. Mollard, *European J. Comb.* **9** (1988), 49–52.] The true value of this limit, however, is probably ∞.

46. Leo Moser (unpublished) has conjectured that it is $\sim n/e$. So far only an upper bound of about $n/\sqrt{2}$ has been established; see the references in the previous answer.

48. If $d(n, k, v)$ of the cycles begin with $g(0) \dots g(k-1)v$, the conjecture implies that $d(n, k, v) \le d(n, k, g(k))$, because the reverse of a Gray cycle is a Gray cycle. Thus the hint follows from $d(n) = d(n, 1)$ and

$$d(n,k) = \sum_v \{ d(n,k,v) \mid v - g(k-1), v \notin S_k \} \le c_{nk} d(n,k,g(k)) = d(n,k+1).$$

Finally, $d(n, 2^n) = 1$, hence $d(n) \le \prod_{k=1}^{2^n-1} c_{nk} = \prod_{k=1}^n k^{\binom{n}{k}} = n \prod_{k=1}^{n-1}(k(n-k))^{\binom{n}{k}/2} \le n \prod_{k=1}^{n-1}(n/2)^{\binom{n}{k}} = n(n/2)^{2^n-2}$. [*IEEE Trans.* **IT-29** (1983), 894–901.]

49. Take any Hamiltonian path P from $0 \ldots 0$ to $1 \ldots 1$ in the $(2n-1)$-cube, such as the Savage–Winkler code, and use $0P$, $1\overline{P}$. (All such cycles are obtained by this construction when $n = 1$ or $n = 2$, but many more possibilities exist when $n > 2$.)

50. $\alpha_1(n+1)\alpha_1^R n \alpha_1 j_1 \alpha_2 n \alpha_2^R (n+1)\alpha_2 \ldots j_{l-1}\alpha_l n \alpha_l^R (n+1)\alpha_l n \alpha_l^R j_{l-1} \ldots j_1 \alpha_1^R n$.

51. We can assume that $n > 3$ and that we have an n-bit Gray cycle with transition counts $c_j = 2\lfloor (2^{n-1}+j)/n \rfloor$; we want to construct an $(n+2)$-bit cycle with transition counts $c_j' = 2\lfloor (2^{n+1}+j)/(n+2) \rfloor$. If $2^{n+1} \bmod (n+2) \ge 2$, we can use Theorem D with $l = 2\lfloor 2^{n+1}/(n+2) \rfloor + 1$, underlining b_j copies of j where $b_j = 4\lfloor (2^{n-1}+j)/n \rfloor - \lfloor (2^{n+1}+j)/(n+2) \rfloor - [j = 0]$ and putting an underlined 0 last. This is always easy to do because $|b_j - 2^{n+2}/n(n+2)| < 5$. A similar construction works if $2^{n+1} \bmod (n+2) \le n$, with $l = 2\lfloor 2^{n+1}/(n+2) \rfloor - 1$ and $b_j = 4\lfloor (2^{n-1}+j)/n \rfloor - \lfloor (2^{n+1}+j+2)/(n+2) \rfloor - [j = 0]$. In fact, $2^{n+1} \bmod (n+2)$ is always $\le n$ [see K. Kedlaya, *Electronic J. Combinatorics* **3** (1996), comment on #R25 (9 April 1997)]. The basic idea of this proof is due to J. P. Robinson and M. Cohn [*IEEE Trans.* **C-30** (1981), 17–23].

52. The number of different code patterns in the smallest j coordinate positions is at most $c_0 + \cdots + c_{j-1}$.

53. Notice that Theorem D produces only cycles with $c_j = c_{j+1}$ for some j, so it cannot produce the counts $(2, 4, 6, 8, 12)$. The extension in exercise 50 gives also $c_j = c_{j+1} - 2$, but it cannot produce $(6, 10, 14, 18, 22, 26, 32)$. The sets of numbers satisfying the conditions of exercise 52 are precisely those obtainable by starting with $\{2, 2, 4, \ldots, 2^{n-1}\}$ and repeatedly replacing some pair $\{c_j, c_k\}$ for which $c_j < c_k$ by the pair $\{c_j + 2, c_k - 2\}$.

54. Suppose the values are $\{p_1, \ldots, p_n\}$, and let x_{jk} be the number of times p_j occurs in $(a_1, \ldots, a_k)$. We must have $(x_{1k}, \ldots, x_{nk}) \equiv (x_{1l}, \ldots, x_{nl})$ (modulo 2) for some $k < l$. But if the p's are prime numbers, varying as the delta sequence of an n-bit Gray cycle, the only solution is $k = 0$ and $l = 2^n$. [*AMM* **60** (1953), 418; **83** (1976), 54.]

56. [*Bell System Tech. J.* **37** (1958), 815–826.] The 112 canonical delta sequences yield

Class	Example	t	Class	Example	t	Class	Example	t
A	0102101302012023	2	D	0102013201020132	4	G	0102030201020302	8
B	0102303132101232	2	E	0102032021202302	4	H	0102101301021013	8
C	0102030130321013	2	F	0102013102010232	4	I	0102013121012132	1

Here B is the balanced code (Fig. 13(b)), G is standard Gray binary (Fig. 10(b)), and H is the complementary code (Fig. 13(a)). Class H is also equivalent to the modular $(4, 4)$ Gray code under the correspondence of exercise 18. A class with t automorphisms corresponds to $32 \times 24/t$ of the 2688 different delta sequences $\delta_0 \delta_1 \ldots \delta_{15}$.

Similarly (see exercise 7.2.3–00), the 5-bit Gray cycles fall into 237,675 different equivalence classes.

57. With Type 1 only, 480 vertices are isolated, namely those of classes D, F, G in the previous answer. With Type 2 only, the graph has 384 components, 288 of which are isolated vertices of classes F and G. There are 64 components of size 9, each containing 3 vertices from E and 6 from A; 16 components of size 30, each with 6 from H and 24 from C; and 16 components of size 84, each with 12 from D, 24 from B, 48 from I. With Type 3 (or Type 4) only, the entire graph is connected. [Similarly, all 91,392 of the 4-bit Gray *paths* are connected if path $\alpha\beta$ is considered adjacent to path $\alpha^R\beta$. Vickers and Silverman, *IEEE Trans.* **C-29** (1980), 329–331, have conjectured that Type 3 changes will suffice to connect the graph of n-bit Gray cycles for all $n \geq 3$.]

58. If some nonempty substring of $\beta\beta$ involves each coordinate an even number of times, that substring cannot have length $|\beta|$, so some cyclic shift of β has a prefix γ with the same evenness property. But then α doesn't define a Gray cycle, because we could change each n of γ back to 0.

59. If α is nonlocal in exercise 58, so is $\beta\beta$, provided that $q > 1$ and that 0 occurs more than $q + 1$ times in α. Therefore, starting with the α of (30) but with 0 and 1 interchanged, we obtain nonlocal cycles for $n \geq 5$ in which coordinate 0 changes exactly 6 times. [Mark Ramras, *Discrete Math.* **85** (1990), 329–331.] On the other hand, a 4-bit Gray cycle cannot be nonlocal because it always has a run of length 2; if $\delta_k = \delta_{k+2}$, elements $\{v_{k-1}, v_k, v_{k+1}, v_{k+2}\}$ form a 2-subcube.

60. Use the construction of exercise 58 with $q = 1$.

61. The idea is to interleave an m-bit cycle $U = (u_0, u_1, u_2, \ldots)$ with an n-bit cycle $V = (v_0, v_1, v_2, \ldots)$, by forming concatenations

$$W = (u_{i_0}v_{j_0},\ u_{i_1}v_{j_1},\ u_{i_2}v_{j_2},\ \ldots),\qquad i_k = \bar{a}_0 + \cdots + \bar{a}_{k-1},\quad j_k = a_0 + \cdots + a_{k-1},$$

where $a_0 a_1 a_2 \ldots$ is a periodic string of control bits $\alpha\alpha\alpha\ldots$; we advance to the next element of U when $a_k = 0$, otherwise to the next element of V.

If α is any string of length $2^m \leq 2^n$, containing s bits that are 0 and $t = 2^m - s$ bits that are 1, W will be an $(m+n)$-bit Gray cycle if s and t are odd. For we have $i_{k+l} \equiv i_k$ (modulo 2^m) and $j_{k+l} \equiv j_k$ (modulo 2^n) only if l is a multiple of 2^m, since $i_k + j_k = k$. Suppose $l = 2^m c$; then $j_{k+l} = j_k + tc$, so c is a multiple of 2^n.

(a) Let $\alpha = 0111$; then runs of length 8 occur in the left 2 bits and runs of length $\geq \lfloor \frac{4}{3} r(n) \rfloor$ occur in the right n bits.

(b) Let s be the largest odd number $\leq 2^m r(m)/(r(m) + r(n))$. Also let $t = 2^m - s$ and $a_k = \lfloor (k+1)t/2^m \rfloor - \lfloor kt/2^m \rfloor$, so that $i_k = \lceil ks/2^m \rceil$ and $j_k = \lfloor kt/2^m \rfloor$. If a run of length l occurs in the left m bits, we have $i_{k+l+1} \geq i_k + r(m) + 1$, hence $l + 1 > 2^m r(m)/s \geq r(m) + r(n)$. And if it occurs in the right n bits we have $j_{k+l+1} \geq j_k + r(n) + 1$, hence

$$l + 1 > 2^m r(n)/t > 2^m r(n)/(2^m r(n)/(r(m) + r(n)) + 2)$$

$$= r(m) + r(n) - \frac{2(r(m) + r(n))^2}{2^m r(n) + 2(r(m) + r(n))} > r(m) + r(n) - 1$$

because $r(m) \leq r(n)$.

The construction often works also in less restricted cases. See the paper that introduced the study of Gray-code runs: L. Goddyn, G. M. Lawrence, and E. Nemeth, *Utilitas Math.* **34** (1988), 179–192.

63. Set $a_k \leftarrow k \bmod 4$ for $0 \leq k < 2^{10}$, except that $a_k = 4$ when $k \bmod 16 = 15$ or $k \bmod 64 = 42$ or $k \bmod 256 = 133$. Also set $(j_0, j_1, j_2, j_3, j_4) \leftarrow (0, 2, 4, 6, 8)$. Then for $k = 0, 1, \ldots, 1023$, set $\delta_k \leftarrow j_{a_k}$ and $j_{a_k} \leftarrow 1 + 4a_k - j_{a_k}$. (This construction generalizes the method of exercise 61.)

64. (a) Each element u_k appears together with $\{v_k, v_{k+2^m}, \ldots, v_{k+2^m(2^{n-1}-1)}\}$ and $\{v_{k+1}, v_{k+1+2^m}, \ldots, v_{k+1+2^m(2^{n-1}-1)}\}$. Thus the permutation $\sigma_0 \ldots \sigma_{2^m-1}$ must be a 2^{n-1}-cycle containing the n-bit vertices of even parity, times an arbitrary permutation of the other vertices. This condition is also sufficient.

(b) Let τ_j be the permutation that takes $v \mapsto v \oplus 2^j$, and let $\pi_j(u, w)$ be the permutation $(uw)\tau_j$. If $u \oplus w = 2^i + 2^j$ then $\pi_j(u, w)$ takes $u \mapsto u \oplus 2^i$ and $w \mapsto w \oplus 2^i$, while $v \mapsto v \oplus 2^j$ for all other vertices v, so it takes each vertex to a neighbor.

If S is any set $\subseteq \{0, \ldots, n-1\}$, let $\sigma(S)$ be the stream of all permutations τ_j for all $j \in \{0, \ldots, n-1\} \setminus S$, in increasing order of j, repeated twice; for example, if $n = 5$ we have $\sigma(\{1,2\}) = \tau_0\tau_3\tau_4\tau_0\tau_3\tau_4$. Then the Gray stream

$$\Sigma(i, j, u) = \sigma(\{i,j\})\pi_j(u, u \oplus 2^i \oplus 2^j)\sigma(\{i,j\})\tau_j\sigma(\{j\})$$

consists of $6n - 8$ permutations whose product is the transposition $(u\ u \oplus 2^i \oplus 2^j)$. Moreover, when this stream is applied to any n-bit vertex v, its runs all have length $n - 2$ or more.

We may assume that $n \geq 5$. Let $\delta_0 \ldots \delta_{2^n-1}$ be the delta sequence for an n-bit Gray cycle $(v_0, v_1, \ldots, v_{2^n-1})$ with all runs of length 3 or more. Then the product of all permutations in

$$\Sigma = \prod_{k=1}^{2^{n-1}-1} \bigl(\Sigma(\delta_{2k-1}, \delta_{2k}, v_{2k-1})\,\Sigma(\delta_{2k}, \delta_{2k+1}, v_{2k})\bigr)$$

is $(v_1\,v_3)(v_2\,v_4)\ldots(v_{2^n-3}\,v_{2^n-1})(v_{2^n-2}\,v_0) = (v_{2^n-1}\ldots v_1)(v_{2^n-2}\ldots v_0)$, so it satisfies the cycle condition of (a).

Moreover, all powers $(\sigma(\emptyset)\Sigma)^t$ produce runs of length $\geq n - 2$ when applied to any vertex v. By repeating individual factors $\sigma(\{i,j\})$ or $\sigma(\{j\})$ in Σ as many times as we wish, we can adjust the length of $\sigma(\emptyset)\Sigma$, obtaining $2n + (2^{n-1} - 1)(12n - 16) + 2(n-2)a + 2(n-1)b$ for any integers $a, b \geq 0$; thus we can increase its length to exactly 2^m, provided that $2^m \geq 2n + (2^{n-1}-1)(12n-16) + 2(n^2 - 5n + 6)$, by exercise 5.2.1–21.

(c) The bound $r(n) \geq n - 4\lg n + 8$ can be proved for $n \geq 5$ as follows. First we observe that it holds for $5 \leq n < 33$ by the methods of exercises 60–63. Then we observe that every integer $N \geq 33$ can be written as $N = m + n$ or $N = m + n + 1$, for some $m \geq 20$, where

$$n = m - \lfloor 4\lg m \rfloor + 10.$$

If $m \geq 20$, 2^m is sufficiently large for the construction in part (b) to be valid; hence

$$\begin{aligned}
r(N) \geq r(m+n) \geq 2\min(r(m), n-2) &\geq 2(m - \lfloor 4\lg m \rfloor + 8) \\
&= m + n + 1 - \lfloor 4\lg(m+n) - 1 + \epsilon \rfloor + 8 \\
&\geq N - 4\lg N + 8
\end{aligned}$$

where $\epsilon = 4\lg(2m/(m+n)) < 1$. [*Electronic Journal of Combinatorics* **10** (2003), #R27, 1–10.] Recursive use of (b) gives, in fact, $r(1024) \geq 1000$.

65. A computer search reveals that eight essentially different patterns (and their reverses) are possible. One of them has the delta sequence 01020314203024041234 214103234103, and it is close to two of the others.

66. (Solution by Mark Cooke.) One suitable delta sequence is 01234560701213243565760710213534626701537412362567017314262065701342146560573102464537 571020435376140736304642737035640271327505412102756415024036542501 36

0254161560431257603257204315762432176045204175163547670356475706 2543
724213262416152341751436714316 4314. (Solutions for $n > 8$ are still unknown.)

67. Let $v_{2k+1} = \bar{v}_{2k}$ and $v_{2k} = 0u_k$, where $(u_0, u_1, \ldots, u_{2^n-1})$ is any $(n-1)$-bit Gray cycle. [See Robinson and Cohn, *IEEE Trans.* **C-30** (1981), 17–23.]

68. Yes. The simplest way is probably to take $(n-1)$-trit modular Gray ternary code and add $0\ldots0$, $1\ldots1$, $2\ldots2$ to each string (modulo 3). For example, when $n = 3$ the code is 000, 111, 222, 001, 112, 220, 002, 110, 221, 012, 120, 201, $\ldots$, 020, 101, 212.

69. (a) We need only verify the change in h when bits $b_{j-1}\ldots b_0$ are simultaneously complemented, for $j = 1, 2, \ldots$; and these changes are respectively $(1110)_2$, $(1101)_2$, $(0111)_2$, $(1011)_2$, $(10011)_2$, $(100011)_2$, $\ldots$. To prove that every n-tuple occurs, note that $0 \le h(k) < 2^n$ when $0 \le k < 2^n$ and $n > 3$; also $h^{[-1]}((a_{n-1}\ldots a_0)_2) = (b_{n-1}\ldots b_0)_2$, where $b_0 = a_0 \oplus a_1 \oplus a_2 \oplus \cdots$, $b_1 = a_0$, $b_2 = a_2 \oplus a_3 \oplus a_4 \oplus \cdots$, $b_3 = a_0 \oplus a_1 \oplus a_3 \oplus \cdots$, and $b_j = a_j \oplus a_{j+1} \oplus \cdots$ for $j \ge 4$.

(b) Let $h(k) = (\ldots a_2 a_1 a_0)_2$ where $a_j = b_j \oplus b_{j+1} \oplus b_0[j \le t] \oplus b_{t-1}[t-1 \le j \le t]$.

70. As in (32) and (33), we can remove a factor of $n!$ by assuming that the strings of weight 1 occur in order. Then there are 14 solutions for $n = 5$ starting with 00000, and 21 starting with 00001. When $n = 6$ there are 46,935 of each type (related by reversal and complementation). When $n = 7$ the number is much, much larger, yet very small by comparison with the total number of 7-bit Gray codes.

71. Suppose that $\alpha_{n(j+1)}$ differs from α_{nj} in coordinate t_j, for $0 \le j < n-1$. Then $t_j = j\pi_n$, by (44) and (38). Now Eq. (34) tells us that $t_0 = n-1$; and if $0 < j < n-1$ we have $t_j = ((j-1)\pi_{n-1})\pi_{n-1}$ by (40). Thus $t_j = j\sigma_n\pi_{n-1}^2$ for $0 \le j < n-1$, and the value of $(n-1)\pi_n$ is whatever is left. (Notations for permutations are notoriously confusing, so it is always wise to check a few small cases carefully.)

72. The delta sequence is 01021324302012340123130 41021323.

73. Let $Q_{nj} = P_{nj}^R$ and denote the sequences (41), (42) by S_n and T_n. Thus $S_n = P_{n0}Q_{n1}P_{n2}\ldots$ and $T_n = Q_{n0}P_{n1}Q_{n2}\ldots$, if we omit the commas; and we have

$$S_{n+1} = 0P_{n0}\, 0Q_{n1}\, 1Q_{n0}^\pi\, 1P_{n1}^\pi\, 0P_{n2}\, 0Q_{n3}\, 1Q_{n2}^\pi\, 1P_{n3}^\pi\, 0P_{n4} \,\ldots,$$
$$T_{n+1} = 0Q_{n0}\, 1P_{n0}^\pi\, 0P_{n1}\, 0Q_{n2}\, 1Q_{n1}^\pi\, 1P_{n2}^\pi\, 0P_{n3}\, 0Q_{n4}\, 1Q_{n3}^\pi \,\ldots,$$

where $\pi = \pi_n$, revealing a reasonably simple joint recursion between the delta sequences Δ_n and E_n of S_n and T_n. Namely, if we write

$$\Delta_n = \phi_1\, a_1\, \phi_2\, a_2 \ldots \phi_{n-1}\, a_{n-1}\, \phi_n, \qquad E_n = \psi_1\, b_1\, \psi_2\, b_2 \ldots \psi_{n-1}\, b_{n-1}\, \psi_n,$$

where each ϕ_j and ψ_j is a string of length $2\binom{n-1}{j-1} - 1$, the next sequences are

$$\Delta_{n+1} = \phi_1\, a_1\, \phi_2\, n\, \psi_1\pi\, b_1\pi\, \psi_2\pi\, n\, \phi_3\, a_3\, \phi_4\, n\, \psi_3\pi\, b_3\pi\, \psi_4\pi\, n \,\ldots$$
$$E_{n+1} = \psi_1\, n\, \phi_1\pi\, n\, \psi_2\, b_2\, \psi_3\, n\, \phi_2\pi\, a_2\pi\, \phi_3\pi\, n\, \psi_4\, b_4\, \psi_5\, n\, \phi_4\pi\, a_4\pi\, \phi_5\pi\, n \,\ldots$$

For example, we have $\Delta_3 = 010210\underline{1}$ and $E_3 = 0\underline{2}12020\underline{2}1$, if we underline the a's and b's to distinguish them from the ϕ's and ψ's; and

$$\Delta_4 = 0\,1\,0\,2\,1\,3\,0\pi\,2\pi\,1\pi\,2\pi\,0\pi\,3\,1\,3\,1\pi = 0\,\underline{1}\,0\,2\,1\,3\,2\,\underline{1}\,0\,1\,2\,3\,1\,\underline{3}\,0,$$
$$E_4 = 0\,3\,0\pi\,3\,1\,2\,0\,2\,1\,3\,0\pi\,2\pi\,1\pi\,0\pi\,1\pi = 0\,\underline{3}\,2\,3\,1\,2\,0\,\underline{2}\,1\,3\,2\,1\,0\,\underline{2}\,0;$$

here $a_3\phi_4$ and $b_3\psi_4$ are empty. Elements have been underlined for the next step.

Thus we can compute the delta sequences in memory as follows. Here $p[j] = j\pi_n$ for $1 \le j < n$; $s_k = \delta_k$, $t_k = \varepsilon_k$, and $u_k = [\delta_k$ and ε_k are underlined], for $0 \le k < 2^n - 1$.

R1. [Initialize.] Set $n \leftarrow 1$, $p[0] \leftarrow 0$, $s_0 \leftarrow t_0 \leftarrow u_0 \leftarrow 0$.

R2. [Advance n.] Perform Algorithm S below, which computes the arrays s', t', and u' for the next value of n; then set $n \leftarrow n + 1$.

R3. [Ready?] If n is sufficiently large, the desired delta sequence Δ_n is in array s'; terminate. Otherwise keep going.

R4. [Compute π_n.] Set $p'[0] = n - 1$, and $p'[j] = p[p[j-1]]$ for $1 \leq j < n$.

R5. [Prepare to advance.] Set $p[j] \leftarrow p'[j]$ for $0 \leq j < n$; set $s_k \leftarrow s'_k$, $t_k \leftarrow t'_k$, and $u_k \leftarrow u'_k$ for $0 \leq k < 2^n - 1$. Return to R2. $\blacksquare$

In the following steps, "Transmit stuff(l, j) while $u_j = 0$" is an abbreviation for "If $u_j = 0$, repeatedly stuff(l, j), $l \leftarrow l + 1$, $j \leftarrow j + 1$, until $u_j \neq 0$."

S1. [Prepare to compute Δ_{n+1}.] Set $j \leftarrow k \leftarrow l \leftarrow 0$ and $u_{2^n - 1} \leftarrow -1$.

S2. [Advance j.] Transmit $s'_l \leftarrow s_j$ and $u'_l \leftarrow 0$ while $u_j = 0$. Then go to S5 if $u_j < 0$.

S3. [Advance j and k.] Set $s'_l \leftarrow s_j$, $u'_l \leftarrow 1$, $l \leftarrow l + 1$, $j \leftarrow j + 1$. Then transmit $s'_l \leftarrow s_j$ and $u'_l \leftarrow 0$ while $u_j = 0$. Then set $s'_l \leftarrow n$, $u'_l \leftarrow 0$, $l \leftarrow l + 1$. Then transmit $s'_l \leftarrow p[t_k]$ and $u'_l \leftarrow 0$ while $u_k = 0$. Then set $s'_l \leftarrow p[t_k]$, $u'_l \leftarrow 1$, $l \leftarrow l + 1$, $k \leftarrow k + 1$. And once again transmit $s'_l \leftarrow p[t_k]$ and $u'_l \leftarrow 0$ while $u_k = 0$.

S4. [Done with Δ_{n+1}?] If $u_k < 0$, go to S6. Otherwise set $s'_l \leftarrow n$, $u'_l \leftarrow 0$, $l \leftarrow l + 1$, $j \leftarrow j + 1$, $k \leftarrow k + 1$, and return to S2.

S5. [Finish Δ_{n+1}.] Set $s'_l \leftarrow n$, $u'_l \leftarrow 1$, $l \leftarrow l + 1$. Then transmit $s'_l \leftarrow p[t[k]]$ and $u'_l \leftarrow 0$ while $u_k = 0$.

S6. [Prepare to compute E_{n+1}.] Set $j \leftarrow k \leftarrow l \leftarrow 0$. Transmit $t'_l \leftarrow t_k$ while $u_k = 0$. Then set $t'_l \leftarrow n$, $l \leftarrow l + 1$.

S7. [Advance j.] Transmit $t'_l \leftarrow p[s_j]$ while $u_j = 0$. Then terminate if $u_j < 0$; otherwise set $t'_l \leftarrow n$, $l \leftarrow l + 1$, $j \leftarrow j + 1$, $k \leftarrow k + 1$.

S8. [Advance k.] Transmit $t'_l \leftarrow t_k$ while $u_k = 0$. Then go to S10 if $u_k < 0$.

S9. [Advance k and j.] Set $t'_l \leftarrow t_k$, $l \leftarrow l + 1$, $k \leftarrow k + 1$. Then transmit $t'_l \leftarrow t_k$ while $u_k = 0$. Then set $t'_l \leftarrow n$, $l \leftarrow l + 1$. Then transmit $t'_l \leftarrow p[s_j]$ while $u_j = 0$. Then set $t'_l \leftarrow p[s_j]$, $l \leftarrow l + 1$, $j \leftarrow j + 1$. Return to S7.

S10. [Finish E_{n+1}.] Set $t'_l \leftarrow n$, $l \leftarrow l + 1$. Then transmit $t'_l \leftarrow p[s_j]$ while $u_j = 0$. $\blacksquare$

To generate the monotonic Savage–Winkler code for fairly large n, one can first generate Δ_{10} and E_{10}, say, or even Δ_{20} and E_{20}. Using these tables, a suitable recursive procedure will then be able to reach higher values of n with very little computational overhead per step, on the average.

74. If the monotonic path is $v_0, \ldots, v_{2^n-1}$ and if v_k has weight j, we have

$$2 \sum_{t>0} \binom{n}{j - 2t} + ((j + \nu(v_0)) \bmod 2) \leq k \leq 2 \sum_{t \geq 0} \binom{n}{j - 2t} + ((j + \nu(v_0)) \bmod 2) - 2.$$

Therefore the maximum distance between vertices of respective weights j and $j + 1$ is $2\left(\binom{n-1}{j-1} + \binom{n-1}{j} + \binom{n-1}{j+1}\right) - 1$. The maximum value, approximately $3 \cdot 2^n / \sqrt{2\pi n}$, occurs when j is approximately $n/2$. [This is only about three times the smallest value achievable in *any* ordering of the vertices, which is $\sum_{j=0}^{n-1} \binom{j}{\lfloor j/2 \rfloor}$ by exercise 7.10–00.]

75. There are only five essentially distinct solutions, all of which turn out in fact to be Gray *cycles*. The delta sequences are

$$0\,1\,2\,3\,0\,1\,2\,4\,2\,1\,0\,3\,2\,1\,0\,1\,2\,1\,0\,3\,2\,1\,0\,4\,0\,1\,2\,3\,0\,1\,2\ (1)$$
$$0\,1\,2\,3\,0\,1\,2\,4\,2\,1\,0\,3\,2\,1\,0\,1\,3\,0\,1\,2\,3\,0\,1\,4\,1\,0\,3\,2\,1\,0\,3\ (1)$$
$$0\,1\,2\,3\,0\,1\,2\,4\,2\,1\,0\,3\,2\,1\,0\,2\,0\,3\,2\,1\,0\,3\,2\,4\,2\,3\,0\,1\,2\,3\,0\ (2)$$
$$0\,1\,2\,3\,0\,1\,2\,4\,2\,3\,0\,1\,2\,3\,0\,2\,0\,1\,2\,3\,0\,1\,2\,4\,2\,3\,0\,1\,2\,3\,0\ (2)$$
$$0\,1\,2\,3\,4\,1\,0\,1\,2\,1\,0\,3\,0\,1\,4\,3\,2\,1\,0\,3\,0\,1\,4\,1\,0\,1\,2\,3\,4\,1\,0\ (3)$$

76. If $v_0, \ldots, v_{2^n-1}$ is trend-free, so is the $(n+1)$-bit cycle $0v_0, 1v_0, 1v_1, 0v_1, 0v_2, 1v_2,$ $\ldots, 1v_{2^n-1}, 0v_{2^n-1}$. Figure 14(g) shows a somewhat more interesting construction, which generalizes the first solution of exercise 75 to an $(n+2)$-bit cycle

$$00\Gamma''^{R},\ 01\Gamma'^{R},\ 11\Gamma',\ 10\Gamma'',\ 10\Gamma,\ 11\Gamma''',\ 01\Gamma'''^{R},\ 00\Gamma^{R}$$

where Γ is the n-bit sequence $g(1), \ldots, g(2^{n-1})$ and $\Gamma' = \Gamma \oplus g(1)$, $\Gamma'' = \Gamma \oplus g(2^{n-1})$, $\Gamma''' = \Gamma \oplus g(2^{n-1}+1)$. [An n-bit trend-free design that is *almost* a Gray code, having just four steps in which $\nu(v_k \oplus v_{k+1}) = 2$, was found for all $n \geq 3$ by C. S. Cheng, *Proc. Berkeley Conf. Neyman and Kiefer* **2** (Hayward, Calif.: Inst. of Math. Statistics, 1985), 619–633.]

77. Replace the array $(o_{n-1}, \ldots, o_0)$ by an array of sentinel values $(s_{n-1}, \ldots, s_0)$, with $s_j \leftarrow m_j - 1$ in step H1. Set $a_j \leftarrow (a_j + 1) \bmod m_j$ in step H4. If $a_j = s_j$ in step H5, set $s_j \leftarrow (s_j - 1) \bmod m_j$, $f_j \leftarrow f_{j+1}$, $f_{j+1} \leftarrow j + 1$.

78. For (50), notice that B_{j+1} is the number of times reflection has occurred in coordinate j, because we bypass coordinate j on steps that are multiples of $m_j \ldots m_0$. Hence, if $b_j < m_j$, an increase of b_j by 1 causes a_j to increase or decrease by 1 as appropriate. Furthermore, if $b_i = m_i - 1$ for $0 \leq i < j$, changing all these b_i to 0 when incrementing b_j will increase each of $B_0, \ldots, B_j$ by 1, thereby leaving the values $a_0, \ldots, a_{j-1}$ unchanged in (50).

For (51), note that $B_j = m_j B_{j+1} + b_j \equiv m_j B_{j+1} + a_j + (m_j - 1)B_{j+1} \equiv a_j + B_{j+1}$ (modulo 2); hence $B_j \equiv a_j + a_{j+1} + \cdots$, and (51) is obviously equivalent to (50).

In the modular Gray code for general radices $(m_{n-1}, \ldots, m_0)$, let

$$\bar{g}(k) = \begin{bmatrix} a_{n-1}, & \ldots, & a_2, & a_1, & a_0 \\ m_{n-1}, & \ldots, & m_2, & m_1, & m_0 \end{bmatrix}$$

when k is given by (46). Then $a_j = (b_j - B_{j+1}) \bmod m_j$, because coordinate j has increased modulo m_j exactly $B_j - B_{j+1}$ times if we start at $(0, \ldots, 0)$. The inverse function, which determines the b's from the modular Gray a's, is $b_j = (a_j + a_{j+1} + a_{j+2} + \cdots) \bmod m_j$ in the special case that each m_j is a divisor of m_{j+1} (for example, if all m_j are equal). But the inverse has no simple form in general; it can be computed by using the recurrences $b_j = (a_j + B_{j+1}) \bmod m_j$, $B_j = m_j B_{j+1} + b_j$ for $j = n-1$, $\ldots, 0$, starting with $B_n = 0$.

[Reflected Gray codes for radix $m > 2$ were introduced by Ivan Flores in *IRE Trans.* **EC-5** (1956), 79–82; he derived (50) and (51) in the case that all m_j are equal. Modular Gray codes with general mixed radices were implicitly discussed by Joseph Rosenbaum in *AMM* **45** (1938), 694–696, but without the conversion formulas; conversion formulas when all m_j have a common value m were published by Martin Cohn, *Info. and Control* **6** (1963), 70–78.]

79. (a) The last n-tuple always has $a_{n-1} = m_{n-1} - 1$, so it is one step from $(0, \ldots, 0)$ only if $m_{n-1} = 2$. And this condition suffices to make the final n-tuple $(1, 0, \ldots, 0)$.

[Similarly, the final subforest output by Algorithm K is adjacent to the initial one if and only if the leftmost tree is an isolated vertex.]

(b) The last n-tuple is $(m_{n-1}-1, 0, \ldots, 0)$ if and only if $m_{n-1} \ldots m_{j+1} \bmod m_j = 0$ for $0 \le j < n - 1$, because $b_j = m_j - 1$ and $B_j = m_{n-1} \ldots m_j - 1$.

80. Run through $p_1^{a_1} \ldots p_t^{a_t}$ using reflected Gray code with radices $m_j = e_j + 1$.

81. The first cycle contains the edge from (x, y) to $(x, (y + 1) \bmod m)$ if and only if $(x + y) \bmod m \ne m - 1$ if and only if the second cycle contains the edge from (x, y) to $((x + 1) \bmod m, y)$.

82. There are two 4-bit Gray cycles $(u_0, \ldots, u_{15})$ and $(v_0, \ldots, v_{15})$ that cover all edges of the 4-cube. (Indeed, the non-edges of classes A, B, D, H, and I in exercise 56 form Gray cycles, in the same classes as their complements.) Therefore with 16-ary modular Gray code we can form the four desired cycles $(u_0 u_0, u_0 u_1, \ldots, u_0 u_{15}, u_1 u_{15}, \ldots, u_{15} u_0)$, $(u_0 u_0, u_1 u_0, \ldots, u_{15} u_0, u_{15} u_1, \ldots, u_0 u_{15})$, $(v_0 v_0, \ldots, v_{15} v_0)$, $(v_0 v_0, \ldots, v_0 v_{15})$.

In a similar way we can show that $n/2$ edge-disjoint n-bit Gray cycles exist when n is 16, 32, 64, etc. [*Abhandlungen Math. Sem. Hamburg* **20** (1956), 13–16.] J. Aubert and B. Schneider [*Discrete Math.* **38** (1982), 7–16] have proved that the same property holds for *all* even values of $n \ge 4$, but no simple construction is known.

83. Mark Cooke found the following totally unsymmetric solution in December, 2002:

    (1) 2737465057320265612316546743610525106052042416314372145101421737
2506246064173213107351607103156205713172463452102434643207054702
4147356146737625047350745130620656415073123731427376432561240264
3016735467532402524637475217640270736065105215106073575463253105;

    (2) 0616713417232175171671540460247164742473202531621673531632736052
6710141503047313570615453627623241426465272021632075363710750740
3157674761545652756510451024023107353424651230406545306213710537
2620501752453406703437343531502602463045627674152752406021610434;

    (3) 3701063751507131236243765735103012042353747207410473621617247324
6505132565057121565024570473247421427640231034362703262764130574
0560620341745613151756314702721725205613212604053506260460173642
6717641743513401245360241730636545061563027414535676432625745051;

    (4) 6706546435672147236210405432054510737405170532145431636430504673
4560621206416201320742373627204506473140171020514126107452343672
1320452752353410515426370601363567307105420163151210535061731236
4272537165617217542510760215462375452674257037346403647376271657.

(Each of these delta sequences should start from the same vertex of the cube.) Is there a symmetrical way to do the job?

84. Calling the initial position $(2, 2)$, the 8-step solution in Fig. A-1 shows how the sequence progresses down to $(0, 0)$. In the first move, for example, the front half of the cord passes around and behind the right comb, then through the large right loop. The middle line should be read from right to left. The generalization to n pairs of loops would, similarly, take $3^n - 1$ steps.

[The origin of this delightful puzzle is obscure. *The Book of Ingenious & Diabolical Puzzles* by Jerry Slocum and Jack Botermans (1994) shows a 2-loop version carved from horn, probably made in China about 1850 [page 101], and a modern 6-loop version made in Malaysia about 1988 [page 93]. Slocum also owns a 4-loop version made from bamboo in England about 1884. He has found it listed in Henry Novra's *Catalogue of*

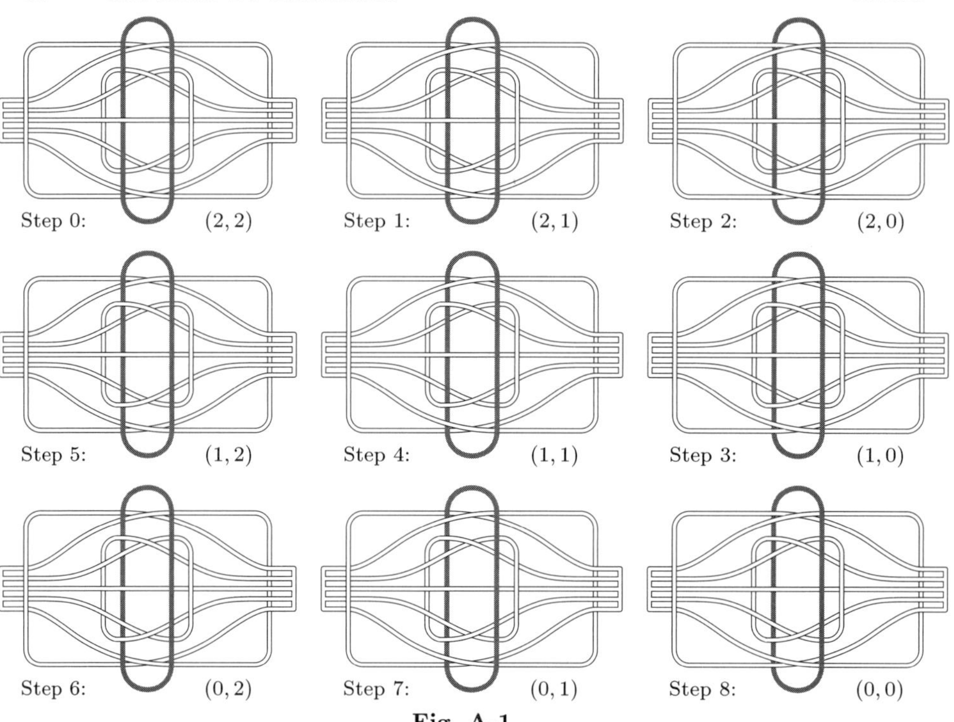

Fig. A-1.

Conjuring Tricks and Puzzles (1858 or 1859) and W. H. Cremer's *Games, Amusements, Pastimes and Magic* (1867), as well as in Hamley's catalog of 1895, under the name "Marvellous Canoe Puzzle." See also *U.S. Patents 2091191* (1937), *D172310* (1954), *3758114* (1973), *D406866* (1999). Dyckman noted its connection to reflected Gray ternary in a letter to Martin Gardner, dated 2 August 1972.]

85. By (50), element $\left[\begin{smallmatrix} b,\ b' \\ t,\ t' \end{smallmatrix}\right]$ of $\Gamma \boxtimes \Gamma'$ is $\alpha_a \alpha'_{a'}$ if $\hat{g}(\left[\begin{smallmatrix} b,\ b' \\ t,\ t' \end{smallmatrix}\right]) = \left[\begin{smallmatrix} a,\ a' \\ t,\ t' \end{smallmatrix}\right]$ in the reflected Gray code for radices (t, t'). We can now show that element $\left[\begin{smallmatrix} b,\ b',\ b'' \\ t,\ t',\ t'' \end{smallmatrix}\right]$ of both $(\Gamma \boxtimes \Gamma') \boxtimes \Gamma''$ and $\Gamma \boxtimes (\Gamma' \boxtimes \Gamma'')$ is $\alpha_a \alpha'_{a'} \alpha''_{a''}$ if $\hat{g}(\left[\begin{smallmatrix} b,\ b',\ b'' \\ t,\ t',\ t'' \end{smallmatrix}\right]) = \left[\begin{smallmatrix} a,\ a',\ a'' \\ t,\ t',\ t'' \end{smallmatrix}\right]$ in the reflected Gray code for radices (t, t', t''). See exercise 4.1–10, and note also the mixed-radix law

$$m_1 \ldots m_n - 1 - \begin{bmatrix} x_1, & \ldots, & x_n \\ m_1, & \ldots, & m_n \end{bmatrix} = \begin{bmatrix} m_1 - 1 - x_1, & \ldots, & m_n - 1 - x_n \\ m_1, & \ldots, & m_n \end{bmatrix}.$$

In general, the reflected Gray code for radices $(m_1, \ldots, m_n)$ is $(0, \ldots, m_1 - 1) \boxtimes \cdots \boxtimes (0, \ldots, m_n - 1)$. [*Information Processing Letters* **22** (1986), 201–205.]

86. Let Γ_{mn} be the reflected m-ary Gray code, which can be defined by $\Gamma_{m0} = \epsilon$ and

$$\Gamma_{m(n+1)} = (0, 1, \ldots, m - 1) \boxtimes \Gamma_{mn}, \qquad n \geq 0.$$

This path runs from $(0, 0, \ldots, 0)$ to $(m-1, 0, \ldots, 0)$ when m is even. Consider the Gray path Π_{mn} defined by $\Pi_{m0} = \emptyset$ and

$$\Pi_{m(n+1)} = \begin{cases} (0, 1, \ldots, m - 1) \boxtimes \Pi_{mn},\ m\Gamma^R_{(m+1)n}, & \text{if } m \text{ is odd}; \\ (0, 1, \ldots, m) \boxtimes \Pi_{mn},\ m\Gamma^R_{mn}, & \text{if } m \text{ is even}. \end{cases}$$

This path traverses all of the $(m + 1)^n - m^n$ nonnegative integer n-tuples for which $\max(a_1, \ldots, a_n) = m$, starting with $(0, \ldots, 0, m)$ and ending with $(m, 0, \ldots, 0)$. The desired infinite Gray path is Π_{0n}, Π_{1n}^R, Π_{2n}, Π_{3n}^R, $\ldots$.

87. This is impossible when n is odd, because the n-tuples with $\max(|a_1|, \ldots, |a_n|) = 1$ include $\frac{1}{2}(3^n + 1)$ with odd parity and $\frac{1}{2}(3^n - 3)$ with even parity. When $n = 2$ we can use a spiral Σ_0, Σ_1, Σ_2, $\ldots$, where Σ_m winds counterclockwise from $(m, 1 - m)$ to $(m, -m)$ when $m > 0$. For even values of $n \geq 2$, if T_m is a path of n-tuples from $(m, 1 - m, m - 1, 1 - m, \ldots, m - 1, 1 - m)$ to $(m, -m, m, -m, \ldots, m, -m)$, we can use $\Sigma_m \boxtimes (T_0, \ldots, T_{m-1})$, $(\Sigma_0, \ldots, \Sigma_m)^R \boxtimes T_m$ for $(n + 2)$-tuples with the same property, where $\boxtimes$ is the dual operation

$$\Gamma \boxtimes \Gamma' = (\alpha_0 \alpha_0', \ldots, \alpha_{t-1} \alpha_0', \alpha_{t-1} \alpha_1', \ldots, \alpha_0 \alpha_1', \alpha_0 \alpha_2', \ldots, \alpha_{t-1} \alpha_2', \alpha_{t-1} \alpha_3', \ldots).$$

[Infinite n-dimensional Gray codes *without* the magnitude constraint were first constructed by E. Vázsonyi, *Acta Litterarum ac Scientiarum*, sectio Scientiarum Mathematicarum **9** (Szeged: 1938), 163–173.]

88. It would visit all the subforests again, but in reverse order, ending with $(0, \ldots, 0)$ and returning to the state it had after the initialization step K1. (This reflection principle is, in fact, the key to understanding how Algorithm K works.)

89. (a) Let $M_0 = \epsilon$, $M_1 = \bullet$, and $M_{n+2} = \bullet\, M_{n+1}^R$, $-M_n^R$. This construction works because the last element of M_{n+1}^R is the first element of M_{n+1}, namely a dot followed by the first element of M_n^R.

(b) Given a string $d_1 \ldots d_l$ where each d_j is $\bullet$ or $-$, we can find its successor by letting $k = l - [d_l = \bullet]$ and proceeding as follows: If k is odd and $d_k = \bullet$, change $d_k d_{k+1}$ to $-$; if k is even and $d_k = -$, change d_k to $\bullet\bullet$; otherwise decrease k by 1 and repeat until either making a change or reaching $k = 0$. The successor of the given word is $\bullet - - \bullet\bullet\bullet - \bullet - \bullet$.

90. A cycle can exist only when the number of code words is even, since the number of dashes changes by ± 1 at each step. Thus we must have $n \bmod 3 = 2$. The Gray paths M_n of exercise 89 are not suitable; they begin with $(\bullet -)^{\lfloor n/3 \rfloor} \bullet^{n \bmod 3}$ and end with $(- \bullet)^{\lfloor n/3 \rfloor} \bullet^{[n \bmod 3 = 1]} -^{[n \bmod 3 = 2]}$. But $M_{3k+1} \bullet$, $M_{3k}^R -$ is a Hamiltonian cycle in the Morse code graph when $n = 3k + 2$.

91. Equivalently, the n-tuples $a_1 \bar{a}_2 a_3 \bar{a}_4 \ldots$ have no two consecutive 1s. Such n-tuples correspond to Morse code sequences of length $n + 1$, if we append 0 and then represent $\bullet$ and $-$ respectively by 0 and 10. Under this correspondence we can convert the path M_{n+1} of exercise 89 into a procedure like Algorithm K, with the fringe containing the indices where each dot or dash begins (except for a final dot):

> **Q1.** [Initialize.] Set $a_j \leftarrow \lfloor ((j - 1) \bmod 6)/3 \rfloor$ and $f_j \leftarrow j$ for $1 \leq j \leq n$. Also set $f_0 \leftarrow 0$, $r_0 \leftarrow 1$, $l_1 \leftarrow 0$, $r_j \leftarrow j + (j \bmod 3)$ and $l_{j+(j \bmod 3)} \leftarrow j$ for $1 \leq j \leq n$, except if $j + (j \bmod 3) > n$ set $r_j \leftarrow 0$ and $l_0 \leftarrow j$. (The "fringe" now contains $1, 2, 4, 5, 7, 8, \ldots$.)

> **Q2.** [Visit.] Visit the n-tuple $(a_1, \ldots, a_n)$.

> **Q3.** [Choose p.] Set $q \leftarrow l_0$, $p \leftarrow f_q$, $f_q \leftarrow q$.

> **Q4.** [Check a_p.] Terminate the algorithm if $p = 0$. Otherwise set $a_p \leftarrow 1 - a_p$ and go to Q6 if $a_p + p$ is now even.

> **Q5.** [Insert $p+1$.] If $p < n$, set $q \leftarrow r_p$, $l_q \leftarrow p+1$, $r_{p+1} \leftarrow q$, $r_p \leftarrow p+1$, $l_{p+1} \leftarrow p$. Go to Q7.

Q6. [Delete $p+1$.] If $p < n$, set $q \leftarrow r_{p+1}$, $r_p \leftarrow q$, $l_q \leftarrow p$.

Q7. [Make p passive.] Set $f_p \leftarrow f_{l_p}$ and $f_{l_p} \leftarrow l_p$. Return to Q2. $\blacksquare$

This algorithm can also be derived as a special case of a considerably more general method due to Gang Li, Frank Ruskey, and D. E. Knuth, which extends Algorithm K by allowing the user to specify either $a_p \geq a_q$ or $a_p \leq a_q$ for each (parent, child) pair (p, q). [See Knuth and Ruskey, *Lecture Notes in Computer Science* **2635** (2004), 183–204.] A generalization in another direction, which produces all strings of length n that do not contain certain substrings, has been discovered by M. B. Squire, *Electronic J. Combinatorics* **3** (1996), #R17, 1–29.

Incidentally, it is amusing to note that the mapping $k \mapsto g(k)/2$ is a one-to-one correspondence between all binary n-tuples with no odd-length runs of 1s and all binary n-tuples with no two consecutive 1s.

92. Yes, because the digraph of all $(n-1)$-tuples $(x_1, \ldots, x_{n-1})$ with $x_1, \ldots, x_{n-1} \leq m$ and with arcs $(x_1, \ldots, x_{n-1}) \to (x_2, \ldots, x_n)$ whenever $\max(x_1, \ldots, x_n) = m$ is connected and balanced; see Theorem 2.3.4.2G. Indeed, we get such a sequence from Algorithm F if we note that the final k^n elements of the prime strings of length dividing n, when subtracted from $m - 1$, are the same for all $m \geq k$. When $n = 4$, for example, the first 81 digits of the sequence Φ_4 are $2 - \alpha^R = 0\,0001\,01\,0011\ldots$, where α is the string (62). [There also are infinite m-ary sequences whose first m^n elements are de Bruijn cycles for all n, given any fixed $m \geq 3$. See L. J. Cummings and D. Wiedemann, *Cong. Numerantium* **53** (1986), 155–160.]

93. The cycle generated by $f()$ is a cyclic permutation of $\alpha 1$, where α has length $m^n - 1$ and ends with 1^{n-1}. The cycle generated by Algorithm R is a cyclic permutation of $\gamma = c_0 \ldots c_{m^{n+1}-1}$, where $c_k = (c_0 + b_0 + \cdots + b_{k-1}) \bmod m$ and $b_0 \ldots b_{m^{n+1}-1} = \beta = \alpha^m 1^m$.

If $x_0 \ldots x_n$ occurs in γ, say $x_j = c_{k+j}$ for $0 \leq j \leq n$, then $y_j = b_{k+j}$ for $0 \leq j < n$, where $y_j = (x_{j+1} - x_j) \bmod m$. [This is the connection with modular m-ary Gray code; see exercise 78.] Now if $y_0 \ldots y_{n-1} = 1^n$ we have $m^{n+1} - m - n < k \leq m^{n+1} - n$; otherwise there is an index k' such that $-n < k' < m^n - n$ and $y_0 \ldots y_{n-1}$ occurs in β at positions $k = (k' + r(m^n - 1)) \bmod m^{n+1}$ for $0 \leq r < m$. In both cases the m choices of k have different values of x_0, because the sum of all elements in α is $m - 1$ (modulo m) when $n \geq 2$. [Algorithm R is valid also for $n = 1$ if $m \bmod 4 \neq 2$, because $m \perp \sum \alpha$ in that case.]

94. $00\underline{1}020304\underline{1}1\underline{21}314\underline{223}243344$. (The underlined digits are effectively inserted into the interleaving of 00112234 with 34. Algorithm D can be used in general when $n = 1$ and $r = m - 2 \geq 0$; but it is pointless to do so, in view of (54).)

95. (a) Let $c_0 c_1 c_2 \ldots$ have period r. If r is odd we have $p = q = r$, so $r = pq$ only in the trivial case when $p = q = 1$ and $a_0 = b_0$. Otherwise $r/2 = \operatorname{lcm}(p, q) = pq/\gcd(p, q)$ by 4.5.2–(10), hence $\gcd(p, q) = 2$. In the latter case the $2n$-tuples $c_l c_{l+1} \ldots c_{l+2n-1}$ that occur are $a_j b_k \ldots a_{j+n-1} b_{k+n-1}$ for $0 \leq j < p$, $0 \leq k < q$, $j \equiv k$ (modulo 2), and $b_k a_j \ldots b_{k+n-1} a_{j+n-1}$ for $0 \leq j < p$, $0 \leq k < q$, $j \not\equiv k$ (modulo 2).

(b) The output would interleave two sequences $a_0 a_1 \ldots$ and $b_0 b_1 \ldots$ whose periods are respectively $m^n + r$ and $m^n - r$; the a's are the cycle of $f()$ with x^n changed to x^{n+1} and the b's are the cycle of $f'()$ with x^n changed to x^{n-1}, for $0 \leq x < r$. By (58) and part (a), the period length is $m^{2n} - r^2$, and every $2n$-tuple occurs with the exception of $(xy)^n$ for $0 \leq x, y < r$.

(c) The real step D6 alters the behavior of (b) by going to D3 when $t \geq n$, $t' = n$, and $0 \leq x' = x < r$; this change emits an extra x at the time when x^{2n-1} has just been output and b is about to be emitted, where b is the digit following x^n in the cycle. D6 also allows control to pass to D7 and then D3 with $t' = n$ in the case that $t \geq n$ and $x < x' < r$; this behavior emits an extra $x'x$ at the time when $(xx')^{n-1}x$ has just been output and b will be next. These r^2 extra bits provide the r^2 missing $2n$-tuples of (b).

96. (a) The recurrences $S_2 = 1$, $S_{2n+1} = S_{2n} = 2S_n$, $R_2 = 0$, $R_{2n+1} = 1 + R_{2n}$, $R_{2n} = 2R_n$, $D_2 = 0$, $D_{2n+1} = D_{2n} = 1 + 2D_n$ have the solution $S_n = 2^{\lfloor \lg n \rfloor - 1}$, $R_n = n - 2S_n$, $D_n = S_n - 1$. Thus $S_n + R_n + D_n = n - 1$.

(b) Each top-level output usually involves $\lfloor \lg n \rfloor - 1$ D-activations and $\nu(n) - 1$ R-activations, plus one basic activation at the bottom level. But there are exceptions: Algorithm R might invoke its $f()$ twice, if the first activation completed a sequence 1^n; and sometimes Algorithm R doesn't need to invoke $f()$ at all. Algorithm D might invoke its $f'()$ twice, if the first activation completed a sequence $(x')^n$; but sometimes Algorithm D doesn't need to invoke either $f()$ or $f'()$.

Algorithm R completes a sequence x^{n+1} if and only if its child $f()$ has just completed a sequence 0^n. Algorithm D completes a sequence x^{2n} for $x < r$ if and only if it has just jumped from D6 to D3 without invoking any child.

From these observations we can conclude that at most $\lfloor \lg n \rfloor + \nu(n) + 1$ activations are possible per top-level output, if $r > 1$; such a case happens when Algorithm D for $n = 6$ goes from D6 to D4. But when $r = 1$ we can have as many as $2\lfloor \lg n \rfloor + 3$ activations, for example when Algorithm R for $n = 25$ goes from R4 to R2.

97. (a) (0011), (00011101), (0000101001111011), and $(00000110001011011111$ $001110101001)$. Thus $j_2 = 2$, $j_3 = 3$, $j_4 = 9$, $j_5 = 15$.

(b) We obviously have $f_{n+1}(k) = \Sigma f_n(k) \bmod 2$ for $0 \leq k < j_n + n$. The next value, $f_{n+1}(j_n + n)$, depends on whether step R4 jumps to R2 after computing $y = f_n(j_n + n - 1)$. If it does (namely, if $f_{n+1}(j_n + n - 1) \neq 0$), we have $f_{n+1}(k) \equiv 1 + \Sigma(k+1)$ for $j_n + n \leq k < 2^n + j_n + n$; otherwise we have $f_{n+1}(k) \equiv 1 + \Sigma(k - 1)$ for those values of k. In particular, $f_{n+1}(k) = 1$ when $2^n \leq k + \delta_n \leq 2^n + n$. The stated formula, which has simpler ranges for the index k, holds because $1 + \Sigma(k \pm 1) \equiv \Sigma(k)$ when $j_n < k < j_n + n$ or $2^n + j_n < k < 2^n + j_n + n$.

(c) The interleaved cycle has $c_n(2k) = f_n^+(k)$ and $c_n(2k+1) = f_n^-(k)$, where

$$f_n^+(k) = \begin{cases} f_n(k-1), & \text{if } 0 < k \leq j_n + 1; \\ f_n(k-2), & \text{if } j_n + 1 < k \leq 2^n + 2; \end{cases} \qquad f_n^-(k) = \begin{cases} f_n(k+1), & \text{if } 0 \leq k < j_n; \\ f_n(k+2), & \text{if } j_n \leq k < 2^n - 2; \end{cases}$$

$f_n^+(k) = f_n^+(k \bmod (2^n + 2))$, $f_n^-(k) = f_n^-(k \bmod (2^n - 2))$. Therefore the subsequence 1^{2n-1} begins at position $k_n = (2^{n-1} - 2)(2^n + 2) + 2j_n + 2$ in the c_n cycle; this will make j_{2n} odd. The subsequence $(01)^{n-1}0$ begins at position $l_n = (2^{n-1} + 1)(j_n - 1)$ if $j_n \bmod 4 = 1$, at $l_n = (2^{n-1} + 1)(2^n + j_n - 3)$ if $j_n \bmod 4 = 3$. Also $k_2 = 6$, $l_2 = 2$.

(d) Algorithm D inserts four elements into the c_n cycle; hence

<table>
<tr><td align="center">when $j_n \bmod 4 < 3$ $(l_n < k_n)$:</td><td align="center">when $j_n \bmod 4 = 3$ $(k_n < l_n)$:</td></tr>
</table>

$$f_{2n}(k) = \begin{cases} c_n(k-1), & \text{if } 0 < k \leq l_n + 2; \\ c_n(k-3), & \text{if } l_n + 2 < k \leq k_n + 3; \\ c_n(k-4), & \text{if } k_n + 3 < k \leq 2^{2n}; \end{cases} = \begin{cases} c_n(k-1), & \text{if } 0 < k \leq k_n + 1; \\ c_n(k-2), & \text{if } k_n + 1 < k \leq l_n + 3; \\ c_n(k-4), & \text{if } l_n + 3 < k \leq 2^{2n}. \end{cases}$$

(e) Consequently $j_{2n} = k_n + 1 + 2[j_n \bmod 4 < 3]$. Indeed, the elements preceding 1^{2n} consist of $2^{n-2} - 1$ complete periods of $f_n^+()$ interleaved with 2^{n-2} complete periods of $f_n^-()$, with one 0 inserted and also with 10 inserted if $l_n < k_n$, followed by $f_n(1)f_n(1)f_n(2)f_n(2)\ldots f_n(j_n-1)f_n(j_n-1)$. The sum of all these elements is odd, unless $l_n < k_n$; therefore $\delta_{2n} = 1 - 2[j_n \bmod 4 = 3]$.

Let $n = 2^t q$, where q is odd and $n > 2$. The recurrences imply that, if $q = 1$, we have $j_n = 2^{n-1} + b_t$ where $b_t = 2^t/3 - (-1)^t/3$. And if $q > 1$ we have $j_n = 2^{n-1} \pm b_{t+2}$, where the $+$ sign is chosen if and only if $\lfloor \lg q \rfloor + [\lfloor 4q/2^{\lfloor \lg q \rfloor} \rfloor = 5]$ is even.

98. If $f(k) = g(k)$ when k lies in a certain range, there's a constant C such that $\Sigma f(k) = C + \Sigma g(k)$ for k in that range. We can therefore continue almost mindlessly to derive additional recurrences: If $n > 1$ we have

$\Sigma f_{2n}(k)$, when $j_n \bmod 4 < 3$ $(l_n < k_n)$:   when $j_n \bmod 4 = 3$ $(k_n < l_n)$:

$$\equiv \begin{cases} \Sigma c_n(k-1), & \text{if } 0 < k \le l_n+2; \\ 1+\Sigma c_n(k-3), & \text{if } l_n+2 < k \le k_n+3; \\ \Sigma c_n(k-4), & \text{if } k_n+3 < k \le 2^{2n}; \end{cases} \equiv \begin{cases} \Sigma c_n(k-1), & \text{if } 0 < k \le k_n+1; \\ 1+\Sigma c_n(k-2), & \text{if } k_n+1 < k \le l_n+3; \\ \Sigma c_n(k-4), & \text{if } l_n+3 < k \le 2^{2n}. \end{cases}$$

$$\Sigma c_n(k) \equiv \Sigma f_n^+(\lceil k/2 \rceil) + \Sigma f_n^-(\lfloor k/2 \rfloor).$$

$$\Sigma f_n^+(k) \equiv \begin{cases} \Sigma f_n(k-1), & \text{if } 0 < k \le j_n+1; \\ 1+\Sigma f_n(k-2), & \text{if } j_n+1 < k \le 2^n+2; \end{cases} \qquad \Sigma f_n^-(k) \equiv \begin{cases} \Sigma f_n(k+1), & \text{if } 0 \le k < j_n; \\ 1+\Sigma f_n(k+2), & \text{if } j_n \le k < 2^n-2; \end{cases}$$

$$\Sigma f_n^\pm(k) \equiv \lfloor k/(2^n \pm 2) \rfloor + \Sigma f_n^\pm(k \bmod (2^n \pm 2)); \quad \Sigma f_n(k) = \Sigma f_n(k \bmod 2^n).$$

$$\Sigma f_{2n+1}(k) \equiv \begin{cases} \Sigma\Sigma f_{2n}(k), & \text{if } 0 < k \le j_{2n} \text{ or } 2^{2n} + j_{2n} < k \le 2^{2n+1}; \\ 1 + k + \Sigma\Sigma f_{2n}(k + \delta_{2n}), & \text{if } j_{2n} < k \le 2^{2n} + j_{2n}. \end{cases}$$

$\Sigma\Sigma f_{2n}(k)$, when $j_n \bmod 4 < 3$ $(l_n < k_n)$:   when $j_n \bmod 4 = 3$ $(k_n < l_n)$:

$$\equiv \begin{cases} \Sigma\Sigma c_n(k-1), & \text{if } 0 < k \le l_n+2; \\ 1+k+\Sigma\Sigma c_n(k-3), & \text{if } l_n+2 < k \le k_n+3; \\ \Sigma\Sigma c_n(k-4), & \text{if } k_n+3 < k \le 2^{2n}; \end{cases} \equiv \begin{cases} \Sigma\Sigma c_n(k-1), & \text{if } 0 < k \le k_n+1; \\ 1+k+\Sigma c_n(k-2), & \text{if } k_n+1 < k \le l_n+3; \\ 1+\Sigma\Sigma c_n(k-4), & \text{if } l_n+3 < k \le 2^{2n}. \end{cases}$$

$$\Sigma\Sigma f_{2n}(k) \equiv [j_n \bmod 4 < 3]\lfloor k/2^{2n} \rfloor + \Sigma\Sigma f_{2n}(k \bmod 2^{2n}).$$

And then, aha, there is closure:

$$\Sigma\Sigma c_n(2k) = \Sigma f_n^+(k), \qquad \Sigma\Sigma c_n(2k+1) = \Sigma f_n^-(k).$$

If $n = 2^t q$ where q is odd, the running time to evaluate $f_n(k)$ by this system of recursive formulas is $O(t + S(q))$, where $S(1) = 1$, $S(2k) = 1 + 2S(k)$, and $S(2k+1) = 1 + S(k)$. Clearly $S(k) < 2k$, so the evaluations involve at most $O(n)$ simple operations on n-bit numbers. In fact, the method is often significantly faster: If we average $S(k)$ over all k with $\lfloor \lg k \rfloor = s$ we get $(3^{s+1} - 2^{s+1})/2^s$, which is less than $3k^{\lg(3/2)} < 3k^{0.59}$. (Incidentally, if $k = 2^{s+1} - 1 - (2^{s-e_1} + 2^{s-e_2} + \cdots + 2^{s-e_t})$ we have $S(k) = s + 1 + e_t + 2e_{t-1} + 4e_{t-2} + \cdots + 2^t e_1$.)

99. A string that starts at position k in $f_n()$ starts at position $k^+ = k+1+[k > j_n]$ in $f_n^+()$ and at position $k^- = k - 1 - [k > j_n]$ in $f_n^-()$, except that 0^n and 1^n occur twice in $f_n^+()$ but not at all in $f_n^-()$.

To find $\gamma = a_0 b_0 \ldots a_{n-1} b_{n-1}$ in the cycle $f_{2n}()$, let $\alpha = a_0 \ldots a_{n-1}$ and $\beta = b_0 \ldots b_{n-1}$. Suppose α starts at position j and β at position k in $f_n()$, and assume that neither α nor β is 0^n or 1^n. If $j^+ \equiv k^+$ (modulo 2), let $l/2$ be a solution to the equation $j^+ + (2^n + 2)x = k^- + (2^n - 2)y$; we may take $l/2 = k + (2^n - 2)(2^{n-3}(j - k) \bmod (2^{n-1} + 1))$ if $j \ge k$, otherwise $l/2 = j + (2^n + 2)(2^{n-3}(k - j) \bmod (2^{n-1} - 1))$. Otherwise let $(l-1)/2 = k^+ + (2^n + 2)x = j^- + (2^n - 2)y$. Then γ starts at position l in the cycle $c_n()$; hence it starts at position $l+1+[l \ge k_n]+2[l \ge l_n]$ in the cycle $f_{2n}()$.

Similar formulas hold when $\alpha \in \{0^n, 1^n\}$ or $\beta \in \{0^n, 1^n\}$ (but not both). Finally, 0^{2n}, 1^{2n}, $(01)^n$, and $(10)^n$ start respectively in positions 0, j_{2n}, $l_n + 1 + [k_n < l_n]$, and $l_n + 2 + [k_n < l_n]$.

To find $\beta = b_0 b_1 \ldots b_n$ in $f_{n+1}()$ when n is even, suppose that the n-bit string $(b_0 \oplus b_1) \ldots (b_{n-1} \oplus b_n)$ starts at position j in $f_n()$. Then β starts at position $k = j - \delta_n[j \geq j_n] + 2^n[j = j_n][\delta_n = 1]$ if $f_{n+1}(k) = b_0$, otherwise at position $k + (2^n - \delta_n, \delta_n, 2^n + \delta_n)$ according as $(j < j_n, j = j_n, j > j_n)$.

The running time of this recursion satisfies $T(n) = O(n) + 2T(\lfloor n/2 \rfloor)$, so it is $O(n \log n)$. [Exercises 97–99 are based on the work of J. Tuliani, who also has developed methods for certain larger values of m; see *Discrete Math.* **226** (2001), 313–336.]

100. No obvious defects are apparent, but extensive testing should be done before any sequence can be recommended. By contrast, the de Bruijn cycle produced implicitly by Algorithm F is a terrible source of supposedly random bits, even though it is n-distributed in the sense of Definition 3.5D, because 0s predominate at the beginning. Indeed, when n is prime, bits $tn + 1$ of that sequence are zero for $0 \leq t < (2^n - 2)/n$.

101. (a) Let β be a proper suffix of $\lambda\lambda'$ with $\beta \leq \lambda\lambda'$. Either β is a suffix of λ', whence $\lambda < \lambda' \leq \beta$, or $\beta = \alpha\lambda'$ and we have $\lambda < \alpha < \beta$.

Now $\lambda < \beta \leq \lambda\lambda'$ implies that $\beta = \lambda\gamma$ for some $\gamma \leq \lambda'$. But γ is a suffix of β with $1 \leq |\gamma| = |\beta| - |\lambda| < |\lambda'|$; hence γ is a proper suffix of λ', and $\lambda' < \gamma$. Contradiction.

(b) Any string of length 1 is prime. Combine adjacent primes by (a), in any order, until no further combination is possible. [See the more general results of M. P. Schützenberger, *Proc. Amer. Math. Soc.* **16** (1965), 21–24.]

(c) If $t \neq 0$, let λ be the smallest suffix of $\lambda_1 \ldots \lambda_t$. Then λ is prime by definition, and it has the form $\beta\gamma$ where β is a nonempty suffix of some λ_j. Therefore $\lambda_t \leq \lambda_j \leq \beta \leq \beta\gamma = \lambda \leq \lambda_t$, so we must have $\lambda = \lambda_t$. Remove λ_t and repeat until $t = 0$.

(d) True. For if we had $\alpha = \lambda\beta$ for some prime λ with $|\lambda| > |\lambda_1|$, we could append the factors of β to obtain another factorization of α.

(e) $3 \cdot 14159265358979323846264338327795 \cdot 02884197$. (An efficient algorithm appears in exercise 106. Knowing more digits of π would not change the first two factors. The infinite decimal expansion of any number that is "normal" in the sense of Borel (see Section 3.5) factors into primes of finite length.)

102. We must have $1/(1 - mz) = 1/\prod_{n=1}^{\infty}(1 - z^n)^{L_m(n)}$. This implies (60) as in exercise 4.6.2–4.

103. When $n = p$ is prime, (59) tells us that $L_m(1) + pL_m(p) = m^p$, and we also have $L_m(1) = m$. [This combinatorial proof provides an interesting contrast to the traditional algebraic proof of Theorem 1.2.4F.]

104. The 4483 nonprimes are `abaca`, `agora`, `ahead`, . . . ; the 1274 primes are . . . , `rusts`, `rusty`, `rutty`. (Since `prime` isn't prime, we should perhaps call prime strings `lowly`.)

105. (a) Let α' be α with its last letter increased, and suppose $\alpha' = \beta\gamma'$ where $\alpha = \beta\gamma$ and $\beta \neq \epsilon$, $\gamma \neq \epsilon$. Let θ be the prefix of α with $|\theta| = |\gamma|$. By hypothesis there is a string ω such that $\alpha\omega$ is prime; hence $\theta \leq \alpha\omega < \gamma\omega$, so we must have $\theta \leq \gamma$. Consequently $\theta < \gamma'$, and we have $\alpha' < \gamma'$.

(b) Let $\alpha = \lambda_1\beta = a_1 \ldots a_n$ where $\lambda_1\beta\omega$ is prime. The condition $\lambda_1\beta\omega < \beta\omega$ implies that $a_j \leq a_{j+r}$ for $1 \leq j \leq n-r$, where $r = |\lambda_1|$. But we cannot have $a_j < a_{j+r}$; otherwise α would begin with a prime longer than λ_1, contradicting exercise 101(d).

(c) If α is the n-extension of both λ and λ', where $|\lambda| > |\lambda'|$, we must have $\lambda = (\lambda')^q\theta$ where θ is a nonempty prefix of λ'. But then $\theta \leq \lambda' < \lambda < \theta$.

106. B1. [Initialize.] Set $a_1 \leftarrow \cdots \leftarrow a_n \leftarrow m - 1$, $a_{n+1} \leftarrow -1$, and $j \leftarrow 1$.

   B2. [Visit.] Visit $(a_1, \ldots, a_n)$ with index j.

   B3. [Subtract one.] Terminate if $a_j = 0$. Otherwise set $a_j \leftarrow a_j - 1$, and $a_k \leftarrow m - 1$ for $j < k \leq n$.

   B4. [Prepare to factor.] (According to exercise 105(b), we now want to find the first prime factor λ_1 of $a_1 \ldots a_n$.) Set $j \leftarrow 1$ and $k \leftarrow 2$.

   B5. [Find the new j.] (Now $a_1 \ldots a_{k-1}$ is the $(k-1)$-extension of the prime $a_1 \ldots a_j$.) If $a_{k-j} > a_k$, return to B2. Otherwise, if $a_{k-j} < a_k$, set $j \leftarrow k$. Then increase k by 1 and repeat this step. ∎

The efficient factoring algorithm in steps B4 and B5 is due to J. P. Duval, *J. Algorithms* **4** (1983), 363–381. For further information, see Cattell, Ruskey, Sawada, Serra, and Miers, *J. Algorithms* **37** (2000), 267–282.

107. The number of n-tuples visited is $P_m(n) = \sum_{j=1}^{n} L_m(j)$. Since $L_m(n) = \frac{1}{n} m^n + O(m^{n/2}/n)$, we have $P_m(n) = Q(m,n) + O(Q(\sqrt{m},n))$, where

$$Q(m,n) = \sum_{k=1}^{n} \frac{m^k}{k} = \frac{m^n}{n} R(m,n);$$

$$R(m,n) = \sum_{k=0}^{n-1} \frac{m^{-k}}{1 - k/n} = \sum_{k=0}^{n/2} \frac{m^{-k}}{1 - k/n} + O(nm^{-n/2})$$

$$= \frac{m}{m-1} \sum_{j=0}^{t-1} \frac{1}{n^j} \sum_{l} \left\{ \begin{matrix} j \\ l \end{matrix} \right\} \frac{l!}{(m-1)^l} + O(n^{-t}).$$

Thus $P_m(n) \sim m^{n+1}/((m-1)n)$. The main contributions to the running time come from the loops in steps F3 and F5, which cost $n - j$ for each prime of length j, hence a total of $nP_m(n) - \sum_{j=1}^{n} j L_m(j) = m^{n+1}(1/((m-1)^2 n) + O(1/(mn^2)))$. This is less than the time needed to output the m^n individual digits of the de Bruijn cycle.

108. (a) If $\alpha \neq 9 \ldots 9$, we have $\lambda_{k+1} \leq \beta 9^{|\alpha|}$, because the latter is prime.

   (b) We can assume that β is not all 0s, since $9^j 0^{n-j}$ is a substring of $\lambda_{t-1} \lambda_t \lambda_1 \lambda_2 = 89^n 0^n 1$. Let k be minimal with $\beta \leq \lambda_k$; then $\lambda_k \leq \beta\alpha$, so β is a prefix of λ_k. Since β is a preprime, it is the $|\beta|$-extension of some prime $\beta' \leq \beta$. The preprime visited by Algorithm F just before β' is $(\beta' - 1)9^{n-|\beta'|}$, by exercise 106, where $\beta' - 1$ denotes the decimal number that is one less than β'. Thus, if β' is not λ_{k-1}, the hint (which also follows from exercise 106) implies that λ_{k-1} ends with at least $n - |\beta'| \geq n - |\beta|$ 9s, and α is a suffix of λ_{k-1}. On the other hand if $\beta' = \lambda_{k-1}$, α is a suffix of λ_{k-2}, and β is a prefix of $\lambda_{k-1} \lambda_k$.

   (c) If $\alpha \neq 9 \ldots 9$, we have $\lambda_{k+1} \leq (\beta\alpha)^{d-1} \beta 9^{|\alpha|}$, because the latter is prime. Otherwise λ_{k-1} ends with at least $(d-1)|\beta\alpha|$ 9s, and $\lambda_{k+1} \leq (\beta\alpha)^{d-1} 9^{|\beta\alpha|}$, so $(\alpha\beta)^d$ is a substring of $\lambda_{k-1} \lambda_k \lambda_{k+1}$.

   (d) Within the primes $135899\,135914$, $787899\,787979$, $129999\,13\,131314$, $09\,090911$, $089999\,09\,090911$, $118999\,119\,119122$.

   (e) Yes: In all cases, the position of $a_1 \ldots a_n$ precedes the position of the substring $a_1 \ldots a_{n-1}(a_n + 1)$, if $0 \leq a_n < 9$ (and if we assume that strings like $9^j 0^{n-j}$ occur at the beginning). Furthermore $9^j 0^{n-j-1}$ occurs only after $9^{j-1} 0^{n-j} a$ has appeared for $1 \leq a \leq 9$, so we must not place 0 after $9^j 0^{n-j-1}$.

109. Suppose we want to locate the submatrix

$$\begin{pmatrix} (w_{n-1}\ldots w_1 w_0)_2 & (x_{n-1}\ldots x_1 x_0)_2 \\ (y_{n-1}\ldots y_1 y_0)_2 & (z_{n-1}\ldots z_1 z_0)_2 \end{pmatrix}.$$

The binary case $n = 1$ is the given example, and if $n > 1$ we can assume by induction that we only need to determine the leading bits a_{2n-1}, a_{2n-2}, b_{2n-1}, and b_{2n-2}. The case $n = 3$ is typical: We must solve

$$\begin{array}{llll}
b_5 = w_2, & b_4 = x_2, & a_5 \oplus b_5 = y_2, & a_4 \oplus b_4 = z_2, \quad \text{if } a_0 = 0,\, b_0 = 0; \\
b_4 = w_2, & b'_5 = x_2, & a_4 \oplus b_4 = y_2, & a_5 \oplus b'_5 = z_2, \quad \text{if } a_0 = 0,\, b_0 = 1; \\
a_5 \oplus b_5 = w_2, & a_4 \oplus b_4 = x_2, & b_5 = y_2, & b_4 = z_2, \quad \text{if } a_0 = 1,\, b_0 = 0; \\
a_4 \oplus b_4 = w_2, & a_5 \oplus b'_5 = x_2, & b_4 = y_2, & b'_5 = z_2, \quad \text{if } a_0 = 1,\, b_0 = 1;
\end{array}$$

here $b'_5 = b_5 \oplus b_4 b_3 b_2 b_1$ takes account of carrying when j becomes $j + 1$.

110. Let $a_0 a_1 \ldots a_{m^2-1}$ be an m-ary de Bruijn cycle, such as the first m^2 elements of (54). If m is odd, let $d_{ij} = a_j$ when i is even, $d_{ij} = a_{(j+(i-1)/2)\bmod m^2}$ when i is odd. [The first of many people to discover this construction seems to have been John C. Cock, who also constructed de Bruijn toruses of other shapes and sizes in *Discrete Math.* **70** (1988), 209–210.]

If $m = m'm''$ where $m' \perp m''$, we use the Chinese remainder theorem to define

$$d_{ij} \equiv d'_{ij}\ (\text{modulo } m') \qquad \text{and} \qquad d_{ij} \equiv d''_{ij}\ (\text{modulo } m'')$$

in terms of matrices that solve the problem for m' and m''. Thus the previous exercise leads to a solution for arbitrary m.

Another interesting solution for even values of m was found by Zoltán Tóth [*2nd Conf. Automata, Languages, and Programming Systems* (1988), 165–172; see also Hurlbert and Isaak, *Contemp. Math.* **178** (1994), 153–160]. The first m^2 elements a_j of the infinite sequence

$$0011\,021331203223\,041524355342514054450\,617263746577564\ldots07667\,08\ldots$$

define a de Bruijn cycle with the property that the distance between the appearances of ab and ba is always even. Then we can let $d_{ij} = a_j$ if $i + j$ is even, $d_{ij} = a_i$ if $i + j$ is odd. For example, when $m = 4$ we have

$$\begin{pmatrix}
0010021220302232 \\
0001020320212223 \\
0111031321312333 \\
1011121330313233 \\
0010021220302232 \\
0203000122232021 \\
0111031321312333 \\
1213101132333031 \\
0010021220302232 \\
2021222300010203 \\
0111031321312333 \\
3031323310111213 \\
0010021220302232 \\
2223202102030001 \\
0111031321312333 \\
3233303112131011
\end{pmatrix} \text{(exercise 109)}; \qquad
\begin{pmatrix}
0010001030203020 \\
0001020301000203 \\
0111011131213121 \\
1011121311101213 \\
0010001030203020 \\
2021222321202223 \\
0111011131213121 \\
3031323331303233 \\
0313031333233323 \\
1011121311101213 \\
0212021232223222 \\
0001020301000203 \\
0313031333233323 \\
2021222321202223 \\
0212021232223222 \\
3031323331303233
\end{pmatrix} \text{(Tóth).}$$

111. (a) Let $d_j = j$ and $0 \leq a_j < 3$ for $1 \leq j \leq 9$, $a_9 \neq 0$. Form sequences s_j, t_j by the rules $s_1 = 0$, $t_1 = d_1$; $t_{j+1} = d_{j+1} + 10t_j[a_j = 0]$ for $1 \leq j < 9$; $s_{j+1} = s_j + (0, t_j, -t_j)$ for $a_j = (0, 1, 2)$ and $1 \leq j \leq 9$. Then s_{10} is a possible result; we need only remember the smallish values that occur. More than half the work is saved by disallowing $a_k = 2$ when $s_k = 0$, then using $|s_{10}|$ instead of s_{10}. Since fewer than $3^8 = 6561$ possibilities need to be tried, brute force via the ternary version of Algorithm M works well; fewer than 24,000 mems and 1600 multiplications are needed to deduce that all integers less than 211 are representable, but 211 is not.

Another approach, using Gray code to vary the signs after breaking the digits into blocks in 2^8 possible ways, reduces the number of multiplications to 255, but at the cost of about 500 additional mems. Therefore Gray code is not advantageous in this application.

(b) Now (with 73,000 mems and 4900 multiplications) we can reach all numbers less than 241, but not 241. There are 46 ways to represent 100, including the remarkable $9 - 87 + 6 + 5 - 43 + 210$.

[H. E. Dudeney introduced his "century" problem in *The Weekly Dispatch* (4 and 18 June 1899). See also *The Numerology of Dr. Matrix* by Martin Gardner, Chapter 6; Steven Kahan, *J. Recreational Math.* **23** (1991), 19–25.]

112. The method of exercise 111 now needs more than 167 million mems and 10 million multiplications, because 3^{16} is so much larger than 3^8. We can do much better (10.4 million mems, 1100 mults) by first tabulating the possibilities obtainable from the first k and last k digits, for $1 \leq k < 9$, then considering all blocks of digits that use the 9. There are 60,318 ways to represent 100, and the first unreachable number is 16,040.

SECTION 7.2.1.2

1. [J. P. N. Phillips, *Comp. J.* **10** (1967), 311.] Assuming that $n \geq 3$, we can replace steps L2–L4 by:

    L2′. [Easiest case?] Set $y \leftarrow a_{n-1}$ and $z \leftarrow a_n$. If $y < z$, set $a_{n-1} \leftarrow z$, $a_n \leftarrow y$, and return to L1.

    L2.1′. [Next easiest case?] Set $x \leftarrow a_{n-2}$. If $x \geq y$, go on to step L2.2′. Otherwise set $(a_{n-2}, a_{n-1}, a_n) \leftarrow (z, x, y)$ if $x < z$, (y, z, x) if $x \geq z$. Return to L1.

    L2.2′. [Find j.] Set $j \leftarrow n - 3$ and $y \leftarrow a_j$. If $y \geq x$, set $j \leftarrow j - 1$, $x \leftarrow y$, $y \leftarrow a_j$, and repeat until $y < x$. Terminate if $j = 0$.

    L3′. [Easy increase?] If $y < z$, set $a_j \leftarrow z$, $a_{j+1} \leftarrow y$, $a_n \leftarrow x$, and go to L4.1′.

    L3.1′. [Increase a_j.] Set $l \leftarrow n - 1$; if $y \geq a_l$, repeatedly decrease l by 1 until $y < a_l$. Then set $a_j \leftarrow a_l$ and $a_l \leftarrow y$.

    L4′. [Begin to reverse.] Set $a_n \leftarrow a_{j+1}$ and $a_{j+1} \leftarrow z$.

    L4.1′. [Reverse $a_{j+1} \ldots a_{n-1}$.] Set $k \leftarrow j + 2$, $l \leftarrow n - 1$. Then, if $k < l$, interchange $a_k \leftrightarrow a_l$, set $k \leftarrow k + 1$, $l \leftarrow l - 1$, and repeat until $k \geq l$. Return to L1.   ▌

The program might run still faster if a_t is stored in memory location $\mathtt{A}[n - t]$ for $0 \leq t \leq n$, or if reverse colex order is used as in the following exercise.

2. Again we assume that $a_1 \leq a_2 \leq \cdots \leq a_n$ initially; the permutations generated from $\{1, 2, 2, 3\}$ will, however, be 1223, 2123, 2213, ..., 2321, 3221. Let a_{n+1} be an auxiliary element, *larger* than a_n.

    L1. [Visit.] Visit the permutation $a_1 a_2 \ldots a_n$.

    L2. [Find j.] Set $j \leftarrow 2$. If $a_{j-1} \geq a_j$, increase j by 1 until $a_{j-1} < a_j$. Terminate if $j > n$.

    L3. [Decrease a_j.] Set $l \leftarrow 1$. If $a_l \geq a_j$, increase l until $a_l < a_j$. Then swap $a_l \leftrightarrow a_j$.

    L4. [Reverse $a_1 \ldots a_{j-1}$.] Set $k \leftarrow 1$ and $l \leftarrow j - 1$. Then, if $k < l$, swap $a_k \leftrightarrow a_l$, set $k \leftarrow k + 1$, $l \leftarrow l - 1$, and repeat until $k \geq l$. Return to L1.   ▌

3. Let $C_1 \ldots C_n = c_{a_1} \ldots c_{a_n}$ be the inversion table, as in exercise 5.1.1–7. Then $\text{rank}(a_1 \ldots a_n)$ is the mixed-radix number $\begin{bmatrix} C_1, & \ldots, & C_{n-1}, & C_n \\ n, & \ldots, & 2, & 1 \end{bmatrix}$. [See H. A. Rothe, *Sammlung combinatorisch-analytischer Abhandlungen* **2** (1800), 263–264; and see also the pioneering work of Nārāyaṇa cited in Section 7.2.1.7.] For example, 314592687 has rank $\begin{bmatrix} 2, & 0, & 1, & 1, & 4, & 0, & 0, & 1, & 0 \\ 9, & 8, & 7, & 6, & 5, & 4, & 3, & 2, & 1 \end{bmatrix} = 2 \cdot 8! + 6! + 5! + 4 \cdot 4! + 1! = 81577$; this is the factorial number system featured in Eq. 4.1–(10).

4. Use the recurrence $\text{rank}(a_1 \ldots a_n) = \frac{1}{n} \sum_{j=1}^{t} n_j [x_j < a_1] \binom{n}{n_1, \ldots, n_t} + \text{rank}(a_2 \ldots a_n)$. For example, $\text{rank}(314159265)$ is

$$\tfrac{3}{9} \binom{9}{2,1,1,1,2,1,1} + 0 + \tfrac{2}{7} \binom{7}{1,1,1,2,1,1} + 0 + \tfrac{1}{5} \binom{5}{1,2,1,1} + \tfrac{3}{4} \binom{4}{1,1,1,1} + 0 + \tfrac{1}{2} \binom{2}{1,1} = 30991.$$

5. (a) Step L2 is performed $n!$ times. The probability that exactly k comparisons are made is $q_k - q_{k+1}$, where q_t is the probability that $a_{n-t+1} > \cdots > a_n$, namely $[t \leq n]/t!$. Therefore the mean is $\sum k(q_k - q_{k+1}) = q_1 + \cdots + q_n = \lfloor n! \, e \rfloor / n! - 1 \approx e - 1 \approx 1.718$, and the variance is

$$\sum k^2 (q_k - q_{k+1}) - \text{mean}^2 = q_1 + 3q_2 + \cdots + (2n-1)q_n - (q_1 + \cdots + q_n)^2 \approx e(3-e) \approx 0.766.$$

[For higher moments, see R. Kemp, *Acta Informatica* **35** (1998), 17–89, Theorem 4.]

Incidentally, the average number of interchange operations in step L4 is therefore $\sum \lfloor k/2 \rfloor (q_k - q_{k+1}) = q_2 + q_4 + \cdots \approx \cosh 1 - 1 = (e + e^{-1} - 2)/2 \approx 0.543$, a result due to R. J. Ord-Smith [*Comp. J.* **13** (1970), 152–155].

(b) Step L3 is performed only $n! - 1$ times, but we will assume for convenience that it occurs once more (with 0 comparisons). Then the probability that exactly k comparisons are made is $\sum_{j=k+1}^{n} 1/j!$ for $1 \le k < n$ and $1/n!$ for $k = 0$. Hence the mean is $\frac{1}{2} \sum_{j=0}^{n-2} 1/j! \approx e/2 \approx 1.359$; exercise 1 reduces this number by $\frac{2}{3}$. The variance is $\frac{1}{3} \sum_{j=0}^{n-3} 1/j! + \frac{1}{2} \sum_{j=0}^{n-2} 1/j! - \text{mean}^2 \approx \frac{5}{6} e - \frac{1}{4} e^2 \approx 0.418$.

6. (a) Let $e_n(z) = \sum_{k=0}^{n} z^k/k!$; then the number of different prefixes $a_1 \ldots a_j$ is $j! \, [z^j] \, e_{n_1}(z) \ldots e_{n_t}(z)$. This is $N = \binom{n}{n_1, \ldots, n_t}$ times the probability q_{n-j} that at least $n - j$ comparisons are made in step L2. Therefore the mean is $\frac{1}{N} w(e_{n_1}(z) \ldots e_{n_t}(z)) - 1$, where $w(\sum x_k z^k/k!) = \sum x_k$. In the binary case the mean is $M/\binom{n}{s} - 1$, where $M = \sum_{l=0}^{s} \sum_{k=l}^{n-s+l} \binom{k}{l} = \sum_{l=0}^{s} \binom{n-s+l+1}{l+1} = \binom{n+2}{s+1} - 1 = \binom{n}{s}(2 + \frac{s}{n-s+1} + \frac{n-s}{s+1}) - 1$.

(b) If $\{a_1, \ldots, a_j\} = \{n_1' \cdot x_1, \ldots, n_t' \cdot x_t\}$, the prefix $a_1 \ldots a_j$ contributes altogether $\sum_{1 \le k < l \le t} (n_k - n_k')[n_l < n_l']$ to the total number of comparisons made in step L3. Thus the mean is $\frac{1}{N} \sum_{1 \le k < l \le t} w(f_{kl}(z))$, where

$$f_{kl}(z) = \left(\prod_{\substack{1 \le m \le t \\ m \ne k, \, m \ne l}} e_{n_m}(z) \right) \left(\sum_{r=0}^{n_k} (n_k - r) \frac{z^r}{r!} \right) e_{n_l - 1}(z)$$

$$= e_{n_1}(z) \ldots e_{n_t}(z)(n_k - z \, r_k(z)) r_l(z), \qquad \text{where } r_k(z) = \frac{e_{n_k - 1}(z)}{e_{n_k}(z)}.$$

In the two-valued case this formula reduces to $\frac{1}{N} w((s e_s(z) - z e_{s-1}(z)) e_{n-s-1}(z)) = \frac{s}{N}(\binom{n+1}{s+1} - 1) - \frac{1}{N}(\binom{n+1}{s+1}(s - \frac{s+1}{n-s+1}) + 1) = \frac{1}{N}(-s - 1 + \binom{n+1}{s}) = \frac{n+1}{n-s+1} - \frac{s+1}{N}$.

7. In the notation of the previous answer, the quantity $\frac{1}{N} w(e_{n_1}(z) \ldots e_{n_t}(z)) - 1$ is

$$\frac{n_1 + \cdots + n_t}{n} + \frac{(n_1 n_2 + n_1 n_3 + \cdots + n_{t-1} n_t) + n_1(n_1 - 1) + \cdots + n_t(n_t - 1)}{n(n-1)} + \cdots - 1.$$

One can show using Eq. 1.2.9–(38) that the limit is $-1 + \exp \sum_{k \ge 1} r_k/k$, where $r_k = \lim_{t \to \infty} (n_1^k + \cdots + n_t^k)/(n_1 + \cdots + n_t)^k$. In cases (a) and (b) we have $r_k = [k = 1]$, so the limit is $e - 1 \approx 1.71828$. In case (c) we have $r_k = 1/(2^k - 1)$, so the limit is $-1 + \exp \sum_{k \ge 1} 1/(k(2^k - 1)) \approx 2.46275$.

8. Assume that j is initially zero, and change step L1 to

L1'. [Visit.] Visit the variation $a_1 \ldots a_j$. If $j < n$, set $j \leftarrow j + 1$ and repeat this step. ∎

This algorithm is due to L. J. Fischer and K. C. Krause, *Lehrbuch der Combinationslehre und der Arithmetik* (Dresden: 1812), 55–57.

Incidentally, the total number of variations is $w(e_{n_1}(z) \ldots e_{n_t}(z))$ in the notation of answer 6. This counting problem was first treated by James Bernoulli in *Ars Conjectandi* (1713), Part 2, Chapter 9.

9. R1. [Visit.] Visit the variation $a_1 \ldots a_r$. (At this point $a_{r+1} \le \cdots \le a_n$.)

R2. [Easy case?] If $a_r < a_n$, interchange $a_r \leftrightarrow a_j$ where j is the smallest subscript such that $j > r$ and $a_j > a_r$, and return to R1.

R3. [Reverse.] Set $(a_{r+1}, \ldots, a_n) \leftarrow (a_n, \ldots, a_{r+1})$ as in step L4.

R4. [Find j.] Set $j \leftarrow r - 1$. If $a_j \geq a_{j+1}$, decrease j by 1 repeatedly until $a_j < a_{j+1}$. Terminate if $j = 0$.

R5. [Increase a_j.] Set $l \leftarrow n$. If $a_j \geq a_l$, decrease l by 1 repeatedly until $a_j < a_l$. Then interchange $a_j \leftrightarrow a_l$.

R6. [Reverse again.] Set $(a_{j+1}, \ldots, a_n) \leftarrow (a_n, \ldots, a_{j+1})$ as in step L4, and return to R1. ∎

The number of outputs is $r! \, [z^r] \, e_{n_1}(z) \ldots e_{n_t}(z)$; this is, of course, n^r when the elements are distinct.

10. $a_1 a_2 \ldots a_n = 213 \ldots n$, $c_1 c_2 \ldots c_n = 010 \ldots 0$, $o_1 o_2 \ldots o_n = 1(-1)1 \ldots 1$, if $n \geq 2$.

11. Step (P1, ..., P7) is performed $(1, n!, n!, n! + x_n, n!, (x_n + 3)/2, x_n)$ times, where $x_n = \sum_{k=1}^{n-1} k!$, because P7 is performed $(j - 1)!$ times when $2 \leq j \leq n$.

12. We want the permutation of rank 999999. The answers are (a) 2783915460, by exercise 3; (b) 8750426319, because the reflected mixed-radix number corresponding to $\left[\begin{smallmatrix} 0, & 0, & 1, & 2, & 3, & 0, & 2, & 7, & 0, & 9 \\ 1, & 2, & 3, & 4, & 5, & 6, & 7, & 8, & 9, & 10 \end{smallmatrix}\right]$ is $\left[\begin{smallmatrix} 0, & 0, & 1, & 3-2, & 3, & 5-0, & 2, & 7, & 8-0, & 9-9 \\ 1, & 2, & 3, & 4, & 5, & 6, & 7, & 8, & 9, & 10 \end{smallmatrix}\right]$ by 7.2.1.1–(50); (c) the product $(0\ 1\ \ldots\ 9)^9 (0\ 1\ \ldots\ 8)^0 (0\ 1\ \ldots\ 7)^7 (0\ 1\ \ldots\ 6)^2 \ldots (0\ 1\ 2)^1$, namely 9703156248.

13. The first statement is true for all $n \geq 2$. But when 2 crosses 1, namely when c_2 changes from 0 to 1, we have $c_3 = 2$, $c_4 = 3$, $c_5 = \cdots = c_n = 0$, and the next permutation when $n \geq 5$ is $432156 \ldots n$. [See *Time Travel* (1988), page 74.]

14. True at the beginning of steps P4, P5, and P6, because exactly $j - 1 - c_j + s$ elements lie to the left of x_j, namely $j - 1 - c_j$ from $\{x_1, \ldots, x_{j-1}\}$ and s from $\{x_{j+1}, \ldots, x_n\}$. (In a sense, this formula is the main point of Algorithm P.)

15. If $\left[\begin{smallmatrix} b_{n-1}, & \ldots, & b_0 \\ 1, & \ldots, & n \end{smallmatrix}\right]$ corresponds to the reflected Gray code $\left[\begin{smallmatrix} c_1, & \ldots, & c_n \\ 1, & \ldots, & n \end{smallmatrix}\right]$, we get to step P6 if and only if $b_k = k - 1$ for $j \leq k \leq n$ and B_{n-j+1} is even, by 7.2.1.1–(50). But $b_{n-k} = k - 1$ for $j \leq k \leq n$ implies that B_{n-k} is odd for $j < k \leq m$. Therefore $s = [c_{j+1} = j] + [c_{j+2} = j + 1] = [o_{j+1} < 0] + [o_{j+2} < 0]$ in step P5. [See *Math. Comp.* **17** (1963), 282–285.]

16. **P1′.** [Initialize.] Set $c_j \leftarrow j$ and $o_j \leftarrow -1$ for $1 \leq j < n$; also set $z \leftarrow a_n$.

P2′. [Visit.] Visit $a_1 \ldots a_n$. Then go to P3.5′ if $a_1 = z$.

P3′. [Hunt down.] For $j \leftarrow n - 1, n - 2, \ldots, 1$ (in this order), set $a_{j+1} \leftarrow a_j$, $a_j \leftarrow z$, and visit $a_1 \ldots a_n$. Then set $j \leftarrow n - 1$, $s \leftarrow 1$, and go to P4′.

P3.5′. [Hunt up.] For $j \leftarrow 1, 2, \ldots, n - 1$ (in this order), set $a_j \leftarrow a_{j+1}$, $a_{j+1} \leftarrow z$, and visit $a_1 \ldots a_n$. Then set $j \leftarrow n - 1$, $s \leftarrow 0$.

P4′. [Ready to change?] Set $q \leftarrow c_j + o_j$. If $q = 0$, go to P6′; if $q > j$, go to P7′.

P5′. [Change.] Interchange $a_{c_j + s} \leftrightarrow a_{q+s}$. Then set $c_j \leftarrow q$ and return to P2′.

P6′. [Increase s.] Terminate if $j = 1$; otherwise set $s \leftarrow s + 1$.

P7′. [Switch direction.] Set $o_j \leftarrow -o_j$, $j \leftarrow j - 1$, and go back to P4′. ∎

17. Initially $a_j \leftarrow a'_j \leftarrow j$ for $1 \leq j \leq n$. Step P5 should now set $t \leftarrow j - c_j + s$, $u \leftarrow j - q + s$, $v \leftarrow a_u$, $a_t \leftarrow v$, $a'_v \leftarrow t$, $a_u \leftarrow j$, $a'_j \leftarrow u$, $c_j \leftarrow q$. (See exercise 14.)

But with the inverse required and available we can actually simplify the algorithm significantly, avoiding the offset variable s and letting the control table $c_1 \ldots c_n$ count only downwards, as noted by G. Ehrlich [*JACM* **20** (1973), 505–506]:

Q1. [Initialize.] Set $a_j \leftarrow a'_j \leftarrow j$, $c_j \leftarrow j - 1$, and $d_j \leftarrow -1$ for $1 \leq j \leq n$. Also set $c_0 = -1$.

Q2. [Visit.] Visit the permutation $a_1 \ldots a_n$ and its inverse $a'_1 \ldots a'_n$.

Q3. [Find k.] Set $k \leftarrow n$. Then if $c_k = 0$, set $c_k \leftarrow k - 1$, $o_k \leftarrow -o_k$, $k \leftarrow k - 1$, and repeat until $c_k \neq 0$. Terminate if $k = 0$.

Q4. [Change.] Set $c_k \leftarrow c_k - 1$, $j \leftarrow a'_k$, and $i = j + o_k$. Then set $t \leftarrow a_i$, $a_i \leftarrow k$, $a_j \leftarrow t$, $a'_t \leftarrow j$, $a'_k \leftarrow i$, and return to Q2. ∎

18. Set $a_n \leftarrow n$, and use $(n-1)!/2$ iterations of Algorithm P to generate all permutations of $\{1, \ldots, n-1\}$ such that 1 precedes 2. [M. K. Roy, *CACM* **16** (1973), 312–313; see also exercise 13.]

19. For example, we can use the idea of Algorithm P, with the n-tuples $c_1 \ldots c_n$ changing as in Algorithm 7.2.1.1H with respect to the radices $(1, 2, \ldots, n)$. That algorithm maintains the directions correctly, although it numbers subscripts differently. The offset s needed by Algorithm P can be computed as in the answer to exercise 15, or the inverse permutation can be maintained as in exercise 17. [See G. Ehrlich, *CACM* **16** (1973), 690–691.] Other algorithms, like that of Heap, can also be implemented looplessly.

(*Note:* In most applications of permutation generation we are interested in minimizing the *total* running time, not the maximum time between successive visits; from this standpoint looplessness is usually undesirable, except on a parallel computer. Yet there's something intellectually satisfying about the fact that a loopless algorithm exists, whether practical or not.)

20. For example, when $n = 3$ we can begin 123, 132, 312, $\overline{3}12$, $1\overline{3}2$, $12\overline{3}$, $21\overline{3}$, $\ldots$, 213, $\overline{2}13$, $\ldots$. If the delta sequence for n is $(\delta_1 \delta_2 \ldots \delta_{2^n n!})$, the corresponding sequence for $n + 1$ is $(\Delta_n \delta_1 \Delta_n \delta_2 \ldots \Delta_n \delta_{2^n n!})$, where Δ_n is the sequence of $2n - 1$ operations n $n{-}1$ $\ldots$ $1 - 1 \ldots n{-}1$ n; here $\delta_k = j$ means $a_j \leftrightarrow a_{j+1}$ and $\delta_k = -$ means $a_1 \leftarrow -a_1$.

(Signed permutations appear in another guise in exercises 5.1.4–43 and 44. The set of all signed permutations is called the octahedral group.)

21. Clearly $\mathtt{M} = 1$, hence $\mathtt{O}$ must be 0 and $\mathtt{S}$ must be $b - 1$. Then $\mathtt{N} = \mathtt{E} + 1$, $\mathtt{R} = b - 2$, and $\mathtt{D} + \mathtt{E} = b + \mathtt{Y}$. This leaves exactly $\max(0, b - 7 - k)$ choices for $\mathtt{E}$ when $\mathtt{Y} = k \geq 2$, hence a total of $\sum_{k=2}^{b-7}(b - 7 - k) = \binom{b-8}{2}$ solutions when $b \geq 8$. [*Math. Mag.* **45** (1972), 48–49. Incidentally, D. Eppstein has proved that the task of solving alphametics with a given radix is NP-complete; see *SIGACT News* **18**, 3 (1987), 38–40.]

22. $(\mathtt{XY})_b + (\mathtt{XX})_b = (\mathtt{XYX})_b$ is solvable only when $b = 2$.

23. Almost true, because the number of solutions will be even, *unless* $[j \in F] \neq [k \in F]$. (Consider the ternary alphametic $\mathtt{X} + (\mathtt{XX})_3 + (\mathtt{YY})_3 + (\mathtt{XZ})_3 = (\mathtt{XYX})_3$.)

24. (a) $9283 + 7 + 473 + 1062 = 10825$. (b) $698392 + 3192 = 701584$. (c) $63952 + 69275 = 133227$. (d) $653924 + 653924 = 1307848$. (e) $5718 + 3 + 98741 = 104462$. (f) $127503 + 502351 + 3947539 + 46578 = 4623971$. (g) $67432 + 704 + 8046 + 97364 = 173546$. (h) $59 + 577404251698 + 69342491650 + 49869442698 + 1504 + 40614 + 82591 + 344 + 41 + 741425 = 5216367650 + 691400684974$. [All solutions are unique. References for (b)–(g): *J. Recreational Math.* **10** (1977), 115; **5** (1972), 296; **10** (1977), 41; **10** (1978), 274; **12** (1979), 133–134; **9** (1977), 207.]

(i) In this case there are $\frac{8}{10}10! = 2903040$ solutions, because *every* permutation of $\{0, 1, \ldots, 9\}$ works except those that assign $\mathtt{H}$ or $\mathtt{N}$ to 0. (A well-written general additive alphametic solver will be careful to reduce the amount of output in such cases.)

25. We may assume that $s_1 \leq \cdots \leq s_{10}$. Let i be the least index $\notin F$, and set $a_i \leftarrow 0$; then set the remaining elements a_j in order of increasing j. A proof like that of Theorem 6.1S shows that this procedure maximizes $a \cdot s$. A similar procedure yields the minimum, because $\min(a \cdot s) = -\max(a \cdot (-s))$.

26. $400739 + 63930 - 2379 - 1252630 + 53430 - 1390 + 738300$.

27. Readers can probably improve upon the following examples: BLOOD + SWEAT + TEARS = LATER; EARTH + WATER + WRATH = HELLO + WORLD; AWAIT + ROBOT + ERROR = SOBER + WORDS; CHILD + THEME + PEACE + ETHIC = IDEAL + ALPHA + METIC. (This exercise was inspired by WHERE + SEDGE + GRASS + GROWS = MARSH [A. W. Johnson, Jr., *J. Recr. Math.* **15** (1982), 51], which would be marvelously pure except that D and O have the same signature.)

28. (a) $11 = 3 + 3 + 2 + 2 + 1$, $20 = 11 + 3 + 3 + 3$, $20 = 11 + 3 + 3 + 2 + 1$, $20 = 11 + 3 + 3 + 1 + 1 + 1$, $20 = 8 + 8 + 2 + 1 + 1$, $20 = 7 + 7 + 6$, $20 = 7 + 7 + 2 + 2 + 2$, $20 = 7 + 7 + 2 + 1 + 1 + 1 + 1$, $20 = 7 + 5 + 5 + 2 + 1$, $20 = 7 + 5 + 2 + 2 + 2 + 1 + 1$, $20 = 7 + 5 + 2 + 2 + 1 + 1 + 1 + 1$, $20 = 7 + 3 + 3 + 2 + 2 + 1 + 1 + 1$, $20 = 7 + 3 + 3 + 1 + 1 + 1 + 1 + 1 + 1 + 1$, $20 = 5 + 3 + 3 + 3 + 3 + 3$. [These fourteen solutions were first computed by Roy Childs in 1999. The next doubly partitionable values of n are 30 (in 20 ways), then 40 (in 94 ways), 41 (in 67), 42 (in 57), 50 (in 190 ways, including $50 = 2 + 2 + \cdots + 2$), etc.]

(b) $51 = 20 + 15 + 14 + 2$, $51 = 15 + 14 + 10 + 9 + 3$, $61 = 19 + 16 + 11 + 9 + 6$, $65 = 17 + 16 + 15 + 9 + 7 + 1$, $66 = 20 + 19 + 16 + 6 + 5$, $69 = 18 + 17 + 16 + 10 + 8$, $70 = 30 + 20 + 10 + 7 + 3$, $70 = 20 + 16 + 12 + 9 + 7 + 6$, $70 = 20 + 15 + 12 + 11 + 7 + 5$, $80 = 50 + 20 + 9 + 1$, $90 = 50 + 12 + 11 + 9 + 5 + 2 + 1$, $91 = 45 + 19 + 11 + 10 + 5 + 1$. [The two 51s are due to Steven Kahan; see his book *Have Some Sums To Solve* (Farmingdale, New York: Baywood, 1978), 36–37, 84, 112. Amazing examples with seventeen distinct terms in Italian and fifty-eight distinct terms in Roman numerals have been found by Giulio Cesare, *J. Recr. Math.* **30** (1999), 63.]

Notes: The beautiful example THREE = TWO + ONE + ZERO [Richard L. Breisch, *Recreational Math. Magazine* **12** (December 1962), 24] is unfortunately ruled out by our conventions. The total number of doubly true partitions into distinct parts is probably finite, in English, although nomenclature for arbitrarily large integers is not standard. Is there an example bigger than NINETYNINENONILLIONNINETYNINESEXTILLIONSIXTYONE = NINETYNINENONILLIONNINETYNINESEXTILLIONNINETEEN + SIXTEEN + ELEVEN + NINE + SIX (suggested by G. González-Morris)?

29. $10 + 7 + 1 - 9 + 6 + 3$, $11 + 10 - 8 + 7 + 6$, $12 + 7 + 6 + 5 - 11 + 10 + 9$, $\ldots$, $19 + 10 + 3 = 14 + 13 + 4 + 1$ (31 examples in all).

30. (a) $567^2 = 321489$, $807^2 = 651249$, or $854^2 = 729316$. (b) $958^2 = 917764$. (c) $96 \times 7^2 = 4704$. (d) $51304/61904 = 7260/8760$. (e) $328509^2 = 4761^3$. [*Strand* **78** (1929), 91, 208; *J. Recr. Math* **3** (1970), 43; **13** (1981), 212; **27** (1995), 137; **31** (2003), 133. The solutions to (b), (c), (d), and (e) are unique. With a right-to-left approach based on Algorithm X, the answers are found in (14, 13, 11, 3423, 42) kilomems, respectively. Nob also noticed that NORTH/SOUTH = WEST/EAST has the unique solution $67104/27504 = 9320/3820$.]

31. $5/34 + 7/68 + 9/12(!)$. One can verify uniqueness with Algorithm X using the side condition A < D < G, in about 265 Kμ. [*Quark Visual Science Magazine*, No. 136 (Tokyo: Kodansha, October 1993).] Curiously, a very similar puzzle also has a unique solution: $1/(3 \times 6) + 5/(8 \times 9) + 7/(2 \times 4) = 1$; see Scot Morris, *Omni* **17**, 4 (January 1995), 97.

32. There are eleven ways, of which the most surprising is $3 + 69258/714$. [See *The Weekly Dispatch* (9 and 23 June 1901); *Amusements in Mathematics* (1917), 158–159.]

33. (a) 1, 2, 3, 4, 15, 18, 118, 146. (b) 6, 9, 16, 20, 27, 126, 127, 129, 136, 145. [*The Weekly Dispatch* (11 and 30 November, 1902); *Amusements in Math.* (1917), 159.]

In this case one suitable strategy is to find all variations where $a_k \ldots a_{l-1}/a_l \ldots a_9$ is an integer, then to record solutions for all permutations of $a_1 \ldots a_{k-1}$. There are exactly 164959 integers with a unique solution, the largest being 9876533. There are solutions for all years in the 21st century except 2091. The most solutions (125) occur when $n = 6443$; the longest stretch of representable n's is $5109 < n < 7060$. Dudeney was able to get the correct answers by hand for small n by "casting out nines."

34. (a) $x = 10^5$, $7378 + 155 + 92467 = 7178 + 355 + 92467 = 1016 + 733 + 98251 = 100000$. (b) $x = 4^7$, $3036 + 455 + 12893 = 16384$ is unique. The fastest way to resolve this problem is probably to start with a list of the 2529 primes that consist of five distinct digits (namely 10243, 10247, $\ldots$, 98731) and to permute the five remaining digits.

Incidentally, the unrestricted alphametic EVEN + ODD = PRIME has ten solutions; both ODD and PRIME are prime in just one of them. [See M. Arisawa, *J. Recr. Math.* **8** (1975), 153.]

35. In general, if $s_k = |S_k|$ for $1 \le k < n$, there are $s_1 \ldots s_{k-1}$ ways to choose each of the nonidentity elements of S_k. Hence the answer is $\prod_{k=1}^{n-1}(\prod_{j=1}^{k-1} s_j^{s_k-1})$, which in this case is $2^2 \cdot 6^3 \cdot 24^{15} = 436196692474023836123136$.

(But if the vertices are renumbered, the s_k values may change. For example, if vertices $(0, 3, 5)$ of (12) are interchanged with $(\mathsf{e}, \mathsf{d}, \mathsf{c})$, we have $s_{14} = 1$, $s_{13} = 6$, $s_{12} = 4$, $s_{11} = 1$, and $4^5 \cdot 24^{15}$ Sims tables.)

36. Since each of $\{0, 3, 5, 6, 9, \mathsf{a}, \mathsf{c}, \mathsf{f}\}$ lies on three lines, but every other element lies on only two, it is clear that we may let $S_\mathsf{f} = \{(), \sigma, \sigma^2, \sigma^3, \alpha, \alpha\sigma, \alpha\sigma^2, \alpha\sigma^3\}$, where $\sigma = (03\mathsf{fc})(17\mathsf{e}4)(2\mathsf{bd}4)(56\mathsf{a}9)$ is a $90°$ rotation and $\alpha = (05)(14)(27)(36)(8\mathsf{d})(9\mathsf{c})(\mathsf{af})(\mathsf{be})$ is an inside-out twist. Also $S_\mathsf{e} = \{(), \beta, \gamma, \beta\gamma\}$, where $\beta = (14)(28)(3\mathsf{c})(69)(\mathsf{be})$ is a transposition and $\gamma = (12)(48)(5\mathsf{a})(69)(7\mathsf{b})(\mathsf{de})$ is another twist; $S_\mathsf{d} = \cdots = S_1 = \{()\}$. (There are $4^7 - 1$ alternative answers.)

37. The set S_k can be chosen in $k!^{k-1}$ ways (see exercise 35), and its nonidentity elements can be assigned to $\sigma(k, 1)$, $\ldots$, $\sigma(k, k)$ in $k!$ further ways. So the answer is $A_n = \prod_{k=1}^{n-1} k!^k = n!^{\binom{n}{2}}/\prod_{k=1}^n k^{\binom{k}{2}}$. For example, $A_{10} \approx 6.256 \times 10^{148}$. We have

$$\sum_{k=1}^{n-1} \binom{k}{2} \ln k = \frac{1}{2} \int_1^n x(x-1) \ln x \, dx + O(n^2 \log n) = \frac{1}{6} n^3 \ln n + O(n^3)$$

by Euler's summation formula; thus $\ln A_n = \frac{1}{3} n^3 \ln n + O(n^3)$.

38. The probability that $\phi(k)$ is needed in step G4 is $1/k! - 1/(k+1)!$, for $1 \le k < n$; the probability is $1/n!$ that we don't get to step G4 at all. Since $\phi(k)$ does $\lceil k/2 \rceil$ transpositions, the average is $\sum_{k=1}^{n-1}(1/k! - 1/(k+1)!)\lceil k/2 \rceil - \sum_{k=1}^{n-1}(\lceil k/2 \rceil - \lceil (k-1)/2 \rceil)/k! - \lceil (n-1)/2 \rceil/n! = \sum_{k \text{ odd}} 1/k! + O(1/(n-1)!)$.

39. (a) 0123, 1023, 2013, 0213, 1203, 2103, 3012, 0312, 1302, 3102, 0132, 1032, 2301, 3201, 0231, 2031, 3021, 0321, 1230, 2130, 3120, 1320, 2310, 3210; (b) 0123, 1023, 2013, 0213, 1203, 2103, 3102, 1302, 0312, 3012, 1032, 0132, 0231, 2031, 3021, 0321, 2301, 3201, 3210, 2310, 1320, 3120, 2130, 1230.

40. By induction we find $\sigma(1, 1) = (0\ 1)$, $\sigma(2, 2) = (0\ 1\ 2)$,

$$\sigma(k, k) = \begin{cases} (0\ k)(k{-}1\ k{-}2\ \ldots\ 1), & \text{if } k \ge 3 \text{ is odd,} \\ (0\ k{-}1\ k{-}2\ 1\ \ldots\ k{-}3\ k), & \text{if } k \ge 4 \text{ is even;} \end{cases}$$

also $\omega(k) = (0\ k)$ when k is even, $\omega(k) = (0\ k{-}2\ \ldots\ 1\ k{-}1\ k)$ when $k \geq 3$ is odd. Thus when $k \geq 3$ is odd, $\sigma(k,1) = (k\ k{-}1\ 0)$ and $\sigma(k,j)$ takes $k \mapsto j-1$ for $1 < j < k$; when $k \geq 4$ is even, $\sigma(k,j) = (0\ k\ k{-}3\ \ldots\ 1\ k{-}2\ k{-}1)^j$ for $1 \leq j \leq k$.

Notes: The first scheme that causes Algorithm G to generate all permutations by single transpositions was devised by Mark Wells [*Math. Comp.* **15** (1961), 192–195], but it was considerably more complicated. W. Lipski, Jr., studied such schemes in general and found a variety of additional methods [*Computing* **23** (1979), 357–365].

41. We may assume that $r < n$. Algorithm G will generate r-variations for any Sims table if we simply change '$k \leftarrow 1$' to '$k \leftarrow n - r$' in step G3, provided that we redefine $\omega(k)$ to be $\sigma(n-r, n-r)\ldots\sigma(k,k)$ instead of using (16).

If $n - r$ is odd, the method of (27) is still valid, although the formulas in answer 40 need to be revised when $k < n-r+2$. The new formulas are $\sigma(k,j) = (k\ j{-}1\ \ldots\ 1\ 0)$ and $\omega(k) = (k\ \ldots\ 1\ 0)$ when $k = n - r$; $\sigma(k,j) = (k\ \ldots\ 1\ 0)^j$ when $k = n - r + 1$.

If $n - r$ is even, we can use (27) with even and odd reversed, if $r \leq 3$. But when $r \geq 4$ a more complex scheme is needed, because a fixed transposition like $(k\ 0)$ can be used for odd k only if $\omega(k - 1)$ is a k-cycle, which means that $\omega(k - 1)$ must be an even permutation; but $\omega(k)$ is odd for $k \geq n - r + 2$.

The following scheme works when $n - r$ is even: Let $\tau(k,j)\omega(k - 1)^- = (k\ k{-}j)$ for $1 \leq j \leq k = n - r$, and use (27) when $k > n - r$. Then, when $k = n - r + 1$, we have $\omega(k - 1) = (0\ 1\ \ldots\ k{-}1)$, hence $\sigma(k,j)$ takes $k \mapsto (2j - 1) \bmod k$ for $1 \leq j \leq k$, and $\sigma(k,k) = (k\ k{-}1\ k{-}3\ \ldots\ 0\ k{-}2\ \ldots\ 1)$, $\omega(k) = (k\ \ldots\ 1\ 0)$, $\sigma(k+1,j) = (k{+}1\ \ldots\ 0)^j$.

42. If $\sigma(k,j) = (k\ j{-}1)$ we have $\tau(k,1) = (k\ 0)$ and $\tau(k,j) = (k\ j{-}1)(k\ j{-}2) = (k\ j{-}1\ j{-}2)$ for $2 \leq j \leq k$.

43. Of course $\omega(1) = \sigma(1,1) = \tau(1,1) = (0\ 1)$. The following construction makes $\omega(k) = (k{-}2\ k{-}1\ k)$ for all $k \geq 2$: Let $\alpha(k,j) = \tau(k,j)\omega(k-1)^-$, where $\alpha(2,1) = (2\ 0)$, $\alpha(2,2) = (2\ 0\ 1)$, $\alpha(3,1) = \alpha(3,3) = (3\ 1)$, $\alpha(3,2) = (3\ 1\ 0)$; this makes $\sigma(2,2) = (0\ 2)$, $\sigma(3,3) = (0\ 3\ 1)$. Then for $k \geq 4$, let

$$
\begin{array}{ccccccc}
 & k \bmod 3 = 0 & & k \bmod 3 = 1 & & k \bmod 3 = 2 & \\
\alpha(k, k{-}2) = & (k\ k{-}2\ 0) & \text{or} & (k\ k{-}3\ 0) & \text{or} & (k\ k{-}1\ 0), & \\
\alpha(k, k{-}1) = & (k\ k{-}2\ k{-}3) & \text{or} & (k\ k{-}3) & \text{or} & (k\ k{-}1\ k{-}3), & \\
\alpha(k, k) = & (k\ k{-}2) & \text{or} & (k\ k{-}3\ k{-}2) & \text{or} & (k\ k{-}2); &
\end{array}
$$

this makes $\sigma(k,k) = (k{-}3\ k\ k{-}2)$ as required.

44. No, because $\tau(k,j)$ is a $(k + 1)$-cycle, not a transposition. (See (19) and (24).)

45. (a) 202280070, since $u_k = \max(\{0, 1, \ldots, a_k - 1\} \setminus \{a_1, \ldots, a_{k-1}\})$. (Actually u_n is never set by the algorithm, but we can assume that it is zero.) (b) 425368917.

46. True (assuming that $u_n = 0$). If either $u_k > u_{k+1}$ or $a_k > a_{k+1}$ we must have $a_k > u_k \geq a_{k+1} > u_{k+1}$.

47. Steps $(X1, X2, \ldots, X6)$ are performed respectively $(1, A, B, A-1, B-N_n, A)$ times, where $A = N_0 + \cdots + N_{n-1}$ and $B = nN_0 + (n - 1)N_1 + \cdots + 1N_{n-1}$.

48. Steps $(X2, X3, X4, X5, X6)$ are performed respectively $A_n + (1, n!, 0, 0, 1)$ times, where $A_n = \sum_{k=1}^{n-1} n^{\underline{k}} = n! \sum_{k=1}^{n-1} 1/k! \approx n!\,(e - 1)$. Assuming that they cost respectively $(1, 1, 3, 1, 3)$ mems, for operations involving a_j, l_j, or u_j, the total cost is about $9e - 8 \approx 16.46$ mems per permutation.

Algorithm L uses approximately $(e, 2 + e/2, 2e + 2e^{-1} - 4)$ mems per permutation in steps $(L2, L3, L4)$, for a total of $3.5e + 2e^{-1} - 2 \approx 8.25$ (see exercise 5).

Algorithm X could be tuned up for this case by streamlining the code when k is near n. But so can Algorithm L, as shown in exercise 1.

49. Order the signatures so that $|s_0| \geq \cdots \geq |s_9|$; also prepare tables $w_0 \ldots w_9$, $x_0 \ldots x_9$, $y_0 \ldots y_9$, so that the signatures $\{s_k, \ldots, s_9\}$ are $w_{x_k} \leq \cdots \leq w_{y_k}$. For example, when $\texttt{SEND} + \texttt{MORE} = \texttt{MONEY}$ we have $(s_0, \ldots, s_9) = (-9000, 1000, -900, 91, -90, 10, 1, -1, 0, 0)$ for the respective letters $(\texttt{M}, \texttt{S}, \texttt{O}, \texttt{E}, \texttt{N}, \texttt{R}, \texttt{D}, \texttt{Y}, \texttt{A}, \texttt{B})$; also $(w_0, \ldots, w_9) = (-9000, -900, -90, -1, 0, 0, 1, 10, 91, 1000)$, and $x_0 \ldots x_9 = 0112233344$, $y_0 \ldots y_9 = 9988776554$. Yet another table $f_0 \ldots f_9$ has $f_j = 1$ if the digit corresponding to w_j cannot be zero; in this case $f_0 \ldots f_9 = 1000000001$. These tables make it easy to compute the largest and smallest values of

$$s_k a_k + \cdots + s_9 a_9$$

over all choices $a_k \ldots a_9$ of the remaining digits, using the method of exercise 25, since the links l_j tell us those digits in increasing order.

This method requires a rather expensive computation at each node of the search tree, but it often succeeds in keeping that tree small. For example, it solves the first eight alphametics of exercise 24 with costs of only 7, 13, 7, 9, 5, 343, 44, and 89 kilomems; this is a substantial improvement in cases (a), (b), (e), and (h), although case (f) comes out significantly worse. Another bad case is the '`CHILD`' example of answer 27, where left-to-right needs 2947 kilomems compared to 588 for the right-to-left approach. Left-to-right does, however, fare better on $\texttt{BLOOD} + \texttt{SWEAT} + \texttt{TEARS}$ (73 versus 360) and $\texttt{HELLO} + \texttt{WORLD}$ (340 versus 410).

50. If α is in a permutation group, so are all its powers α^2, α^3, $\ldots$, including $\alpha^{m-1} = \alpha^-$, where m is the order of α (the least common multiple of its cycle lengths). And (32) is equivalent to $\alpha^- = \sigma_1 \sigma_2 \ldots \sigma_{n-1}$.

51. False. For example, $\sigma(k, i)^-$ and $\sigma(k, j)^-$ might both take $k \mapsto 0$.

52. $\tau(k, j) = (k{-}j \ \ k{-}j{+}1)$ is an adjacent interchange, and

$$\omega(k) = (n{-}1 \ \ldots \ 0)(n{-}2 \ \ldots \ 0) \ldots (k \ \ldots \ 0) = \phi(n-1)\phi(k-1)$$

is a k-flip followed by an n-flip. The permutation corresponding to control table $c_0 \ldots c_{n-1}$ in Algorithm H has c_j elements to the right of j that are less than j, for $0 \leq j < n$; so it is the same as the permutation corresponding to $c_1 \ldots c_n$ in Algorithm P, except that subscripts are shifted by 1.

The only essential difference between Algorithm P and this version of Algorithm H is that Algorithm P uses a reflected Gray code to run through all possibilities of its control table, while Algorithm H runs through those mixed-radix numbers in ascending (lexicographic) order.

Indeed, Gray code can be used with any Sims table, by modifying either Algorithm G or Algorithm H. Then all transitions are by $\tau(k, j)$ or by $\tau(k, j)^-$, and the permutations $\omega(k)$ are irrelevant.

53. The text's proof that $n! - 1$ transpositions cannot be achieved for $n = 4$ also shows that we can reduce the problem from n to $n - 2$ at the cost of a single transposition $(n{-}1 \ n{-}2)$, which was called '$(3\,c)$' in the notation of that proof.

Thus we can generate all permutations by making the following transformation in step H4: If $k = n - 1$ or $k = n - 2$, transpose $a_{j \bmod n} \leftrightarrow a_{(j-1) \bmod n}$, where $j = c_{n-1} - 1$. If $k = n - 3$ or $k = n - 4$, transpose $a_{n-1} \leftrightarrow a_{n-2}$ and also $a_{j \bmod (n-2)} \leftrightarrow a_{(j-1) \bmod (n-2)}$, where $j = c_{n-3} - 1$. And in general if $k = n - 2t - 1$ or $k = n - 2t - 2$, transpose $a_{n-2i+1} \leftrightarrow a_{n-2i}$ for $1 \leq i \leq t$ and also $a_{j \bmod (n-2t)} \leftrightarrow a_{(j-1) \bmod (n-2t)}$, where $j = c_{n-2t-1} - 1$. [See *CACM* **19** (1976), 68–72.]

The corresponding Sims table permutations can be written down as follows, although they don't appear explicitly in the algorithm itself:

$$\sigma(k,j)^- = \begin{cases} (0 \ 1 \ \ldots \ j{-}1 \ k), & \text{if } n - k \text{ is odd}; \\ (0 \ 1 \ \ldots \ k)^j, & \text{if } n - k \text{ is even}. \end{cases}$$

The value of $a_{j \bmod (n-2t)}$ will be $n - 2t - 1$ after the interchange. For efficiency we can also use the fact that k usually equals $n - 1$. The total number of transpositions is $\sum_{t=0}^{\lfloor n/2 \rfloor} (n - 2t)! - \lfloor n/2 \rfloor - 1$.

54. Yes; the transformation can be any k-cycle on positions $\{1, \ldots, k\}$.

55. (a) Since $\rho_!(m) = \rho_!(m \bmod n!)$ when $n > \rho_!(m)$, we have $\rho_!(n! + m) = \rho_!(m)$ for $0 < m < n \cdot n! = (n + 1)! - n!$. Therefore $\beta_{n!+m} = \sigma_{\rho_!(n!+m)} \cdots \sigma_{\rho_!(n!+1)} \beta_{n!} = \sigma_{\rho_!(m)} \cdots \sigma_{\rho_!(1)} \beta_{n!} = \beta_m \beta_{n!}$ for $0 \leq m < n \cdot n!$, and we have in particular

$$\beta_{(n+1)!} = \sigma_{n+1} \beta_{(n+1)!-1} = \sigma_{n+1} \beta_{n!-1} \beta_{n!}^n = \sigma_{n+1} \sigma_n^- \beta_{n!}^{n+1}.$$

Similarly $\alpha_{n!+m} = \beta_{n!}^- \alpha_m \beta_{n!} \alpha_{n!}$ for $0 \leq m < n \cdot n!$.

Since $\beta_{n!}$ commutes with τ_n and τ_{n+1} we find $\alpha_{n!} = \tau_n \alpha_{n!-1}$, and

$$\begin{aligned} \alpha_{(n+1)!} = \tau_{n+1} \alpha_{(n+1)!-1} &= \tau_{n+1} \beta_{n!}^- \alpha_{(n+1)!-1-n} \beta_{n!} \alpha_{n!} = \cdots \\ &= \tau_{n+1} \beta_{n!}^{-n} \alpha_{n!-1} (\beta_{n!} \alpha_{n!})^n \\ &= \beta_{n!}^{-n-1} \tau_{n+1} \tau_n^- (\beta_{n!} \alpha_{n!})^{n+1} \\ &= \beta_{(n+1)!}^- \sigma_{n+1} \sigma_n^- \tau_{n+1} \tau_n^- (\beta_{n!} \alpha_{n!})^{n+1}. \end{aligned}$$

(b) In this case $\sigma_{n+1} \sigma_n^- = (n \ n{-}1 \ \ldots \ 1)$ and $\tau_{n+1} \tau_n^- = (n{+}1 \ n \ 0)$, and we have $\beta_{(n+1)!} \alpha_{(n+1)!} = (n{+}1 \ n \ \ldots \ 0)$ by induction. Therefore $\alpha_{jn!+m} = \beta_{n!}^{-j} \alpha_m (n \ \ldots \ 0)^j$ for $0 \leq j \leq n$ and $0 \leq m < n!$. All permutations of $\{0, \ldots, n\}$ are achieved because $\beta_{n!}^{-j} \alpha_m$ fixes n and $(n \ \ldots \ 0)^j$ takes $n \mapsto n - j$.

56. If we set $\sigma_k = (k{-}1 \ k{-}2)(k{-}3 \ k{-}4) \ldots$ in the previous exercise, we find by induction that $\beta_{n!} \alpha_{n!}$ is the $(n+1)$-cycle $(0 \ n \ n{-}1 \ n{-}3 \ \ldots \ (2 \text{ or } 1) \ (1 \text{ or } 2) \ \ldots \ n{-}4 \ n{-}2)$.

57. Arguing as in answer 5, we obtain $\sum_{k=2}^{n-1} [k \text{ odd}]/k! - (\lfloor n/2 \rfloor - 1)/n! = \sinh 1 - 1 - O(1/(n-1)!)$.

58. True. By the formulas of exercise 55 we have $\alpha_{n!-1} = (0 \ n) \beta_{n!}^- (n \ \ldots \ 0)$, and this takes $0 \mapsto n - 1$ because $\beta_{n!}$ fixes n. (Consequently Algorithm E will define a Hamiltonian *cycle* on the graph of exercise 66 if and only if $\beta_{n!} = (n{-}1 \ \ldots \ 2 \ 1)$, and this holds if and only if the length of every cycle of $\beta_{(n-1)!}$ is a divisor of n. The latter is true for $n = 2$, 3, 4, 6, 12, 20, and 40, but for no other $n \leq 250{,}000$.)

59. The Cayley graph with generators $(\alpha_1, \ldots, \alpha_k)$ in the text's definition is isomorphic to the Cayley graph with generators $(\alpha_1^-, \ldots, \alpha_k^-)$ in the alternative definition, since $\pi \to \alpha_j \pi$ in the former if and only if $\pi^- \to \pi^- \alpha_j^-$ in the latter.

60. There are 88 delta sequences, which reduce to four classes: $P = (32131231)^3$ (plain changes, represented by 8 different delta sequences); $Q = (32121232)^3$ (a doubly Gray variant of plain changes, with 8 representatives); $R = (121232321232)^2$ (a doubly Gray code with 24 representatives); $S = 2\alpha 3\alpha^R$, $\alpha = 12321312121$ (48 representatives). Classes P and Q are cyclic shifts of their complements; classes P, Q, and S are shifts of their reversals; class R is a shifted reversal of its complement. [See A. L. Leigh Silver, *Math. Gazette* **48** (1964), 1–16.]

61. There are respectively $(26, 36, 20, 26, 28, 40, 40, 20, 26, 28, 28, 26)$ such paths ending at $(1243, 1324, 1432, 2134, 2341, 2413, 3142, 3214, 3421, 4123, 4231, 4312)$.

62. There are only two paths when $n = 3$, ending respectively at 132 and 213. But when $n \geq 4$ there are Gray codes leading from $12\ldots n$ to any odd permutation $a_1 a_2 \ldots a_n$. Exercise 61 establishes this when $n = 4$, and we can prove it by induction for $n > 4$ as follows.

Let $A(j)$ be the set of all permutations that begin with j, and let $A(j, k)$ be those that begin with jk. If $(\alpha_0, \alpha_1, \ldots, \alpha_n)$ are any odd permutations such that $\alpha_j \in A(x_j, x_{j+1})$, then $(1\,2)\alpha_j$ is an even permutation in $A(x_{j+1}, x_j)$. Consequently, if $x_1 x_2 \ldots x_n$ is a permutation of $\{1, 2, \ldots, n\}$, there is at least one Hamiltonian path of the form

$$(1\,2)\alpha_0 \;\text{—}\cdots\text{—}\; \alpha_1 \;\text{—}\; (1\,2)\alpha_1 \;\text{—}\cdots\text{—}\; \alpha_2 \;\text{—}\cdots\text{—}\; (1\,2)\alpha_{n-1} \;\text{—}\cdots\text{—}\; \alpha_n;$$

the subpath from $(1\,2)\alpha_{j-1}$ to α_j includes all elements of $A(x_j)$.

This construction solves the problem in at least $(n-2)!^n / 2^{n-1}$ distinct ways when $a_1 \neq 1$, because we can take $\alpha_0 = 2\,1\ldots n$ and $\alpha_n = a_1 a_2 \ldots a_n$; there are $(n-2)!$ ways to choose $x_2 \ldots x_{n-1}$, and $(n-2)!/2$ ways to choose each of $\alpha_1, \ldots, \alpha_{n-1}$.

Finally, if $a_1 = 1$, take any path $12\ldots n \;\text{—}\cdots\text{—}\; a_1 a_2 \ldots a_n$ that runs through all of $A(1)$, and choose any step $\alpha \;\text{—}\; \alpha'$ with $\alpha \in A(1, j)$ and $\alpha' \in A(1, j')$ for some $j \neq j'$. Replace that step by

$$\alpha \;\text{—}\; (1\,2)\alpha_1 \;\text{—}\cdots\text{—}\; \alpha_2 \;\text{—}\cdots\text{—}\; (1\,2)\alpha_{n-1} \;\text{—}\cdots\text{—}\; \alpha_n \;\text{—}\; \alpha',$$

using a construction like the Hamiltonian path above but now with $\alpha_1 = \alpha$, $\alpha_n = (1\,2)\alpha'$, $x_1 = 1$, $x_2 = j$, $x_n = j'$, and $x_{n+1} = 1$. (In this case the permutations $\alpha_1, \ldots, \alpha_n$ might all be even.)

63. Monte Carlo estimates using the techniques of Section 7.2.3 suggest that the total number of equivalence classes will be roughly 1.2×10^{21}; most of those classes will contain 480 Gray cycles.

64. Exactly 2,005,200 delta sequences have the doubly Gray property; they belong to 4206 equivalence classes under cyclic shift, reversal, and/or complementation. Nine classes, such as the code $2\alpha 2\alpha^R$ where

$$\alpha = 12343234321232121232321232121234343212123432123432121232321,$$

are shifts of their reversal; 48 classes are composed of repeated 60-cycles. One of the most interesting of the latter type is $\alpha\alpha$ where

$$\alpha = \beta 2\beta 4\beta 4\beta 4\beta 4, \qquad \beta = 32121232123.$$

65. Such a path exists for any given $N \leq n!$: Let the Nth permutation be $\alpha = a_1 \ldots a_n$, and let $j = a_1$. Also let Π_k be the set of all permutations $\beta = b_1 \ldots b_n$ for which $b_1 = k$ and $\beta \leq \alpha$. By induction on N there is a Gray path P_1 for Π_j. We can then construct Gray paths P_k for $\Pi_j \cup \Pi_1 \cup \cdots \cup \Pi_{k-1}$ for $2 \leq k \leq j$, successively combining P_{k-1} with a Gray cycle for Π_{k-1}. (See the "absorption" construction of answer 62. In fact, P_j will be a Gray *cycle* when N is a multiple of 6.)

66. Defining the delta sequence by the rule $\pi_{(k+1)\bmod n!} = (1\,\delta_k)\pi_k$, we find exactly 36 such sequences, all of which are cyclic shifts of a pattern like $(xyzyzyxzyzyz)^2$. (The next case, $n = 5$, probably has about 10^{18} solutions that are inequivalent with respect to cyclic shifting, reversal, and permutation of coordinates, thus about 6×10^{21} different delta sequences.) Incidentally, Igor Pak has shown that the Cayley graph generated by star transpositions is an $(n-2)$-dimensional torus in general.

67. If we let π be equivalent to $\pi(12345)$, we get a reduced graph on 24 vertices that has 40768 Hamiltonian cycles, 240 of which lead to delta sequences of the form α^5 in which α uses each transposition 6 times (for example, $\alpha = 35423253423453 2454352452$). The total number of solutions to this problem is probably about 10^{16}.

68. If A isn't connected, neither is G. If A is connected, we can assume that it is a free tree. Moreover, in this case we can prove a generalization of the result in exercise 62: For $n \geq 4$ there is a Hamiltonian path in G from the identity permutation to any odd permutation. For we can assume without loss of generality that A contains the edge $1 \text{---} 2$ where 1 is a leaf of the tree, and a proof like that of exercise 62 applies.

[This elegant construction is due to M. Tchuente, *Ars Combinatoria* **14** (1982), 115–122. Extensive generalizations have been discussed by Ruskey and Savage in *SIAM J. Discrete Math.* **6** (1993), 152–166. See also the original Russian publication in *Kibernetika* **11**, 3 (1975), 17–25; English translation, *Cybernetics* **11** (1975), 362–366.]

69. Following the hint, the modified algorithm behaves like this when $n = 5$:

```
1234     1243     1423     4123     4132     1432     1342     1324     3124     3142     3412     4312
 ↓        ↑        ↓        ↑        ↓        ↑        ↓        ↑        ↓        ↑        ↓        ↑
54321    24351    24153    54123    14523    14325    24315    24513    54213    14253    14352    54312
12345    15342    35142    32145    32541    52341    51342    31542    31245    35241    25341    21345
15342    12435    32415    35412←31452    51432    52431    32451←35421    31425    21435    25431
23451    53421    51423    21453→25413    23415    13425    15423→12453    52413    53412    13452
21543    51243    53241    23541    23145    25143    15243    13245    13542    53142    52143    12543
34512    34215    14235    14532    54132    34152    34251    54231    24531    24135    34125    34521
32154→35124    15324→12354    52314    32514←31524    51324    21354→25314    35214→31254
45123←42153    42351←45321    41325    41523→42513    42315    45312←41352    41253←45213
43215    43512←41532    41235    45231→43251    43152→45132    42135    42531←43521    43125
51234    21534→23514    53214    13254←15234    25134←23154    53124    13524→12534    52134
 ↓        ↑        ↓        ↑        ↓        ↑        ↓        ↑        ↓        ↑        ↓        ↑
```

Here the columns represent sets of permutations that are cyclically rotated and/or reflected in all $2n$ ways; therefore each column contains exactly one "rosary permutation" (exercise 18). We can use Algorithm P to run through the rosary permutations systematically, knowing that the pair xy will occur before yx in its column, at which time τ' instead of ρ' will move us to the right or to the left. Step Z2 omits the interchange $a_1 \leftrightarrow a_2$, thereby causing the permutations $a_1 \ldots a_{n-1}$ to repeat themselves going backwards. (We implicitly use the fact that $t[k] = t[n! - k]$ in the output of Algorithm T.)

Now if we replace $1 \ldots n$ by $24 \ldots 31$ and change $A_1 \ldots A_n$ to $A_1 A_n A_2 A_{n-1} \ldots$, we get the unmodified algorithm whose results are shown in Fig. 22(b).

This method was inspired by a (nonconstructive) theorem of E. S. Rapoport, *Scripta Math.* **24** (1959), 51–58. It illustrates a more general fact observed by Carla Savage in 1989, namely that the Cayley graph for *any* group generated by three involutions ρ, σ, τ has a Hamiltonian cycle when $\rho\tau = \tau\rho$ [see I. Pak and R. Radoičić, "Hamiltonian paths in Cayley graphs," to appear].

70. No; the longest cycle in that digraph has length 358. But there do exist pairs of disjoint 180-cycles from which a Hamiltonian path of length 720 can be derived. For example, consider the cycles $\alpha\sigma\beta\sigma$ and $\gamma\sigma\sigma$ where

$$\alpha = \tau\sigma^5\tau\sigma^5\tau\sigma^3\tau\sigma^2\tau\sigma^5\tau\sigma^3\tau\sigma^2\tau\sigma^5\tau\sigma^5\tau\sigma^2\tau\sigma^3\tau\sigma^1\tau\sigma^5\tau\sigma^5\tau\sigma^5\tau\sigma^3\tau\sigma^1\tau\sigma^1\tau\sigma^3\tau\sigma^2\tau\sigma^1\tau\sigma^1;$$

$$\beta = \sigma^3\tau\sigma^5\tau\sigma^2\tau\sigma^2\tau\sigma^5\tau\sigma^2\tau\sigma^3\tau\sigma^1\tau\sigma^1\tau\sigma^5\tau\sigma^1\tau\sigma^3\tau\sigma^5\tau\sigma^5\tau\sigma^3\tau\sigma^2\tau\sigma^1\tau\sigma^2\tau\sigma^3\tau\sigma^1\tau\sigma^1\tau\sigma^3\tau\sigma^2\tau\sigma^4;$$

$$\gamma = \sigma\tau\sigma^5\tau\sigma^5\tau\sigma^3\tau\sigma^1\tau\sigma^1\tau\sigma^3\tau\sigma^2\tau\sigma^5\tau\sigma^2\tau\sigma^3\tau\sigma^5\tau\sigma^1\tau\sigma^5\tau\sigma^3\tau\sigma^2\tau\sigma^1\tau\sigma^2\tau\sigma^3\tau\sigma^1\tau\sigma^1\tau\sigma^3\tau\sigma^2$$
$$\tau\sigma^5\tau\sigma^5\tau\sigma^5\tau\sigma^3\tau\sigma^5\tau\sigma^2\tau\sigma^5\tau\sigma^2\tau\sigma^3\tau\sigma^1\tau\sigma^1\tau\sigma^5\tau\sigma^1\tau\sigma^3\tau\sigma^3\tau\sigma^5\tau\sigma^5\tau\sigma^1\tau\sigma^5\tau\sigma^2\tau\sigma^3\tau\sigma^1\tau\sigma^2.$$

If we start with 134526 and follow $\alpha\sigma\beta\tau$ we reach 163452; then follow $\gamma\sigma\tau$ and reach 126345; then follow $\sigma\gamma\tau$ and reach 152634; then follow $\beta\sigma\alpha$, ending at 415263.

71. Brendan McKay and Frank Ruskey have found such cycles by computer when $n = 7$, 9, and 11, but no nice structure was apparent.

72. Any Hamiltonian path includes $(n-1)!$ vertices that take $y \mapsto x$, each of which (if not the last) is followed by a vertex that takes $x \mapsto x$. So one must be last; otherwise $(n-1)! + 1$ vertices would take $x \mapsto x$.

73. (a) Assume first that β is the identity permutation (). Then every cycle of α that contains an element of A lies entirely within A. Hence the cycles of σ are obtained by omitting all cycles of α that contain no element of A. All remaining cycles have odd length, so σ is an even permutation.

If β is not the identity, we apply this argument to $\alpha' = \alpha\beta^-$, $\beta' = ()$, and $\sigma' = \sigma\beta^-$, concluding that σ' is an even permutation; thus σ and β have the same sign.

Similarly, σ and α have the same sign, because $\beta\alpha^- = (\alpha\beta^-)^-$ has the same order as $\alpha\beta^-$.

(b) Let X be the vertices of the Cayley graph in Theorem R, and let α be the permutation of X that takes a vertex π into $\alpha\pi$; this permutation has g/a cycles of length a. Define the permutation β similarly. Then $\alpha\beta^-$ has g/c cycles of length c. If c is odd, any Hamiltonian cycle in the graph defines a cycle σ that contains all the vertices and satisfies the hypotheses of (a). Therefore α and β have an odd number of cycles, because the sign of a permutation on n elements with r cycles is $(-1)^{n-r}$ (see exercise 5.2.2–2).

[This proof, which shows that X cannot be the union of any odd number of cycles, was presented by Rankin in *Proc. Cambridge Phil. Soc.* **62** (1966), 15–16.]

74. The representation $\beta^j\gamma^k$ is unique if we require $0 \le j < g/c$ and $0 \le k < c$. For if we had $\beta^j = \gamma^k$ for some j with $0 < j < g/c$, the group would have at most jc elements. It follows that $\beta^{g/c} = \gamma^t$ for some t.

Let σ be a Hamiltonian cycle, as in the previous answer. If $x\sigma = x\alpha$ then $x\gamma\sigma$ must be $x\gamma\alpha$, because $x\gamma\beta = \alpha$. And if $x\sigma = x\beta$ then $x\gamma\sigma$ cannot be $x\gamma\alpha$, because that would imply $x\gamma^c\sigma = x\gamma^c\alpha$. Thus the elements $x\gamma^k$ all have equivalent behavior with respect to their successors in σ.

Notice that if $j \ge 0$ there is a $k \le j$ such that $x\sigma^j = x\alpha^k\beta^{j-k} = x\beta^j\gamma^k$. Therefore $x\sigma^{g/c} = x\gamma^{t+k}$ is equivalent to x, and the same behavior will repeat. We return to x for the first time in g steps if and only if $t + k$ is relatively prime to c.

75. Apply the previous exercise with $g = mn$, $a = m$, $b = n$, $c = mn/d$. The number t satisfies $t \equiv 0$ (modulo m), $t + d \equiv 0$ (modulo n); and it follows that $k + t \perp c$ if and only if $(d - k)m/d \perp kn/d$.

Notes: The modular Gray code of exercise 7.2.1.1–78 is a Hamiltonian path from $(0, 0)$ to $(m - 1, (-m) \bmod n)$, so it is a Hamiltonian cycle if and only if m is a multiple of n. It is natural to conjecture (falsely) that at least one Hamiltonian cycle exists whenever $d > 1$. But P. Erdős and W. T. Trotter have observed [*J. Graph Theory* **2**

(1978), 137–142] that if p and $2p+1$ are odd prime numbers, no suitable k exists when $m = p(2p+1)(3p+1)$ and $n = (3p+1)\prod_{q=1}^{3p} q^{[q \text{ is prime}][q\neq p][q\neq 2p+1]}$.

See J. A. Gallian, *Mathematical Intelligencer* **13**, 3 (Summer 1991), 40–43, for interesting facts about other kinds of cycles in $C_m \times C_n$.

76. We may assume that the tour begins in the lower left corner. There are no solutions when m and n are both divisible by 3, because 2/3 of the cells are unreachable in that case. Otherwise, letting $d = \gcd(m, n)$ and arguing as in the previous exercise but with $(x,y)\alpha = ((x+2) \bmod m, (y+1) \bmod n)$ and $(x,y)\beta = ((x+1) \bmod m, (y+2) \bmod n)$, we find the answer

$$\sum_{k=1}^{d-1} \binom{d}{k} \left[\gcd((2d-k)m, (k+d)n) = d \text{ or } (mn \perp 3 \text{ and } \gcd((2d-k)m, (k+d)n) = 3d)\right].$$

77.

```
01   * Permutation generator \`a la Heap
02 N     IS    10               The value of n (3 or more, not large)
03 t     IS    $255
04 j     IS    $0               8j
05 k     IS    $1               8k
06 ak    IS    $2
07 aj    IS    $3

08       LOC   Data_Segment
09 a     GREG  @                Base address for a0...an-1
10 A0    IS    @
11 A1    IS    @+8
12 A2    IS    @+16
13       LOC   @+8*N            Space for a0...an-1
14 c     GREG  @-8*3            Location of 8c0
15       LOC   @-8*3+8*N        8c3...8cn-1, initially zero
16       OCTA  -1               8cn = -1, a convenient sentinel
17 u     GREG  0                Contents of a0, except in inner loop
18 v     GREG  0                Contents of a1, except in inner loop
19 w     GREG  0                Contents of a2, except in inner loop

20       LOC   #100
21 1H    STCO  0,c,k            B - A   ck <- 0.
22       INCL  k,8              B - A   k <- k + 1.
23 0H    LDO   j,c,k            B       j <- ck.
24       CMP   t,j,k            B
25       BZ    t,1B             B       Loop if ck = k.
26       BN    j,Done           A       Terminate if ck < 0 (k = n).
27       LDO   ak,a,k           A - 1   Fetch ak.
28       ADD   t,j,8            A - 1
29       STO   t,c,k            A - 1   ck <- j + 1.
30       AND   t,k,#8           A - 1
31       CSZ   j,t,0            A - 1   Set j <- 0 if k is even.
32       LDO   aj,a,j           A - 1   Fetch aj.
33       STO   ak,a,j           A - 1   Replace it by ak.
34       CSZ   u,j,ak           A - 1   Set u <- ak if j = 0.
35       SUB   j,j,8            A - 1   j <- j - 1.
36       CSZ   v,j,ak           A - 1   Set v <- ak if j = 0.
```

37		SUB	j,j,8	$A-1$	$j \leftarrow j - 1$.
38		CSZ	w,j,ak	$A-1$	Set $w \leftarrow a_k$ if $j = 0$.
39		STO	aj,a,k	$A-1$	Replace a_k by what was a_j.
40	Inner	PUSHJ	0,Visit	A	
		...			(See (42))
55		PUSHJ	0,Visit	A	
56		SET	t,u	A	Swap $u \leftrightarrow w$.
57		SET	u,w	A	
58		SET	w,t	A	
59		SET	k,8*3	A	$k \leftarrow 3$.
60		JMP	0B	A	
61	Main	LDO	u,A0	1	
62		LDO	v,A1	1	
63		LDO	w,A2	1	
64		JMP	Inner	1	∎

78. Lines 31–38 become $2r - 1$ instructions, lines 61–63 become r, and lines 56–58 become $3 + (r - 2)[r \text{ even}]$ instructions (see $\omega(r - 1)$ in answer 40). The total running time is therefore $\big((2r!+2)A+2B+r-5\big)\mu+\big((2r!+2r+7+(r-2)[r \text{ even}])A+7B-r-4\big)v$, where $A = n!/r!$ and $B = n!(1/r! + \cdots + 1/n!)$.

79. SLU u,[#f],t; SLU t,a,4; XOR t,t,a; AND t,t,u; SRU u,t,4; OR t,t,u; XOR a,a,t; here, as in the answer to exercise 1.3.1′–34, the notation '[#f]' denotes a register that contains the constant value $^\#\text{f}$.

80. SLU u,a,t; MXOR u,[#8844221188442211],u; AND u,u,[#ff000000]; SRU u,u,t; XOR a,a,u. This cheats, since it transforms $^\#12345678$ to $^\#13245678$ when $t = 4$, but (45) still works.

Even faster and trickier would be a routine analogous to (42): Consider

```
PUSHJ 0,Visit;  MXOR a,a,c1;  PUSHJ 0,Visit;  ... MXOR a,a,c5;  PUSHJ 0,Visit
```

where c1, ..., c5 are constants that would cause $^\#12345678$ to become successively $^\#12783456$, $^\#12567834$, $^\#12563478$, $^\#12785634$, $^\#12347856$. Other instructions, executed only 1/6 or 1/24 as often, can take care of shuffling nybbles within and between bytes. Very clever, but it doesn't beat (46) in view of the PUSHJ/POP overhead.

81.
```
     t  IS  $255 ;k IS $0 ;kk IS $1 ;c IS $2 ;d IS $3
        SET  k,1        k ← 1.
     3H SRU  d,a,60      d ← leftmost nybble.
        SLU  a,a,4       a ← 16a mod 16^16.
        CMP  c,d,k
        SLU  kk,k,2
        SLU  d,d,kk
        OR   t,t,d       t ← t + 16^k d.
        PBNZ c,1B        Return to main loop if d ≠ k.
        INCL k,1         k ← k + 1.
        PBNZ a,3B        Return to second loop if k < n.
```

82. $\mu + (5n! + 11A - (n-1)! + 6)v = \big((5 + 10/n)v + O(n^{-2})\big)n!$, plus the visiting time, where $A = \sum_{k=1}^{n-1} k!$ is the number of times the loop at 3H is used.

83. With suitable initialization and a 13-octabyte table, only about a dozen MMIX instructions are needed:

```
magic  GREG #8844221188442211
OH     ⟨Visit register a⟩
       PBN   c,Sigma
Tau    MXOR  t,magic,a; ANDNL t,#ffff;  JMP 1F
Sigma  SRU   t,a,20; SLU a,a,4; ANDNML a,#f00
1H     XOR   a,a,t; SLU c,c,1
2H     PBNZ  c,0B; INCL p,8
3H     LDOU  c,p,0; PBNZ c,0B                        ▮
```

84. Assuming that the processors all have essentially the same speed, we can let the kth processor generate all permutations of rank r for $(k-1)n!/p \le r < kn!/p$, using any method based on control tables $c_1 \ldots c_n$. The starting and ending control tables are easily computed by converting their ranks to mixed-radix notation (exercise 12).

85. We can use a technique like that of Algorithm 3.4.2P: To compute $k = r(\alpha)$, first set $a'_{a_j} \leftarrow j$ for $1 \le j \le n$ (the inverse permutation). Then set $k \leftarrow 0$, and for $j = n$, $n-1$, $\ldots$, 2 (in this order) set $t \leftarrow a'_j$, $k \leftarrow kj + t - 1$, $a_t \leftarrow a_j$, $a'_{a_j} \leftarrow t$. To compute $r^{[-1]}(k)$, start with $a_1 \leftarrow 1$. Then for $j = 2, \ldots, n-1, n$ (in this order) set $t \leftarrow (k \bmod j) + 1$, $a_j \leftarrow a_t$, $a_t \leftarrow j$, $k \leftarrow \lfloor k/j \rfloor$. [See S. Pleszczyński, *Inf. Proc. Letters* **3** (1975), 180–183; W. Myrvold and F. Ruskey, *Inf. Proc. Letters* **79** (2001), 281–284.]

Another method is preferable if we want to rank and unrank only the $n^{\underline{m}}$ *variations* $a_1 \ldots a_m$ of $\{1, \ldots, n\}$: To compute $k = r(a_1 \ldots a_m)$, start with $b_1 \ldots b_n \leftarrow b'_1 \ldots b'_n \leftarrow 1 \ldots n$; then for $j = 1, \ldots, m$ (in this order) set $t \leftarrow b'_{a_j}$, $b_t \leftarrow b_{n+1-j}$, and $b'_{b_t} \leftarrow t$; finally set $k \leftarrow 0$ and for $j = m, \ldots, 1$ (in this order) set $k \leftarrow k \times (n+1-j) + b'_{a_j} - 1$. To compute $r^{[-1]}(k)$, start with $b_1 \ldots b_n \leftarrow 1 \ldots n$; then for $j = 1, \ldots, m$ (in this order) set $t \leftarrow (k \bmod (n+1-j)) + 1$, $a_j \leftarrow b_t$, $b_t \leftarrow b_{n+1-j}$, $k \leftarrow \lfloor k/(n+1-j) \rfloor$. (See exercise 3.4.2–15 for cases with large n and small m.)

86. If $x \prec y$ and $y \prec z$, the algorithm will never move y to the left of x, nor z to the left of y, so it will never test x versus z.

87. They appear in lexicographic order; Algorithm P used a reflected Gray order.

88. Generate inverse permutations with $a'_0 < a'_1 < a'_2$, $a'_3 < a'_4 < a'_5$, $a'_6 < a'_7$, $a'_8 < a'_9$, $a'_0 < a'_3$, $a'_6 < a'_8$.

89. (a) Let $d_k = \max\{j \mid 0 \le j \le k$ and j is nontrivial$\}$, where 0 is considered nontrivial. This table is easily precomputed, because j is trivial if and only if it must follow $\{1, \ldots, j-1\}$. Set $k \leftarrow d_n$ in step V2 and $k \leftarrow d_{k-1}$ in step V5. (Assume $d_n > 0$.)

(b) Now $M = \sum_{j=1}^{n} t_j [j$ is nontrivial$]$.

(c) There are at least two topological sorts $a_j \ldots a_k$ of the set $\{j, \ldots, k\}$, and either of them can be placed after any topological sort $a_1 \ldots a_{j-1}$ of $\{1, \ldots, j-1\}$.

(d) Algorithm 2.2.3T repeatedly outputs minimal elements (elements with no predecessors), removing them from the relation graph. We use it in reverse, repeatedly removing and giving the highest labels to *maximal* elements (elements with no successors). If only one maximal element exists, it is trivial. If k and l are both maximal, they both are output before any element x with $x \prec k$ or $x \prec l$, because steps T5 and T7 keep maximal elements in a queue (not a stack). Thus if k is nontrivial and output first, element l might become trivial, but the next nontrivial element j will not be output before l; and k is unrelated to l.

(e) Let the nontrivial t's be $s_1 < s_2 < \cdots < s_r = N$. Then we have $s_j \ge 2s_{j-2}$, by (c). Consequently $M = s_2 + \cdots + s_r \le s_r(1 + \frac{1}{2} + \frac{1}{4} + \cdots) + s_{r-1}(1 + \frac{1}{2} + \frac{1}{4} + \cdots) < 4s_r$.

(A sharper estimate is in fact true, as observed by M. Peczarski: Let $s_0 = 1$, let the nontrivial indices be $0 = k_1 < k_2 < \cdots < k_r$, and let $k'_j = \max\{k \mid 1 \le k < k_j,$ $k \not\prec k_j\}$ for $j \ge 1$. Then $k'_j \ge k_{j-1}$. There are s_j topological sorts of $\{1, \ldots, k_{j+1}\}$ that end with k_{j+1}; and there are at least s_{j-1} that end with k'_{j+1}, since each of the s_{j-1} topological sorts of $\{1, \ldots, k_j - 1\}$ can be extended. Hence

$$s_{j+1} \ge s_j + s_{j-1} \qquad \text{for } 1 \le j < r.$$

Now let $y_0 = 0$, $y_1 = F_2 + \cdots + F_r$, and $y_j = y_{j-2} + y_{j-1} - F_{r+1}$ for $1 < j < r$. Then

$$F_{r+1}(s_1 + \cdots + s_r) + \sum_{j+1}^{r-1} y_j(s_{r+1-j} - s_{r-j} - s_{r-1-j}) = (F_2 + \cdots + F_{r+1})s_r,$$

and each $y_j = F_{r+1} - 2F_j + (-1)^j F_{r+1-j}$ is nonnegative. Hence $s_1 + \cdots + s_r \le ((F_2 + \cdots + F_{r+1})/F_{r+1})s_r \approx 2.6 s_r$. The following exercise shows that this bound is best possible.)

90. The number N of such permutations is F_{n+1} by exercise 5.2.1–25. Therefore $M = F_{n+1} + \cdots + F_2 = F_{n+3} - 2 \approx \phi^2 N$. Notice incidentally that all such permutations satisfy $a_1 \ldots a_n = a'_1 \ldots a'_n$. They can be arranged in a Gray path (exercise 7.2.1.1–89).

91. Since $t_j = (j-1)(j-3) \ldots (2 \text{ or } 1)$, we find $M = (1 + 2/\sqrt{\pi n} + O(1/n))N$.

Note: The inversion tables $c_1 \ldots c_{2n}$ for permutations satisfying (49) are characterized by the conditions $c_1 = 0$, $0 \le c_{2k} \le c_{2k-1}$, $0 \le c_{2k+1} \le c_{2k-1} + 1$.

92. The total number of pairs (R, S), where R is a partial ordering and S is a linear ordering that includes R, is equal to P_n times the expected number of topological sorts; it is also Q_n times $n!$. So the answer is $n! \, Q_n / P_n$.

We will discuss the computation of P_n and Q_n in Section 7.2.3. For $1 \le n \le 12$ the expectation turns out to be approximately

$$(1,\ 1.33,\ 2.21,\ 4.38,\ 10.1,\ 26.7,\ 79.3,\ 262,\ 950,\ 3760,\ 16200,\ 74800).$$

Asymptotic values as $n \to \infty$ have been deduced by Brightwell, Prömel, and Steger [*J. Combinatorial Theory* **A73** (1996), 193–206], but the limiting behavior is quite different from what happens when n is in a practical range. The values of Q_n were first determined for $n \le 5$ by S. P. Avann [*Æquationes Math.* **8** (1972), 95–102].

93. The basic idea is to introduce dummy elements $n + 1$ and $n + 2$ with $j \prec n + 1$ and $j \prec n + 2$ for $1 \le j \le n$, and to find all topological sorts of such an extended relation via adjacent interchanges; then take every *second* permutation, suppressing the dummy elements. An algorithm similar to Algorithm V can be used, but with a recursion that reduces n to $n - 2$ by inserting $n - 1$ and n among $a_1 \ldots a_{n-2}$ in all possible ways, assuming that $n - 1 \not\prec n$, occasionally swapping $n + 1$ with $n + 2$. [See G. Pruesse and F. Ruskey, *SICOMP* **23** (1994), 373–386. A loopless implementation has been described by Canfield and Williamson, *Order* **12** (1995), 57–75.]

94. The case $n = 3$ illustrates the general idea of a pattern that begins with $1 \ldots (2n)$ and ends with $1(2n)2(2n-1) \ldots n(n+1)$: 123456, 123546, 123645, 132645, 132546, 132456, 142356, 142536, 142635, 152634, 152436, 152346, 162345, 162435, 162534.

Matchings can also be regarded as involutions of $\{1, \ldots, 2n\}$ that have n cycles. With that representation this pattern involves two transpositions per step.

Notice that the C inversion tables of the permutations just listed are respectively 000000, 000100, 000200, 010200, 010100, 010000, 020000, 020100, 020200, 030200, 030100, 030000, 040000, 040100, 040200. In general, $C_1 = C_3 = \cdots = C_{2n-1} = 0$

and the n-tuples $(C_2, C_4, \ldots, C_{2n})$ run through a reflected Gray code on the radices $(2n - 1, 2n - 3, \ldots, 1)$. Thus the generation process can easily be made loopless if desired. [See Timothy Walsh, *J. Combinatorial Math. and Combinatorial Computing* **36** (2001), 95–118, Section 1.]

Note: Algorithms to generate all matchings go back to J. F. Pfaff [*Abhandlungen Akad. Wissenschaften* (Berlin: 1814–1815), 124–125], who described two such procedures: His first method was lexicographic, which also corresponds to lexicographic order of the C inversion tables; his second method corresponds to *colex* order of those tables. Even and odd permutations alternate in both cases.

95. Generate inverse permutations with $a'_1 < a'_n > a'_2 < a'_{n-1} > \cdots$, using Algorithm V. (See exercise 5.1.4–23 for the number of solutions.)

96. For example, we can start with $a_1 \ldots a_{n-1} a_n = 2 \ldots n1$ and $b_1 b_2 \ldots b_n b_{n+1} = 12 \ldots n1$, and use Algorithm P to generate the $(n - 1)!$ permutations $b_2 \ldots b_n$ of $\{2, \ldots, n\}$. Just after that algorithm swaps $b_i \leftrightarrow b_{i+1}$, we set $a_{b_{i-1}} \leftarrow b_i$, $a_{b_i} \leftarrow b_{i+1}$, $a_{b_{i+1}} \leftarrow b_{i+2}$, and visit $a_1 \ldots a_n$.

97. Use Algorithm X, with $t_k(a_1, \ldots, a_k) = {}'a_k \neq k'$.

98. Using the notation of exercise 47, we have $N_k = \sum \binom{k}{j}(-1)^j (n - j)^{\underline{k-j}}$ by the method of inclusion and exclusion (exercise 1.3.3–26). If $k = O(\log n)$ then $N_{n-k} = (n!\, e^{-1}/k!)(1 + O(\log n)^2/n)$; hence $A/n! \approx (e - 1)/e$ and $B/n! \approx 1$. The number of memory references, under the assumptions of answer 48, is therefore $\approx A + B + 3A + B - N_n + 3A \approx n!\,(9 - \frac{8}{e}) \approx 6.06n!$, about 16.5 per derangement. [See S. G. Akl, *BIT* **20** (1980), 2–7, for a similar method.]

99. Suppose L_n generates $D_n \cup D_{n-1}$, beginning with $(1\ 2\ \ldots\ n)$, then $(2\ 1\ \ldots\ n)$, and ending with $(1\ \ldots\ n{-}1)$; for example, $L_3 = (1\ 2\ 3), (2\ 1\ 3), (1\ 2)$. Then we can generate D_{n+1} as $K_{nn}, \ldots, K_{n2}, K_{n1}$, where $K_{nk} = (1\ 2\ \ldots\ n)^{-k}(n\ n{+}1)L_n(1\ 2\ \ldots\ n)^k$; for example, D_4 is

$$(1\,2\,3\,4),\ (2\,1\,3\,4),\ (1\,2)(3\,4),\ (3\,1\,2\,4),\ (1\,3\,2\,4),\ (3\,1)(2\,4),\ (2\,3\,1\,4),\ (3\,2\,1\,4),\ (2\,3)(1\,4).$$

Notice that K_{nk} begins with the cycle $(k{+}1\ \ldots\ n\ 1\ \ldots\ k\ n{+}1)$ and ends with $(k{+}1\ \ldots\ n\ 1\ \ldots\ k{-}1)(k\ n{+}1)$; so premultiplication by $(k{-}1\ k)$ takes us from K_{nk} to $K_{n(k-1)}$. Also, premultiplication by $(1\ n)$ will return from the last element of D_{n+1} to the first. Premultiplication by $(1\ 2\ n{+}1)$ takes us from the last element of D_{n+1} to $(2\ 1\ 3\ \ldots\ n)$, from which we can return to $(1\ 2\ \ldots\ n)$ by following the cycle for D_n backwards, thereby completing the list L_{n+1} as desired.

100. Use Algorithm X, with $t_k(a_1, \ldots, a_k) = {}'p > 0\ \text{or}\ l[q] \neq k + 1'$.

Notes: The number of indecomposable permutations is $[z^n]\left(1 - 1/\sum_{k=0}^{\infty} k!\, z^k\right)$; see L. Comtet, *Comptes Rendus Acad. Sci.* **A275** (Paris, 1972), 569–572. It appears likely that the indecomposable permutations can be generated by adjacent transpositions; for example, when $n = 4$ they are 3142, 3412, 3421, 3241, 2341, 2431, 4231, 4321, 4312, 4132, 4123, 4213, 2413.

101. Here is a lexicographic involution generator analogous to Algorithm X.

Y1. [Initialize.] Set $a_k \leftarrow k$ and $l_{k-1} \leftarrow k$ for $1 \leq k \leq n$. Then set $l_n \leftarrow 0$, $k \leftarrow 1$.

Y2. [Enter level k.] If $k > n$, visit $a_1 \ldots a_n$ and go to Y3. Otherwise set $p \leftarrow l_0$, $u_k \leftarrow p$, $l_0 \leftarrow l_p$, $k \leftarrow k + 1$, and repeat this step. (We have decided to let $a_p = p$.)

Y3. [Decrease k.] Set $k \leftarrow k - 1$, and terminate if $k = 0$. Otherwise set $q \leftarrow u_k$ and $p \leftarrow a_q$. If $p = q$, set $l_0 \leftarrow q$, $q \leftarrow 0$, $r \leftarrow l_p$, and $k \leftarrow k + 1$ (preparing to make $a_p > p$). Otherwise set $l_{u_{k-1}} \leftarrow q$, $r \leftarrow l_q$ (preparing to make $a_p > q$).

Y4. [Increase a_p.] If $r = 0$ go to Y5. Otherwise set $l_q \leftarrow l_r$, $u_{k-1} \leftarrow q$, $u_k \leftarrow r$, $a_p \leftarrow r$, $a_q \leftarrow q$, $a_r \leftarrow p$, $k \leftarrow k + 1$, and go to Y2.

Y5. [Restore a_p.] Set $l_0 \leftarrow p$, $a_p \leftarrow p$, $a_q \leftarrow q$, $k \leftarrow k - 1$, and return to Y3. ▮

Let $t_{n+1} = t_n + nt_{n-1}$, $a_{n+1} = 1 + a_n + na_{n-1}$, $t_0 = t_1 = 1$, $a_0 = 0$, $a_1 = 1$. (See Eq. 5.1.4–(40).) Step Y2 is performed t_n times with $k > n$ and a_n times with $k \leq n$. Step Y3 is performed a_n times with $p = q$ and $a_n + t_n$ times altogether. Step Y4 is performed $t_n - 1$ times; step Y5, a_n times. The total number of mems for all t_n outputs is therefore approximately $11a_n + 12t_n$, where $a_n < 1.25331414t_n$. (Optimizations are clearly possible if speed is essential.)

102. We construct a list L_n that begins with () and ends with $(n-1 \ n)$, starting with $L_3 = ()$, (1 2), (1 3), (2 3). If n is odd, L_{n+1} is L_n, K_{n1}^R, K_{n2}, ..., K_{nn}^R, where $K_{nk} = (k \ \ldots \ n)^- L_{n-1}(k \ \ldots n)(k \ n+1)$. For example,

$$L_4 \; = \; (), \ (1 \ 2), \ (1 \ 3), \ (2 \ 3), \ (2 \ 3)(1 \ 4), \ (1 \ 4), \ (2 \ 4), \ (1 \ 3)(2 \ 4), \ (1 \ 2)(3 \ 4), \ (3 \ 4).$$

If n is even, L_{n+1} is L_n, $K_{n(n-1)}$, $K_{n(n-2)}^R$, ..., K_{n1}, $(1 \ n-2)L_{n-1}^R(1 \ n-2)(n \ n+1)$.

For further developments, see the article by Walsh cited in answer 94.

103. The following elegant solution by Carla Savage needs only $n - 2$ different operations ρ_j, for $1 < j < n$, where ρ_j replaces $a_{j-1}a_ja_{j+1}$ by $a_{j+1}a_{j-1}a_j$ when j is even, $a_ja_{j+1}a_{j-1}$ when j is odd. We may assume that $n \geq 4$; let $A_4 = (\rho_3\rho_2\rho_2\rho_3)^3$. In general A_n will begin and end with ρ_{n-1}, and it will contain $2n - 2$ occurrences of ρ_{n-1} altogether. To get A_{n+1}, replace the kth ρ_{n-1} of A_n by $\rho_n A_n' \rho_n$, where $k = 1, 2, 4, \ldots, 2n - 2$ if n is even and $k = 1, 3, \ldots, 2n - 3, 2n - 2$ if n is odd, and where A_n' is A_n with its first or last element deleted. Then, if we begin with $a_1 \ldots a_n = 1 \ldots n$, the operations ρ_{n-1} of A_n will cause position a_n to run through the successive values $n \to p_1 \to n \to p_2 \to \cdots \to p_{n-1} \to n$, where $p_1 \ldots p_{n-1} = (n-1 - [n\,\text{even}]) \ldots 4213 \ldots (n-1 - [n\,\text{odd}])$; the final permutation will again be $1 \ldots n$.

104. (a) A well-balanced permutation has $\sum_{k=1}^n ka_k = n(n + 1)^2/4$, an integer.

(b) Replace k by a_k when summing over k.

(c) A fairly fast way to count, when n is not too large, can be based on the streamlined plain-change algorithm of exercise 16, because the quantity $\sum ka_k$ changes in a simple way with each adjacent interchange, and because $n - 1$ of every n steps are "hunts" that can be done rapidly. We can save half the work by considering only permutations in which 1 precedes 2. The values for $1 \leq n \leq 15$ are 0, 0, 0, 2, 6, 0, 184, 936, 6688, 0, 420480, 4298664, 44405142, 0, 6732621476.

105. (a) For each permutation $a_1 \ldots a_n$, insert $\prec$ between a_j and a_{j+1} if $a_j > a_{j+1}$; insert either $\equiv$ or $\prec$ between them if $a_j < a_{j+1}$. (A permutation with k "ascents" therefore yields 2^k weak orders. Weak orders are sometimes called "preferential arrangements; exercise 5.3.1–4 shows that there are approximately $n!/(2(\ln 2)^{n+1})$ of them. A Gray code for weak orders, in which each step changes $\prec \leftrightarrow \equiv$ and/or $a_j \leftrightarrow a_{j+1}$, can be obtained by combining Algorithm P with Gray binary code at the ascents.

(b) Start with $a_1 \ldots a_n a_{n+1} = 0 \ldots 00$ and $a_0 = -1$. Perform Algorithm L until it stops with $j = 0$. Find k such that $a_1 > \cdots > a_k = a_{k+1}$, and terminate if $k = n$. Otherwise set $a_l \leftarrow a_{k+1} + 1$ for $1 \leq l \leq k$ and go to step L4. [See M. Mor and A. S. Fraenkel, *Discrete Math.* **48** (1984), 101–112. Weak ordering sequences are characterized by the property that, if k appears and $k > 0$, then $k - 1$ also appears.]

106. All weak ordering sequences can be obtained by a sequence of elementary operations $a_i \leftrightarrow a_j$ or $a_i \leftarrow a_j$. (Perhaps one could actually restrict the transformations further, allowing only $a_j \leftrightarrow a_{j+1}$ or $a_j \leftarrow a_{j+1}$ for $1 \le j < n$.)

107. Every step increases the quantity $\sum_{k=1}^{n} 2^k [a_k = k]$, as noted by H. S. Wilf, so the game must terminate. At least three approaches to the solution are plausible: one bad, one good, and one better.

The bad one is to play the game on all 13! shuffles and to record the longest. This method does produce the correct answer; but 13! is 6,227,020,800, and the average game lasts ≈ 8.728 steps.

The good one [A. Pepperdine, *Math. Gazette* **73** (1989), 131–133] is to play backwards, starting with the final position $1*\ldots*$ where $*$ denotes a card that is face down; we will turn a card up only when its value becomes relevant. To move backward from a given position $a_1 \ldots a_n$, consider all $k > 1$ such that either $a_k = k$ or $a_k = *$ and k has not yet turned up. Thus the next-to-last positions are $21*\ldots*$, $3*1*\ldots*$, $\ldots$, $n*\ldots*1$. Some positions (like $6**213$ for $n = 6$) have no predecessors, even though we haven't turned all the cards up. It is easy to explore the tree of potential backwards games systematically, and one can in fact show that the number of nodes with t $*$'s is exactly $(n-1)!/t!$. Hence the total number of nodes considered is exactly $\lfloor (n-1)!\,e \rfloor$. When $n = 13$ this is 1,302,061,345.

The better one is to play forwards, starting with initial position $*\ldots*$ and turning over the top card when it is face down, running through all $(n-1)!$ permutations of $\{2, \ldots, n\}$ as cards are turned. If the bottom $n - m$ cards are known to be equal to $(m+1)(m+2)\ldots n$, in that order, at most $f(m)$ further moves are possible; thus we need not pursue a line of play any further if it cannot last long enough to be interesting. A permutation generator like Algorithm X allows us to share the computation for all permutations with the same prefix and to reject unimportant prefixes. The card in position j need not take the value j when it is turned. When $n = 13$ this method needs to consider only respectively $(1, 11, 940, 6960, 44745, 245083, 1118216, 4112676, 11798207, 26541611, 44380227, 37417359)$ branches at levels $(1, 2, \ldots, 12)$ and to make a total of only 482,663,902 forward moves. Although it repeats some lines of play, the early cutoffs of unprofitable branches make it run more than 11 times faster than the backward method when $n = 13$.

The unique way to attain length 80 is to start with 2 9 4 5 11 12 10 1 8 13 3 6 7.

108. This result holds for any game in which

$$a_1 \ldots a_n \to a_k a_{p(k,2)} \cdots a_{p(k,k-1)} a_1 a_{k+1} \ldots a_n$$

when $a_1 = k$, where $p(k,2) \ldots p(k,k-1)$ is an arbitrary permutation of $\{2, \ldots, k-1\}$. Suppose a_1 takes on exactly m distinct values $d(1) < \cdots < d(m)$ during a play of the game; we will prove that at most F_{m+1} permutations occur, including the initial shuffle. This assertion is obvious when $m = 1$.

Let $d(j)$ be the initial value of $a_{d(m)}$, where $j < m$, and suppose $a_{d(m)}$ changes on step r. If $d(j) = 1$, the number of permutations is $r + 1 \le F_m + 1 \le F_{m+1}$. Otherwise $r \le F_{m-1}$, and at most F_m further permutations follow step r. [*SIAM Review* **19** (1977), 239–241.]

The values of $f(n)$ for $1 \le n \le 16$ are $(0, 1, 2, 4, 7, 10, 16, 22, 30, 38, 51, 65, 80, 101, 113, 139)$, and they are attainable in respectively $(1, 1, 2, 2, 1, 5, 2, 1, 1, 1, 1, 1,$

1, 4, 6, 1) ways. The unique longest-winded permutation for $n = 16$ is

$$9\ 12\ 6\ 7\ 2\ 14\ 8\ 1\ 11\ 13\ 5\ 4\ 15\ 16\ 10\ 3.$$

109. The forward method of answer 107 suggests that $f(n)$ probably grows at least as fast as $n \log n$ (by comparison with coupon collecting).

110. For $0 \le j \le 9$ construct the bit vectors $A_j = [a_j \in S_1] \ldots [a_j \in S_m]$ and $B_j = [j \in S_1] \ldots [j \in S_m]$. Then the number of j such that $A_j = v$ must equal the number of k such that $B_k = v$, for all bit vectors v. And if so, the values $\{a_j \mid A_j = v\}$ should be assigned to permutations of $\{k \mid B_k = v\}$ in all possible ways.

For example, the bit vectors in the given problem are

$$(A_0, \ldots, A_9) = (9, 6, 8, \mathrm{b}, 5, 4, 0, \mathrm{a}, 2, 0), \qquad (B_0, \ldots, B_9) = (5, 0, 8, 6, 2, \mathrm{a}, 4, \mathrm{b}, 9, 0),$$

in hexadecimal notation; hence $a_0 \ldots a_9 = 8327061549$ or 8327069541.

In a larger problem we would keep the bit vectors in a hash table. It would be better to give the answer in terms of equivalence classes, not permutations; indeed, this problem has comparatively little to do with permutations.

111. In the directed graph with $n!/2$ vertices $a_1 \ldots a_{n-2}$ and $n!$ arcs $a_1 \ldots a_{n-2} \to a_2 \ldots a_{n-1}$ (one for each permutation $a_1 \ldots a_n$), each vertex has in-degree 2 and out-degree 2. Furthermore, from paths like $a_1 \ldots a_{n-2} \to a_2 \ldots a_{n-1} \to a_3 \ldots a_n \to a_4 \ldots a_n a_2 \to a_5 \ldots a_n a_2 a_1 \to \cdots \to a_2 a_1 a_3 \ldots a_{n-2}$, we can see that any vertex is reachable from any other. Therefore an Eulerian trail exists by Theorem 2.3.4.2D, and such a trail clearly is equivalent to a universal cycle of permutations. The lexicographically smallest example when $n = 4$ is $(123124132134214324314234)$.

[G. Hurlbert and G. Isaak, in *Discrete Math.* **149** (1996), 123–129, have suggested another appealing approach: Let's say that a *modular universal cycle of permutations* is a cycle of $n!$ digits $\{0, \ldots, n\}$ with the property that each permutation $a_1 \ldots a_n$ of $\{1, \ldots, n\}$ arises from consecutive digits $u_1 \ldots u_n$ by letting $a_j = (u_j - c) \bmod (n+1)$, where c is the "missing" digit in $\{u_1, \ldots, u_n\}$. For example, the modular universal cycle (012032) is essentially unique for $n = 3$; and the lexicographically smallest for $n = 4$ is $(012301420132014321430243)$. If vertices $a_1 \ldots a_{n-2}$ and $a'_1 \ldots a'_{n-2}$ in the digraph of the previous paragraph are considered equivalent when $a_1 - a'_1 \equiv \cdots \equiv a_{n-2} - a'_{n-2}$ (modulo n), we get a digraph of $(n-1)!/2$ vertices whose Eulerian trials correspond to the modular universal cycles of permutations for $\{1, \ldots, n-1\}$.]

112. By exercise 2.3.4.2–22 it suffices to count the oriented trees rooted at $12 \ldots (n-2)$, in the digraph of the preceding answer; and those trees can be counted by exercise 2.3.4.2–19. For $n \le 6$ the numbers U_n turn out to be tantalizingly simple: $U_2 = 1$, $U_3 = 3$, $U_4 = 2^7 \cdot 3$, $U_5 = 2^{33} \cdot 3^8 \cdot 5^3$, $U_6 = 2^{190} \cdot 3^{49} \cdot 5^{33}$. (Here we consider (121323) to be the same cycle as (213231), but different from (131232).)

Mark Cooke has discovered the following instructive way to compute these values efficiently: Notice first that a universal cycle of permutations is also equivalent to a *Hamiltonian* cycle on the Cayley graph with generators $\sigma = (1\ 2\ \ldots\ n)$ and $\rho = (1\ 2\ \ldots\ n{-}1)$. For example, the cycle in the previous answer for $n = 4$ corresponds to the cycle $\sigma^3 \rho^2 \sigma \rho \sigma^2 \rho^2 \sigma^3 \rho \sigma^2 \rho^2 \sigma \rho \sigma^2 \rho$.

Now consider the $n! \times n!$ matrix $M = 2I - R - S$, where $R_{\pi\pi'} = [\pi' = \pi\rho]$ and $S_{\pi\pi'} = [\pi' = \pi\sigma]$. There is a matrix H such that $H^- R H$ and $H^- S H$ each have block diagonal form consisting of k_λ copies of $k_\lambda \times k_\lambda$ matrices R_λ and S_λ, for each partition λ of n, where k_λ is $n!$ divided by the product of the hook lengths of shape λ (Theorem 5.1.4H), and where R_λ and S_λ are matrix representations of ρ and σ based on Young tableaux. [A proof can be found in Bruce Sagan, *The Symmetric Group* (Pacific Grove, Calif.: Wadsworth & Brooks/Cole, 1991).] For example, when $n = 3$ we have

$$R = \begin{pmatrix} 0 & 0 & 0 & 1 & 0 & 0 \\ 0 & 0 & 0 & 0 & 0 & 1 \\ 0 & 0 & 0 & 0 & 1 & 0 \\ 1 & 0 & 0 & 0 & 0 & 0 \\ 0 & 0 & 1 & 0 & 0 & 0 \\ 0 & 1 & 0 & 0 & 0 & 0 \end{pmatrix}, \quad S = \begin{pmatrix} 0 & 1 & 0 & 0 & 0 & 0 \\ 0 & 0 & 1 & 0 & 0 & 0 \\ 1 & 0 & 0 & 0 & 0 & 0 \\ 0 & 0 & 0 & 0 & 1 & 0 \\ 0 & 0 & 0 & 0 & 0 & 1 \\ 0 & 0 & 0 & 1 & 0 & 0 \end{pmatrix}, \quad H = \begin{pmatrix} 1 & 1 & 1 & -1 & 1 & 0 \\ 1 & 1 & -1 & 0 & 0 & -1 \\ 1 & 1 & 0 & 1 & -1 & 1 \\ 1 & -1 & -1 & 1 & 0 & 1 \\ 1 & -1 & 1 & 0 & 1 & -1 \\ 1 & -1 & 0 & -1 & -1 & 0 \end{pmatrix},$$

$$H^- R H = \begin{pmatrix} 1 & 0 & 0 & 0 & 0 & 0 \\ 0 & -1 & 0 & 0 & 0 & 0 \\ 0 & 0 & 0 & 1 & 0 & 0 \\ 0 & 0 & 1 & 0 & 0 & 0 \\ 0 & 0 & 0 & 0 & 0 & 1 \\ 0 & 0 & 0 & 0 & 1 & 0 \end{pmatrix}, \quad H^- S H = \begin{pmatrix} 1 & 0 & 0 & 0 & 0 & 0 \\ 0 & 1 & 0 & 0 & 0 & 0 \\ 0 & 0 & 0 & -1 & 0 & 0 \\ 0 & 0 & 1 & -1 & 0 & 0 \\ 0 & 0 & 0 & 0 & 0 & -1 \\ 0 & 0 & 0 & 0 & 1 & -1 \end{pmatrix}$$

when rows and columns are indexed by the respective permutations 1, σ, σ^2, ρ, $\rho\sigma$, $\rho\sigma^2$; here $k_3 = k_{111} = 1$ and $k_{21} = 2$. Therefore the eigenvalues of M are the union, over λ, of k_λ-fold repeated eigenvalues of the $k_\lambda \times k_\lambda$ matrices $2I - R_\lambda - S_\lambda$. In the example, the eigenvalues of (0), (2), and $\left(\begin{smallmatrix} 2 & 0 \\ -2 & 3 \end{smallmatrix} \right)$ twice are $\{0\}$, $\{2\}$, and $\{2, 3\}$ twice.

The eigenvalues of M are directly related to those of the matrix A in exercise 2.3.4.2–19. Indeed, each eigenvector of A yields an eigenvector of M, if we equate the components for permutations π and $\pi\rho\sigma^-$, because rows π and $\pi\rho\sigma^-$ of $R + S$ are equal. For example,

$$A = \begin{pmatrix} 2 & -1 & -1 \\ -1 & 2 & -1 \\ -1 & -1 & 2 \end{pmatrix} \text{ has eigenvectors } \begin{pmatrix} 1 \\ 1 \\ 1 \end{pmatrix}, \begin{pmatrix} 1 \\ -1 \\ 0 \end{pmatrix}, \begin{pmatrix} 1 \\ 0 \\ -1 \end{pmatrix} \text{ for eigenvalues } 0, 3, 3,$$

yielding the eigenvectors $(1, 1, 1, 1, 1, 1)^T$, $(1, -1, 0, 0, -1, 1)^T$, $(1, 0, -1, -1, 0, 1)^T$ of M for the same eigenvalues. And M has $n!/2$ additional eigenvectors, with all components zero except those indexed by π and $\pi\sigma^-\rho$ for some π, because only rows $\pi\rho^-$ and $\pi\sigma^-$ of $R+S$ have nonzero entries in columns π and $\pi\sigma^-\rho$; such vectors yield $n!/2$ additional eigenvalues, all equal to 2.

Therefore U_n, which is $2/n!$ times the product of the nonzero eigenvalues of A, is $2^{1-n!/2}/n!$ times the product of the nonzero eigenvalues of M.

Unfortunately the small-prime-factor phenomenon does not continue; U_7 equals $2^{1217} 3^{123} 5^{119} 7^5 11^{28} 43^{35} 73^{20} 79^{21} 109^{35}$, and U_9 is divisible by 59229013196333^{168}.

At least one of these cycles must almost surely be easy to describe and to compute, as we did for de Bruijn cycles in Section 7.2.1.1. But no simple construction has yet been found.

INDEX AND GLOSSARY

When an index entry refers to a page containing a relevant exercise, see also the *answer* to that exercise for further information. An answer page is not indexed here unless it refers to a topic not included in the statement of the exercise.